Claret and Blue Blood

CLARET and BLUE BLOOD

Pumping Life Into West Ham United

**Kirk Blows
and Ben Sharratt**

MAINSTREAM
PUBLISHING

EDINBURGH AND LONDON

Copyright © Kirk Blows and Ben Sharratt, 2002
All rights reserved
The moral right of the authors has been asserted

First published in Great Britain in 2002 by
MAINSTREAM PUBLISHING (EDINBURGH) LTD
7 Albany Street
Edinburgh EH1 3UG

ISBN 1 84018 489 2

A catalogue record for this book is available from the British Library

Typeset in Frutiger and Stone Print

Printed in Great Britain by
Creative Print and Design Wales

ACKNOWLEDGEMENTS

Archive consultants: Terry Connelly and Tony Hogg

THE AUTHORS WOULD LIKE TO THANK: Paul Allen, John Ayris, Bobby Barnes, Jimmy Barrett, Peter Bennett, Eddie Bovington, Ronnie Boyce, Martin Britt, Trevor Brooking, Paul Brush, Jack Burkett, Dennis Burnett, Lynda Bickles, Noel Cantwell, Tony Carr, Michael Carrick, John Charles, Joe Cole, Tony Cottee, Alan Curbishley, Mervyn Day, Brian Dear, Jermain Defoe, Alan Dickens, John Green, Peter Grotier, Pat Holland, Bobby Howe, Kevin Keen, Joe Kirkup, Frank Lampard, Jimmy Lindsay, Kevin Lock, Alvin Martin, John McDowell, Nicky Morgan, George Parris, Geoff Pike, Steve Potts, Harry Redknapp, Matthew Rush, John Sissons, Stuart Slater; also Jeanette Earl (Charlton Athletic) and Peter Stewart (West Ham United)

Special thanks to: Kaz and Lily, Karen Glaseby, Michael and Alex Sharratt, Patricia Laker, Brita Burns, Tony Fowles, Dave Pitchford, Jo Davies, Chris Wilkinson, Kris Raistrick, Ben Koski, Craig Willoughby, Robin Sorflaten, Joe Sach, Gerry Levey, John Raven

Contents

FOREWORD

IN AN AGE WHEN FOREIGN STARS DOMINATE THE BRITISH GAME, many supporters cling to the hope that it is still possible for 'one of their own' to climb over the mountain of passports and succeed at first-team level. That is not to deride the contribution of talents such as Paolo Di Canio and Tomas Repka; it is merely to point out that football is nothing without input from local people, whether they sell programmes at the side of the pitch or dummies on it.

West Ham United's unerring ability to produce its own top players continues to make the club the envy of the football world, with midfielders Joe Cole and Michael Carrick reaching the international stage and striker Jermain Defoe also tipped for great things. Defoe is from Beckton, just a wayward shot away from Upton Park – indeed, he is one of no fewer than 34 homegrown Hammers among the 48 whose stories you are about to read who were either born or raised in east London or Essex.

Many of those players have a deep affinity with the club; some even stood on the terraces themselves, singing the same songs and experiencing the same agonies and ecstasies as the rest of us. Likewise, Hammers supporters have always reserved special affection for boys brought up the West Ham way, whether they be world-beaters from Barking or flash-in-the-pans from Plaistow.

That a club like West Ham continues to develop such talents is a direct result of forward-thinking initiatives taken nearly half a century ago – and that is where our story starts. Using the late, great Bobby Moore's debut as a starting point, the criterion for a chapter in *Claret & Blue Blood* is that the player must have emerged through the ranks to have made a minimum of 25 first-team appearances. They should also have played a sufficient number of games for the youths to merit being considered a 'product' of the club (hence the exclusion of 1970s striker Clyde Best).

Although the vast majority of players included are Cockneys, our definition of the term 'homegrown' is not exclusive: West Ham's scouts have tempted Scots, Scousers, Geordies and country boys over the years, as well as lads from all over London. Some became Hammers heroes – some even became West Ham managers – while others blew their chance in dramatic fashion.

Here, for the very first time, the players who genuinely bleed claret and blue blood talk of how they helped to pump life into the heart of West Ham United.

PART ONE

Dawn of a New Era

1

A MOOD FOR CHANGE

IN ESSENCE, THE SEQUENCE OF EVENTS THAT TRANSFORMED WEST Ham in the 1950s from a run-of-the-mill Second Division outfit to an 'academy' and Mecca for youth talent went something like this:

1. Hungary create shockwaves by beating England 6–3 at Wembley in 1953. Playing in a fluid, calculating style, they put English football to shame. Malcolm Allison, West Ham's charismatic captain, is spellbound by the 'magnificent Magyars'.
2. Allison becomes the driving force for wholesale changes in attitude towards training and coaching at the club. Technique and skill replace fitness at the head of the Upton Park coaching manual. The youth section, established by ex-striker Bill Robinson in the early '50s, expands to incorporate Tuesday and Thursday night training sessions for local youngsters.
3. Cassettari's café, on the Barking Road close to the Boleyn Ground, becomes the focal point for meetings of the academy, whose members include Allison and team-mates Noel Cantwell, John Bond, Frank O'Farrell, Dave Sexton and Malcolm Musgrove. Doorstep sandwiches are consumed before sauce bottles and cruet are used to debate tactics.

Former left-back Cantwell tells a story that speaks volumes about the mood for change among members of the café society. 'We'd be at Cassettari's for two to three hours talking football, then sometimes we'd go back to Upton Park in the afternoon. We were a nightmare for the groundsman. There was a running track at that time, but Malcolm would insist we went onto the pitch. It would have been prepared for the Saturday, but we'd go out and cut it up. The groundsman would go up to manager Ted Fenton's office and ask him what he was going to do about it. Ted couldn't very well come down and tell us to get off the pitch because we were only doing it for his benefit.

'Malcolm thought what we were doing in training was a load of crap, saying we should be able to bend the ball with the outside of the foot and to get rid of these big old boots. Ted must have thought that the way things were improving, he'd better leave well alone.'

This quest for self-improvement was a major factor behind the club's Second Division Championship success of 1957–58. And with chief scout Wally St Pier working overtime to scour the Home Counties for youth prospects, West Ham's future was looking rosy too. Word began to spread about the quality of the twice-weekly training sessions run primarily by Allison and Cantwell. As a result, the standard of boys attracted to the club improved markedly. Many were England Schoolboy stars. Some turned their backs on junior training at bigger clubs such as Arsenal, Tottenham and Chelsea, simply because of the good things they heard about West Ham.

'Coaching had suddenly become important,' explains Cantwell, 'and West Ham became known as a club that developed young players. Malcolm's time was demanded by a lot of people, so Ted Fenton asked me if I would do the coaching. I got 35 bob a week for the two sessions.'

A few talented local boys slipped through the net, among them Jimmy Greaves and Terry Venables, who both went to Chelsea. 'I had Terry with me,' says Noel. 'He was a good player, but all of a sudden he went missing. Some clubs were reputed to be giving parents fridges and things like that.'

Most of the lads who attended the sessions, held in the forecourt at Upton Park, were from the council estates of Canning Town, Barking and Dagenham, Plaistow, East Ham and Stratford. The East End had always provided its biggest club with a steady stream of talent. Now that stream turned into a torrent. The first tangible sign of West Ham's progress at youth level came with an appearance against Manchester United in the 1957 FA Youth Cup final, with a side featuring future manager John Lyall at left-back. The Hammers lost the final and did so again two years later against Blackburn Rovers, with a young half-back called Bobby Moore in the line-up.

Little did Fenton, Allison or Cantwell know then that the pensive, blond kid from Barking would prove to such a dramatic effect how fruitful West Ham's youth policy could be.

2

FIRST AMONG EQUALS: Bobby Moore OBE

Born: 12 April 1941; Barking, London
Debut: v. Manchester United (h), 8 September 1958
Apps/Goals: 642/27
Final app.: v. Hereford United (h), 5 January 1974

MUCH HAS HAPPENED AT UPTON PARK SINCE BOBBY MOORE'S TRAGIC death, aged just 51, from cancer of the colon in February 1993. It would have been fascinating to hear his thoughts on the managerial partnership of his former playing colleagues Harry Redknapp and Frank Lampard. Redknapp and Moore briefly worked together as the management team at non-league Oxford City in 1980, while Bobby had his old room-mate Lampard under him during his time as boss of Southend United between 1984 and 1986. Redknapp once said he would have found a role at West Ham for the man he called the 'Guv'nor' if circumstances had permitted. Many believe that's the least the club owed him.

It would have been equally fascinating to discover his thoughts on classy defender Rio Ferdinand, arguably the closest the club has come to finding and developing a new Bobby Moore.

If he took a stroll around modern-day Upton Park, Moore would find swanky hotel bedrooms above the places where he swept up Woodbine butts as a member of the 1950s groundstaff. He'd find a stand in his name, a bronze bust in his image and a museum packed with memorabilia about his achievements. He'd also see dedicated souls standing in the drizzle on matchdays, raising thousands of pounds for the Bobby Moore Fund for Imperial Cancer Research. Among the diseases of which the Fund raises awareness is testicular cancer, from which Moore suffered in 1964. It is one of the wonders of the man that, around the same time as having to deal with the trauma of losing a testicle, he was captaining West Ham to FA Cup final glory against Preston and establishing himself as England's youngest ever skipper, having been awarded the job aged 22 in 1963.

Yes, a lot has changed at Upton Park. But the fierce level of affection for the club's greatest ever son remains the same.

Eulogising about Moore comes easily to anyone with West Ham connections. Former colleagues will tell you he was not just the best player. He also had the best manners (Frank Lampard: 'He knew how to handle himself. He never said too much or anything bad'); was the best trainer and the best drinker (Jimmy Lindsay: 'He'd be in every Sunday morning training on his own with a great big wetsuit under his kit. He must've sweated out ten gallons of beer'); was the best connected (Lampard again: 'We went to America where they didn't know much about English football but within five or six days everybody knew who he was'); and was the best fun (Jimmy Greaves: 'Bobby wasn't Mr Perfect – he always lived with a bit of danger and everybody respected that').

Old pals also admit that Bobby had his weaknesses, from his business dealings to his difficulty expressing emotion. In that respect he was no different from most people. But in so many others, he was.

Noel Cantwell was one of Moore's early Hammers mentors after local teacher Tom Russell recommended the Leyton Schools and Essex defender to Jack Turner, one of chief scout Wally St Pier's staff. 'I suppose, being older, I was a little bit of an influence on Bobby and he always looked up to the captain, Malcolm Allison,' says '50s full-back Cantwell. 'He used to ask me if it was possible to be a great player if you were slow. I didn't want to destroy his ambition, so I used to relate his situation to the great Johnny Haynes of Fulham and England. He wasn't fast but had a very good brain. That consoled him. There were a lot of good young players at West Ham at the time and not many people could have guessed that Bobby was going to be the outstanding one.'

It remains eternally puzzling how a boy born with only moderate natural footballing talent could develop such effortless powers of timing and positioning. Hard work and application seem inadequate as the answers, yet according to Cantwell there were certainly no heaven-sent bolts of lightning down West Ham way in the late 1950s. 'It was a gradual thing. When the great improvement came I don't think anybody could say. But he was a good passer of a ball, always curious and had terrific self-belief. He was always asking questions. "What would you do here? Why do you do that?" It was almost like he was insecure. People like that want people to help them.'

Cantwell could see that. So could Allison, without whom it is possible Moore would never have developed in the way he did. In Jeff Powell's book, *Bobby Moore, The Life and Times of a Sporting Hero*, Moore explains how Allison told him: 'Keep forever asking yourself: "If I get the ball now, who will I give it to?" I carried that with me into the middle of Wembley, Maracana, Hampden Park. It was like suddenly looking into the sunshine.'

The first step on the ladder to England immortality came with a youth cap against Holland in October 1957. Ironically, his record haul of 18 youth caps was eventually smashed by another Hammers starlet, Paul Allen. Signing professional forms for West Ham in May 1958, Moore was in the Hammers side beaten 2–1 on aggregate by Blackburn in the FA Youth Cup final in 1958–59. The club's youth policy was working well, but then Bobby had proved that earlier in the season by making his first-team debut aged 17.

The plot and the characters involved on Monday, 8 September 1958 make the event sound more like an epic Western than a football game. Promoted as Second Division champions and in excellent early season form, West Ham took on Manchester United at home. The Hammers won 3–2 and Moore played competently, but the real drama went on behind the scenes. Says Cantwell: 'Manager Ted Fenton said he had a dilemma picking the team for the United game and asked me who I'd play at left-half. Malcolm was my best pal and Bobby was the young prodigy. Malcolm – a centre-half – didn't have the ball skills for that midfield/left-half role. He had never played a First Division game for West Ham, so I plumped for Bobby.

'I don't know how, but Malcolm got to know that I'd influenced the selection of the team. He gave me a bollocking, saying he could have played with his ankles tied together. And we fell out over it, which was sad.'

Allison's fury was compounded by the fact that he had only recently battled back to fitness from tuberculosis. Continues Cantwell: 'After a while he realised I'd only done it in the interests of the team. I didn't know at the time that he'd played his last game. Malcolm trained very hard after his TB, but no matter how hard you train you don't get fast if you're a slow player. Bobby was a slow runner, but not slow in any other way.'

Pupil may have ousted teacher, but it took two more seasons for Moore to make the No. 6 shirt his own. By then, Cantwell had played his last game for West Ham, securing a dream move to Manchester United in September 1960. Many would query why a player as ambitious as Moore didn't get to display his talents on a bigger club stage too. Cantwell says: 'We were on yearly contracts and if the club wanted you, you stayed. And if someone wanted to buy you, your club needn't and wouldn't tell you.

'Sir Matt Busby (United's manager) and I spoke about Bobby. I would have loved him to come to Old Trafford, but in actual fact I don't think he was the type of player Matt would have enjoyed as a defender. The priority in Matt's mind was that you had to be able to defend well. He wouldn't give you many marks if you were a great passer but couldn't stop the opposition. Although Bobby could do those things, you might have thought that generally about the style of West Ham. Anyway, back then it was very rare you got a London player moving north. Instead they'd move within London. Bobby would have been ideal for Spurs or another top quality side.'

In fact, Moore later revealed he'd been itching for a move to Tottenham, who he regarded as *the* team of the 1960s, after his contract expired just days before the start of the World Cup finals in 1966. Bobby's itchiness cut no ice with manager Ron Greenwood, whose relationship with Moore dated back to his time as national youth boss. With England manager Alf Ramsey impressing upon Greenwood the urgent need to get Moore registered in time for the World Cup, a new contract was hastily agreed and the transfer never materialised.

Neither did a switch to Derby County after Brian Clough expressed an interest in taking Moore and midfielder Trevor Brooking to the Baseball Ground in 1973. Again Greenwood blocked the move, despite the fact that his relationship with his captain had deteriorated badly after the infamous 'Blackpool affair' of January 1971. For the crime of having a couple of lagers in a nightclub on the eve of a 4–0

FA Cup drubbing by the Seasiders, Greenwood handed Moore a two-week suspension and a fine of two weeks' wages. The manager, humiliated by yet another FA Cup embarrassment, felt utterly let down by a player he had long hailed the ultimate role model. Moore felt his treatment was ridiculous.

There is no question that there were some major lows during Moore's playing career, particularly towards the end. There was the kidnap threat to his first wife Tina and their two children in 1970, the same year he was falsely accused of stealing a bracelet in Colombia. There was the uncharacteristic defensive slip-up in defeat to Poland in World Cup qualification failure in 1973 that precipitated the end of his international career. And there was the humiliation of playing his last game for West Ham in a reserve match against Plymouth in March 1974, five days before being sold to Second Division Fulham for £25,000.

Yet the major highs were far greater in number. Footballer of the Year (1964); Hammer of the Year (four times); FA Cup and European Cup Winners' Cup winner; Ramsey's General – Moore playing a record 108 times for England, including, of course, in victory over West Germany in the 1966 World Cup final; Pelé's equal – a fact never better illustrated than in the captivating 1–0 defeat against Brazil in the 1970 World Cup finals, a game widely regarded as Moore's best ever.

Although essentially a defender, Bobby was fundamental to the attacking flow that made West Ham so successful and entertaining in the 1960s. Says ex-striker Martin Britt: 'The wonderful thing about Bobby was his passing ability. As a player up front, you would know if somebody was tight on you or if you had space by the way he played the ball to you. He was fantastic.'

In purely footballing terms, the respect Moore and Greenwood afforded one another was immense. Moore worked tirelessly, learned quickly and executed brilliantly; Greenwood coached with vision, applied his astonishing knowledge of world football on the training ground and regarded Moore as living proof that simplicity was genius.

The result was Bobby Moore, superstar. No Englishman before or since has had his sense of timing on the pitch or his aura off it. But many would be inspired by his achievements as the West Ham production line gathered pace.

3

THE OUTSIDER: Joe Kirkup

Born: 17 December 1939; Hexham, Northumberland
Debut: v. Manchester City (a), 13 December 1958
Apps/Goals: 187/6
Final app.: v. Newcastle United (a), 8 January 1966

BY A QUIRK OF COINCIDENCE, JOE KIRKUP'S WEST HAM CAREER ENDED with a game at Newcastle United, just up the road from where he was born and raised. By that time, he'd made nearly 200 appearances across a seven-year period – not bad for somebody who described himself as 'an outsider'.

That's not to say that Kirkup wasn't fully integrated into the Hammers' set-up after making that long journey down from the Northeast at the age of 16 – far from it. He may have finished school but his footballing education took place in the East End, with his second manager Ron Greenwood, youth-team coach Bill Robinson and fellow full-backs Noel Cantwell and George Wright introducing Kirkup to a West Ham philosophy still wearing short trousers itself. He tagged along with the Cassettari's brigade, chewing the fat about football with the likes of Malcolm Allison, and even met future wife Jill at the popular Barking Road café. He was close to colleagues Ronnie Boyce, Geoff Hurst, Martin Peters, Jackie Burkett and John Sissons. But at a time when the majority of youngsters were recruited locally, Kirkup could almost have been considered a foreigner.

Joe followed the fortunes of Newcastle and Sunderland as a boy and, despite playing rugby at grammar school (going so far as to represent his county), he pursued his footballing instincts with West Tyne Boys and Northumberland Boys.

He attracted interest from several northern clubs but rejected Newcastle's overtures on the grounds of their 'signing loads of kids, playing them a few times and then dropping most of them'.

However, a member of Wally St Pier's network of scouts had already started keeping tabs on Kirkup's progress and a chance meeting with the youngster's father resulted in an invitation to start training with West Ham. 'My dad was going home after watching me play one day and got chatting to somebody on the bus, having no idea he was a scout. The bloke started talking about the game he'd just seen and said he liked the look of me. My dad turned round and said: "That's my son!"

'Luckily my sister lived in Dagenham, so I came down during the school holidays a couple of times to train with West Ham. They welcomed me with open arms and I loved it.'

Winning a place on the groundstaff in 1956, Joe avoided living in digs by moving in with his sister Joyce in Sterry Road – bringing his mum down a year later following the death of his father. 'I can't say I missed my roots at all,' he admits.

Initially a right-half, Kirkup didn't get off to the best of starts by allowing the player he was marking in his first Hammers youth game – a fellow by the name of Jimmy Greaves – to score twice. 'They moved me to right-back immediately after that game,' he says, half in jest.

It was a position that suited Joe comfortably – although he always felt that attacking was the best part of his game. 'I was fairly quick – that was one of my biggest assets – and I used to do a good sliding tackle as well.'

Kirkup was part of the Hammers side that crashed to an 8–2 aggregate defeat to Manchester United in the FA Youth Cup final in 1957 – a 3–2 home loss leaving West Ham sufficiently demoralised to collapse 5–0 in the second leg. Creating symmetry in the other full-back position in both games was a player whose arrival at the club coincided with Joe's – John Lyall. He says: 'John was one of my best mates. When we each got married we bought houses in Abridge in Essex and so we lived about 50 yards apart.' Their long-term careers were to take very different paths, however.

Kirkup earned just one England youth cap, having 'a nightmare' in the 6–2 win against Ireland at Leyton Orient's ground. 'My West Ham boss Ted Fenton asked if he could get into the dressing room at half-time and started telling me off, saying: "What are you worried about? Get back out there and play your normal game." Two days later I turned professional for the Hammers.'

Bill Robinson may have been the youth-team coach but full-back George Wright – who played 161 games between 1951 and 1958 – proved the biggest influence on Kirkup during his early days at the club. 'He took me under his wing and helped me a lot, as did Noel Cantwell when I was breaking into the first team. A lot of coaching was done by the senior players such as Noel, John Bond and Malcolm Allison.'

A defensive reshuffle as West Ham tried to adjust to life back in the top flight during 1958–59 after an absence of 26 years saw Joe make his debut just four days short of his 19th birthday. 'Bondy had been in the side for years and it was just a case of getting in and doing the best I could. And when he was fit he generally used to get back in,' says Kirkup.

His tally of games increased in each of his first four seasons, culminating with 44 appearances during the 1961–62 campaign (which also saw him win three England U23 caps) following the arrival of Ron Greenwood as a replacement for the sacked Fenton. Says Joe: 'I thought Ron was the best thing since sliced bread when he came to the club. His knowledge of football was second to none and he wanted us to be an attacking side. But we were always liable to leak goals because lots of players wanted to get forward. We'd always score a few but the most successful teams were the ones keeping clean sheets – and we rarely did that.'

In fact, despite finishing eighth in Greenwood's first full season, the Hammers kept the opposition out just five times in 45 games – leaving much to debate over a fry-up and mug of tea at Cassettari's after training each day. 'There might have been 10, 15 or 20 of the players upstairs in a room and they'd sit there and talk football for a couple of hours,' he says.

As it turned out, West Ham were about to embark on their most successful period, winning the FA Cup and European Cup Winners' Cup in successive years. A slipped disc sustained during the team's run to the final of the invitational American Challenge Cup in 1963 undermined Kirkup's claim to a first-team place and hence he had no involvement in the Hammers' cup run in 1964. 'I was sick about it – and so was Martin Peters because Eddie Bovington played in the cup games instead of him. We both watched the final against Preston from the

Wembley touchline and Ron Greenwood came up to us at the end and said: "Never mind, the pair of you could be back here next year for the final of the Cup Winners' Cup." Of course, he was right and we both played against TSV Munich 1860.'

The 2–0 win against the Germans, widely regarded as one of the best games ever played at Wembley, represented the pinnacle of Kirkup's career. Ten months later he found himself signing for Chelsea in a £27,000 transfer, his relationship with Greenwood having deteriorated badly. He admits: 'Ron and I had a few arguments. When the maximum wage was lifted he spoke to the players about it and I calculated that we were going to be about £2 a week better off. Yet Ron was making it sound as if we were going to be earning the earth. I pointed it out to him – and he didn't like it.

'That was the beginning of the end for me at West Ham. Every time we lost or didn't play very well, it seemed that I was the one who was dropped. I didn't ask for a transfer as such but I did tell Ron to let me know if anybody came in for me. I heard nothing until a reporter rang me up one evening and told me that Chelsea were interested in me.

'The story appeared in the next day's paper and Ron called me into his office, saying: "You put that in the paper, didn't you?" And we had another big row. In the end he said: "Well, you can go and talk to Chelsea – you and their manager Tommy Docherty deserve one another." He didn't think much of Docherty and obviously didn't think very much of me either.'

Kirkup's playing career took him from Chelsea to Southampton before he emigrated to South Africa in 1975 to succeed former Hammer Johnny Byrne as manager of Durban City. Returning a year later after differences with the chairman led to 'an experience I could have done without', Joe once again settled in the south of England to lead a life away from football. Yet 'the outsider' retained a deep affection for the Hammers, insisting: 'I never wanted to leave West Ham; I thought it was a great club.'

4

ON A WING AND A PRAYER: Tony Scott

Born: 1 April 1941; Tottenham, London
Debut: v. Chelsea (h), 6 February 1960
Apps/Goals: 97/19
Final app.: v. Leicester City (h), 11 September 1965

A TEN-GOAL HAUL IN 1962–63, MAKING HIM THE THIRD-HIGHEST scorer after forwards Geoff Hurst and Johnny Byrne, should have been the factor that cemented winger Tony Scott's place in West Ham's golden era side of the mid-1960s. Unfortunately for the featherweight 5ft 7in. attacker, John Sissons – soccer's latest boy wonder who played in the same position – was about to emerge from his chrysalis.

Manager Ron Greenwood pinned his hopes on Sissons, so Scott – hampered, too, by cartilage problems – gradually disappeared out of the picture. After quitting the game he emigrated to Australia where he disappeared altogether – he would be one of the few former colleagues gregarious '60s striker Brian Dear would lose contact with. 'We were real buddies, me and Scotty,' says Dear. 'I saw him in 1999 and he's not been in touch since. I think he got divorced and then married a girl who had a house with all these Christian people in and God knows what. All of a sudden he phoned me up and said: "The Lord's called me."'

Of a posse of boys lured from Spurs' north London heartland in the late-1950s, Scott won the race for a first-team place. Midfielder Eddie Bovington was one of the group. 'Scott was from Tottenham and I was from Edmonton, so I knew him from youth football. He played for Middlesex and London Schoolboys. We used to travel to West Ham on the bus together.'

Signing professional forms in May 1958, the dark-haired attacker played with Bobby Moore at England youth level, earning 12 caps. The two would also appear in West Ham's defeat by Blackburn in the FA Youth Cup final in May 1959. The following February manager Ted Fenton was forced to shuffle his pack due to a catalogue of injuries. Against Chelsea at Upton Park, future manager John Lyall made his debut in place of Noel Cantwell at left-back, while 18-year-old Scott filled in for winger Mike Grice.

It turned out to be quite a day all round, as 29,500 spectators saw emergency centre-forward John Bond – the club's long-serving right-back – score a hat-trick in a thrilling 4–2 victory. Scott played on the right, but he would eventually find his niche on the opposite flank. 'He was right-footed but he taught himself to kick with both feet,' says Bovington. 'He'd get to the byline and pull it back, forcing the defenders to face the same way as the forwards. In terms of crossing the ball on the run he was probably one of the best around.'

That view is upheld by author and West Ham historian Tony Hogg. 'He was a very good crosser. The ball used to float over, just hang in the air. It was a curious way of kicking that some players had.'

On the flipside, Scott's build put him at a disadvantage against more physical opponents. He wasn't the fastest of wingers either. 'He was very lightweight and not very broad,' says Bovington, who made his debut against Manchester United in April 1960 in a crazy 5–3 defeat at Old Trafford in which Scott scored his first goal for the club. 'He could be easily knocked off the ball. He could beat people, but he never had the pace to get away from them once he'd beaten them.'

With Malcolm Musgrove a certainty on the left wing, Scott had to content himself by picking up games wherever he could for the next couple of seasons. He made 24 appearances in 1961–62 as new boss Ron Greenwood took an increasing shine to him. Bagging the first goal in a pulsating 2–1 home win against newly crowned 'Double' winners Tottenham added to his popularity.

When Musgrove was sold to Orient in November 1962, Scott was shifted to the left side. The new No. 11 blossomed. Appearing 34 times, his awareness was a major factor behind the growing understanding between Hurst and Byrne. Meanwhile, his habit of drifting in from the wing and taking aim with carefully placed low shots was rewarded with a double figures tally, including another against Tottenham in a classic 4–4 draw at White Hart Lane just before Christmas 1963. Says Tony Hogg: 'Scott was a member of Greenwood's "new order", one of his disciples. Greenwood was able to get him to play exactly as he wanted. He liked players he could mould, people who weren't set in their ways. With the advent of the 4–4–2 formation, Scott epitomised the modern player.'

Not as modern, it seems, as John Sissons. A much-vaunted star of England's Little World Cup win and West Ham's FA Youth Cup victory over Liverpool – both in 1963 – the clamour for the prodigy to be given a run in the first team was deafening. Yet Scott couldn't revert to the right side as England's Peter Brabrook held the position. As Sissons' stock rocketed during the 1963–64 FA Cup run to Wembley, Scott's plummeted.

He made just ten league appearances that season. Greenwood offered him solace in the League Cup, Scott scoring once as West Ham reached the semi-final, losing to Leicester City. Just eight league starts in the following two seasons led to an inevitable parting of the ways. Early in 1965–66, three games short of 100 appearances, he was sold to Aston Villa for £25,000. Scott later played for Bournemouth – under John Bond – and Torquay.

With cruel irony, this homegrown Hammer had, at the age of just 24, fallen victim to the success of the club's flourishing youth policy. Says Bovington: 'Once Greenwood made up his mind about somebody, that was it. He thought a lot of John Sissons, so Tony Scott really had no chance.'

5

LOYAL TO THE CORE: John Lyall

Born: 24 February 1940; Ilford, Essex
Debut: v. Chelsea (h), 6 February 1960
Apps/Goals: 35/0
Final app.: v. Blackburn Rovers (h), 4 May 1963

IF EVER A WORD NEEDED ADAPTING FOR THE WEST HAM UNITED dictionary, it is loyalty respelt 'L-y-a-l-l-t-y'. Our new word recognises the wide-reaching influence of John Lyall who, in 34 years' service with the Hammers, practised and preached the characteristic with unwavering belief. It was a vital aspect of his personal ethos, not just as a football man but as a human being. And as his character cemented itself into the foundations of West Ham during the 1970s and '80s, loyalty came to be considered a key characteristic of life at Upton Park.

The club remained loyal to John when his playing career was brought to a premature end in 1964; he remained loyal to the club's cause having risen through the coaching ranks to become first-team manager in 1974; the club stood by him following relegation in 1978 and he stuck by them in return after receiving a lucrative offer to move elsewhere in 1984.

He showed loyalty to his players and, by and large, it was repaid. Ultimately, however, John discovered that the two-way street had become one way. His faith in certain players went unrewarded and eventually undermined his position as West Ham suffered relegation in 1989. His faith in the board of directors also proved to be misplaced as his involvement with the club he loved was swiftly terminated that summer.

Typical of the man's character, he thought not of himself but of those around him, including the players he'd developed a close relationship with and to whom he wrote letters of gratitude following his dismissal. 'Those lads kept me in work and it was just nice to say thanks for what they did and that I was grateful,' he says. 'Relegation is such a disappointment because it affects so many people's lives. Managers and players end up leaving a club and when you consider their families as well it can create a tremendous amount of problems for people.'

John was taught the value of honesty, hard work and integrity from Scottish parents who'd met in London and settled in Ilford in Essex prior to his birth as the second of three boys. His father James, a police officer, had a soft spot for Tottenham Hotspur, but next-door neighbour Frank Whale was an avid follower of Second Division West Ham and would often say to young Lyall: 'Come on, I'll take you to see the Hammers.'

Football became John's great love and he quickly established his playing credentials with Ilford County High and Ilford Schoolboys to the extent that, at the age of 14, a schoolteacher friend of the family by the name of John Cunningham recommended him to West Ham boss Ted Fenton. The manager and his chief scout Wally St Pier watched Lyall in action several times and, following a game at Walthamstow, Fenton confirmed: 'Yes, we'll take him.'

Rather than joining the club's groundstaff, John agreed an office position that allowed him to train, play and study on a day-release basis while earning £4 a week. At the end of his two-year apprenticeship, the 17-year-old played in the two legs of the 1957 FA Youth Cup final against Manchester United in a side that included fellow full-back Joe Kirkup. The 8–2 aggregate defeat was disappointing but Fenton and chairman Reg Pratt considered reaching the final as confirmation of the wisdom of a sound youth policy. By that time John had already won his sole England youth cap, in a 7–1 win against Luxembourg, but in 1958 early signs of a problem with his left knee became evident.

He recovered from his first ligament operation at the age of 18 and, having learnt much from playing with veteran defender Dick Walker in the A-team and reserves, Lyall made his First Division debut in February 1960, marking Chelsea's Peter Brabrook (later of the Hammers) in a 4–2 win.

A twisted knee in his second game a few weeks later saw John stretchered off and ruled out for the rest of the season, but his form in the early part of the

1960–61 campaign – in which he played 25 times – enabled the club to sell Noel Cantwell to Manchester United for £29,500, a British record fee for a full-back. By the following season, with new manager Ron Greenwood installed, it became obvious to Lyall that there was a serious weakness in his knee and he played just four first-team games. It was the same story in 1962–63, the year of his final four appearances – the first of which saw John scoring an own-goal in a demoralising 6–1 home defeat by Spurs.

With his knee repeatedly coming out of its joint, he was forced to concede his professional career was over after one final attempt at a comeback ended in failure, in an A-team game against the Metropolitan Police in January 1964. 'It was a devastating moment,' admitted Lyall, still one month short of his 24th birthday.

Any vague doubts he may have had about rejecting a move to Brighton a few years earlier were dispelled when West Ham organised a testimonial game for him (the 1964 FA Cup final side v. an All-stars XI) and made it clear they would keep him at the club. The match attracted 18,000 people and Lyall later reflected: 'The actions of the club and fans that night underlined the sense of loyalty that existed at Upton Park.' Eleven years later, when the manager showed off the FA Cup to an adoring East End faithful, he said: 'It was worth getting to Wembley just to share the joy of the local people.'

The years in between had seen Lyall progress from the wages department and through the club's coaching ranks to succeed Ron Greenwood as first-team boss in 1974. He'd taken his preliminary FA coaching badge at the age of 20, his full badge at the age of 24 and, having taught youngsters the basics of the game throughout his playing years, assumed the part-time role of youth-team manager from Tom Russell shortly after hanging up his boots. Peter Grotier, a teenage goalkeeper at the time, remembers Lyall's early days as a coach. 'It was obvious there was something special about him. John knew how to talk to players and the more he mixed with senior names the more you could see the respect he was getting.'

Greenwood appointed Lyall as his assistant in 1971 and even recommended his protégé to Manchester United boss (and former Hammer) Frank O'Farrell when they were looking for a coach. Preferring to learn his trade from his mentor, John rejected the opportunity and he would later acknowledge those years as being 'the most exciting and stimulating period of my career'. After agreeing to take control of first-team affairs while remaining on the same wage of £80 per week (as

Greenwood moved 'upstairs' to become general manager), Lyall followed up his 1975 FA Cup success by steering the Hammers to the final of the European Cup Winners' Cup in 1976, which they lost 4–2 to Anderlecht.

Defender Frank Lampard, who has particularly bad memories of the Anderlecht defeat, remembers detecting subtle differences in the approaches of his two former bosses. 'John was quite a hard player and, as a former defender, he may have put a bit more grit into the situation. He liked people who would have a go for him, whereas Ron Greenwood was more of a tactician.' Ronnie Boyce, who played under Greenwood in the 1960s and acted as Lyall's first-team coach in the '70s and '80s, observes: 'The two men may not have been different in their ideas; perhaps just a bit different in their approach. John would always invite people into his office, whereas that wasn't so much the case with Ron.'

And Alvin Martin, who played under Lyall for a dozen years after emerging through the ranks in the late 1970s, says: 'It didn't matter if you were the best youth-team player or the worst, you got the same treatment from John. Everybody had so much respect for him – no manager would ever dare tap up one of John's players because of the respect he commanded.' Striker Tony Cottee – given a debut as a 17-year-old by Lyall in 1983 – concurs: 'John's man-management was excellent. He was very powerful and when discussing contracts with him there'd only be one winner. But he was caring, would talk to you if you weren't playing well and wanted to know if you had any problems.'

By the time Cottee had come through the ranks Lyall had won the FA Cup for a second time (against Arsenal in 1980), three years after taking full responsibility of the club following Greenwood's appointment as England manager. West Ham had been relegated in 1978 but they returned to the First Division three years later in sensational style, gaining a record number of points on the way to the Second Division championship and reaching the final of the 1981 League Cup.

Striker David Cross scored 33 goals during the 1980–81 season and Ronnie Boyce cites the big front man as an example of Lyall's ability to coach players to their full potential. 'Cross improved no end under John. He would come up with individual practices to get the best out of players and training under him was terrific.'

The Hammers finished in the top half of the First Division in three successive years (1982, 1983 and 1984) for the first time in their history and Lyall's achievement was noted by QPR chairman Jim Gregory, who sought to replace departing manager Terry Venables with the West Ham boss. John could easily have interpreted his chairman Len Cearns' willingness to allow him to talk to Rangers as a sign of not being wanted, but he discussed the vacancy with Gregory purely to see what they had to offer. He discovered that by practically doubling his West Ham salary he would be around £200,000 better off after the five-year deal expired.

Putting his family first, Lyall decided to accept the offer, only to change his mind when realising that West Ham would seek some £150,000 in compensation from Rangers rather than release him from the remaining year of his contract. Rather than encourage two clubs to fight over him in a tug of war, the dignified Lyall opted to stay put. He negotiated a new four-year deal in the summer of 1985 and engineered a genuine assault on the league championship during the 1985–86 season when the club finished in a best-ever third place.

The failure to build on that success ultimately resulted in John not being offered another contract in 1989, but Alvin Martin, who captained the side during the championship challenge, refuses to accept any criticism of his former boss. 'You have to understand the restrictions he had. If John had had the budget I'm sure he'd have gone out and bought the players he needed. But West Ham have never had the finance to pay for the best.'

Back in 1979, Lyall had splashed a world-record £565,000 on a goalkeeper in QPR's Phil Parkes and he returned to the same club a year later with a cheque for £800,000 to recruit striker Paul Goddard. Towards the end of the 1980s, however, hotshots such as Tony Cottee and Frank McAvennie were being allowed to leave the club – with Lyall feeling he couldn't deny them 'their chance to fulfil their ambitions' – while their successors David Kelly and Leroy Rosenior were being dug out of the Third Division. Insists John: 'That's the way West Ham had to do things then. Kelly and Rosenior were replacing two international footballers and that was never going to be easy for them.'

The team also suffered from injuries to key defenders Martin and Tony Gale, as well as keeper Parkes, while the players bought to fill their boots – such as Gary Strodder, Tommy McQueen and Allen McKnight – simply weren't good enough. One exception was left-back Julian Dicks, who arrived in March 1988, with Lyall saying: 'From the start I would have looked at Julian as a West Ham type of lad. He was loyal, wanted to do well and would make his own decisions.' Some felt the tenacious hardman was atypical of West Ham signings, but Lyall insists: 'The game is about the physical aspect as well. You can't make the game all technical because it then loses passion. Players such as Trevor Brooking and Billy Bonds were so different from each other, but you needed both qualities because one without the other wouldn't have survived.'

Survival proved too much for West Ham in 1989 and they were relegated following a 5–1 defeat at Liverpool. The Merseysiders had been a constant thorn in Lyall's side during his career, having sent the Hammers down in 1978, beaten them in the 1981 League Cup final and ended his title ambitions in 1986. 'The biggest disappointment of the 1988–89 season was our final game at Liverpool,' remembers John. 'You fight so hard to try and succeed and when you fail it's a great frustration.'

Throughout the demise, under-pressure Lyall continued to offer emotional support to his team. 'You've got to try and lift the players – that's one of many things I learned from Ron Greenwood. You have to try and give them belief that they're good enough.' They weren't and it was Lyall who carried the can.

Summoned to chairman Len Cearns' house on 5 June 1989, he was informed that his contract was not being renewed. It was John who'd suggested that any contract talks towards the end of the campaign be shelved until the close-season, and he later revealed: 'I never sensed that my position was under threat. My priority was to get the team playing well again. I felt my own future could wait.'

Lyall rejected the offer of another testimonial from the club, feeling that the West Ham supporters had done enough for him. 'If anything, I owed them for all the loyalty they had shown me.' His players, meanwhile, were shocked that the club had sacked only the fifth manager in its history. Says Alvin Martin: 'Everyone assumed John would remain at the club and eventually step onto the board. I phoned him when I heard the news but didn't know what to say apart from that I was devastated. He was the club's most successful manager and I believe he would have turned things round had he stayed. But now we'll never know.'

6

FAME OF TWO HALVES: Sir Geoff Hurst

Born: 8 December 1941; Ashton-Under-Lyne, Lancs
Debut: v. Nottingham Forest (a), 27 February 1960
Apps/Goals: 499/248
Final app.: v. Liverpool (h), 15 April 1972

AROUND 40 CHEERFUL CHAPS CONGREGATED FOR A UNIQUE photograph at Upton Park on the evening of 8 April 2002, united in the joy of what they'd collectively and individually achieved in the name of West Ham United. The occasion was tagged 'The Last 50 Years of West Ham' and saw the likes of Martin Peters, Ronnie Boyce, Jimmy Barrett, Noel Cantwell and John Bond wag a chin or two in the direction of Trevor Brooking, Frank Lampard, Alvin Martin, Ray Stewart and Alan Devonshire, among others, to raise money for the Bobby Moore Fund for Imperial Cancer Research.

Stephanie Moore was present on behalf of her late husband's cause, along with a whole host of claret 'n' blue-minded souls – most of whom had paid over £100 a head for the privilege. Sky TV's Jeff Stelling hosted the affair and even ventriloquist Roger De Courcey and pal Nookie Bear managed to show their faces. Yet there was a certain knight missing from one of West Ham's round tables – Sir Geoff Hurst, England's hat-trick hero in the 1966 World Cup final and three-times Hammer of the Year after claiming nearly 250 goals to finish as the club's second-highest scorer of all time.

His absence left a significant void in the function suite, not to mention a space in many autograph books. Sir Geoff was apparently 'otherwise engaged', but the joke among some attendees was that the lack of an appropriate appearance fee may have been a contributing factor. For Hurst is unlike any other surviving ex-Hammer. *That* hat-trick catapulted him into superstardom – although he is the first to admit that dealing with sudden fame in the mid-1960s presented him with a far tougher obstacle than any opposing defence. As he acknowledged in his autobiography, *1966 and All That*, 'Many elements of personal fame are beneficial, but there is also a price to pay.'

The biggest one was seeing how, after he'd played such a key role in England's World Cup triumph, people around him – including members of his family – changed their perception of him. Geoff admitted in his book that even his own parents found his new celebrity status hard to handle, to the point that they stopped visiting him and ostracised themselves from the lives of their young grandchildren.

No doubt Hurst was left feeling that he just couldn't win, a situation he could relate to from his days as a struggling wing-half. 'My wife Judith became an expert at pelting my abusers with peanuts from her seat in the West Stand,' he says.

After graduating through the club's youth ranks under manager Ted Fenton to whom he'd been recommended by a pal of his dad's when growing up in Chelmsford, Geoff found himself trying to impress new Hammers boss Ron Greenwood in 1961 – unsuccessfully at first. 'Hurst was just an ordinary wing-half, happy when going forward but terrible when defending,' Greenwood admitted in his autobiography, *Yours Sincerely*, many years later. 'He was useless at accepting responsibility and I told him he was a horrible defender.'

Greenwood is widely credited with having the foresight to switch Hurst to the striking role that would eventually create English footballing history. But the reality is that previous boss Fenton had first pushed the player up front for a Southern Floodlight Cup semi-final – regarded as a first-team fixture despite its stats not generally being included in players' records – against Arsenal in April 1960. Ron had been the Gunners' assistant manager at the time and he acknowledged that the match played a key role in his thinking when arriving at West Ham – even though he remembered it as a 'friendly'.

Geoff's first league appearance in attack – following 37 previous outings – came in the 1–0 home win against Liverpool in September 1962. He finished the campaign as the Hammers' top marksman with 15 goals and from there he never looked back, scoring a phenomenal 232 goals for the club in the next nine seasons.

Between the summers of 1962 and 1967 Hurst formed a partnership with John 'Budgie' Byrne that produced 249 goals. 'I was the pupil and Budgie was the master,' he said. But those goals were as much a reward for sheer graft – a characteristic inherited from his father, an ex-pro with Oldham, Bristol Rovers and Rochdale – as they were for natural talent. Reflected Greenwood in *Yours Sincerely*: 'Nobody could have worked harder. Geoff listened and practised and the improvement in his game in his first years in attack was remarkable.'

Geoff felt that he had to repay Ron for the time the manager spent developing his game, especially in terms of exploiting the near-post cross. And in doing so everybody gained – Hurst, Greenwood, West Ham (for whom he scored in the 3–2 win against Preston in the 1964 FA Cup final) and, of course, England (who he represented at youth, U23 and full levels). Top of the victims' list was Germany, with the striker indelibly stamping his name on world football with those three Wembley goals (the first and last resulting from instinctive long passes from Hammers' team-mate Bobby Moore).

Life was never the same again for Hurst after 30 July 1966. Despite making a conscious decision to shun the show-business set, he still found himself relying on the help of good friend Moore as he came to grips with a status that left him feeling decidedly uncomfortable. He later insisted that the native East Enders would 'never let any of it go to my head' although manager Greenwood declared that all three of his World Cup winners – Moore, Hurst and Peters – 'changed as men'. Yet the Hammers boss was talking in a positive sense, certainly in the case of Hurst. 'Those three goals reshaped his whole career and personality,' he said. 'He grew in stature as a player and person.'

Geoff's new assurance helped him to secure a £140-a-week, six-year contract with the Hammers (without the help of an agent), but his naivety showed when he failed to knit in regular wage increases to allow for inflation. He traded in his second-hand Morris 1100 and splashed out £12,750 on a new house in Chigwell, in the same road as West Ham vice-chairman Len Cearns.

All the time he continued banging in the goals, hitting six (a throwback to his days as a young Essex cricketer) in an 8–0 home massacre of Sunderland in October 1968. 'I could do little wrong that day, although I did knock one in with my hand,' remembers Geoff, who claimed match balls for six league and cup hat-tricks for the Hammers. 'I've given them all away to various charities over the years, as well as quite a few international caps (of the 49 he won which reaped 24 goals) and even the shirt I wore when we won the European Cup Winners' Cup in 1965.' The memorabilia that survived three house burglaries was auctioned at Christie's in the late 1990s, raising around £250,000.

Another ball that had slipped from his grasp had been the one used in the World Cup final but he was finally reunited with it in 1996, prompting him to claim: 'It's like winning the cup all over again.' That particular year was a busy one for Hurst, with England staging a major tournament – the European Championships – for the first time in 30 years. 'At times like this they roll people like Martin Peters and I out of the cupboards. We've recently been guests of honour at three 1966 World Cup reunion dinners,' he told West Ham's official magazine, before admitting: 'I'm not allowed to talk in any great detail about 1966 or Euro '96 because I'm contracted to a national newspaper.'

He did plenty of that as hospitality host of Upton Park's '66' Club on matchdays – despite his insistence that he disliked promoting himself. The role brought Geoff back to the club he left in 1972 at the age of 30, when he signed for Stoke City in a surprise £80,000 deal. Ron Greenwood had considered it a good move for the striker – especially after denying him a transfer to Manchester United in the late '60s – but Hurst was disappointed that he'd not had a proper chance to say goodbye to the Hammers fans he considered 'special people' in his life.

Confirmation of Hurst's position as a special person himself came in 1998 when he appeared in the Queen's birthday honours list. The words 'Arise, Sir Geoffrey' could be imagined drifting from Buckingham Palace as he received the ultimate accolade. 'I'm just thrilled to bits,' he said of his knighthood when speaking to West Ham's official magazine. 'Yet this isn't just about my hat-trick against West Germany but for my services to the FA and the soccer industry as a whole.'

Hurst assisted his old mentor Greenwood when he was England boss between 1977 and 1982, also taking charge of Chelsea for a two-year spell during that time. Many years later, having spent a long period away from the pressures of the game working for a motor insurance firm, his diplomatic skills were put to the test when he became an England Bid Ambassador for the 2006 World Cup. Although his efforts were ultimately unsuccessful, Hurst played the part with his usual sense of decorum. 'I've always been a level-headed sort of character and nothing will change me,' he insisted.

7

MADE TO MEASURE: Eddie Bovington

Born: 23 April 1941; Edmonton, London
Debut: v. Manchester United (a), 18 April 1960
Apps/Goals: 183/2
Final app.: v. Sheffield Wednesday (a), 16 December 1967

TUCKED AWAY IN WHAT SEEMS LIKE AN ENDLESS LIST OF 1960s players whose surnames began with the letter B was right-half Eddie Bovington. As a sleeves rolled up, muck 'n' nettles type of player, this B had few rivals. Unfortunately for Eddie, playing it tough did not always fit into manager Ron Greenwood's game plan.

Aged just 26, Bovington took the remarkable step of packing up football once his Hammers career hit the skids. Rather than find a club lower down the leagues, he simply shelved his shinpads, wrapped a tape measure round his neck and started working for his in-laws' clothing business instead. 'Manchester United didn't want to sign me, so there was only one way to go after being at West Ham and that was down,' he says.

United would figure large in the highlights of Bovington's Hammers career. Unsatisfactory relations with Greenwood would be the key downside. 'I respected him as a coach but not as a person,' says Eddie. 'I never felt that he treated me properly with regards to playing in the side.' Equally, he concedes: 'If I'd been at West Ham when Martin Peters and Bobby Moore hadn't been there I'd probably have played a lot more games. Unfortunately I played in the same position as two men who played for England.'

Bovington joined the club's groundstaff in 1957. A North Londoner, he was recommended to West Ham by the manager of his local youth club side. Many of his new colleagues seemed streets ahead of the new boy. 'I was in awe of the schoolboy internationals on the groundstaff. There was Mickey Brooks, Bobby Keetch, who was a big schoolboy star in those days, Derek Woodley, Johnny Cartwright. None of them really made it at West Ham, although who knows why?'

All except Keetch would play in the 1959 FA Youth Cup final against Blackburn Rovers. Young Hammers drew the first leg 1–1 at Upton Park but lost 1–0 in front of 25,000 screaming Lancastrians in the return game. Bovington would get sweet revenge on Rovers four years later.

Escaping National Service by the skin of his teeth – 'actually, I wouldn't have minded doing it as the units were all football mad' – he signed professional in May 1959. The following April, manager Ted Fenton gave him and several other youngsters their debuts in a 5–3 mauling by Manchester United at Old Trafford. Keeping hold of the No. 4 shirt was never going to be easy, though. Established hardman Andy Malcolm reclaimed it for the whole of 1960–61. Then youth team colleague Geoff Hurst wore it for a while before converting to a forward. Finally, the versatile Peters overtook Bovington in new manager Greenwood's affections.

Bovington's progress would be painfully slow – just 17 league games in three seasons – until 1963–64, when another Hammers mauling changed his luck for the better.

On Boxing Day 1963, league leaders Blackburn knocked the turkey stuffing right out of West Ham with an 8–2 victory at Upton Park. Ominously, the return fixture in the frozen north was just two days later. Greenwood was seething but made just one change, adding a touch of steel by replacing Peters with Bovington and telling him to stick like a limpet to Rovers' danger man Bryan Douglas. He did just that, helping West Ham to secure an improbable 3–1 victory at Ewood Park.

Bovington's mettle had made the difference and he held his place in the side for the next game – an FA Cup third-round tie against Charlton Athletic – as West Ham embarked on a fantastic journey to the 1964 Wembley final. Things were looking up. Bovington kept his place at right-half for all but one FA Cup and league game that season, while Peters was used as emergency cover in other positions.

For Eddie, the 3–2 Wembley win over Preston was a blur. 'I sat in the dressing room afterwards, clutching my medal, laughing and joking, but deep down inside thinking: "What was that all about?"'

More vivid were his memories of the semi-final against Man Utd, played on a quagmire at Hillsborough. Many would regard it as Bovington's finest ever game as he stubbornly nullified the threat posed by England's Bobby Charlton with a man-marking performance par excellence. West Ham won 3–1 in front of 65,000 rain-sodden fans, a victory few had believed possible. 'We were rank outsiders, especially as they'd beaten us 2–0 the week before at Upton Park with a virtual reserve side. The greatest thrill of that cup run was winning the semi and knowing we were in the final. You just cannot believe that you are going to be in it.'

Having been a valuable member of the first Hammers side to win a major trophy, Bovington felt more secure about his first-team fortunes. Off the pitch, he was also cementing his place in the West Ham social club. Although a regular on Bobby Moore's West End forays, he preferred less glitzy shindigs. 'The best drinks were after games on away trips, going to clubs in the midlands and the north. A lot of the time players from the other clubs would be there, so you'd have a good chinwag.

'The camaraderie, the mickey taking – it's the first thing you miss when you pack up. There were no cliques. If you're getting in the same bath as someone you've got to get on together. It brings you down to one level when you've got no clothes on.'

Bovington would have just three more seasons in which to enjoy banter in the buff. In March 1965 in a 3–2 home defeat by Sunderland shortly before the team was due to fly to Switzerland for a European Cup Winners' Cup tie against Lausanne, he smashed his knee-cap just three minutes into the game. West Ham beat Lausanne and progressed to the final, but Bovington's season was over. Eddie felt sure he'd have been picked for the epic 2–0 Wembley win over TSV Munich 1860 if fully fit.

He made it back into Greenwood's plans in 1965–66, but suffered another blow in the League Cup. Having scored a rare goal in the 10–3 aggregate semi-final thrashing of Cardiff City, he found himself surplus to requirements come the first leg of the final against West Bromwich Albion. 'I was choked, but no reason was given. Greenwood just thought there'd be a better balance to the side without me. That was his assessment and I thought it was wrong. I played in the second leg but they beat us and won 5–3 over the two games.'

By 1967–68 he was well and truly back in the shadows. Peters, a World Cup winner in 1966, was now an automatic choice, while several promising homegrown midfielders were putting the squeeze on their academy forerunners. Bovington's last game for West Ham was a 4–1 December 1967 loss at Sheffield Wednesday's Hillsborough, the ground where he'd ruffled Bobby Charlton's wispy feathers four years earlier. Rotherham, Blackpool and Portsmouth all enquired about him as he toiled in the reserves, but Eddie, already working part-time in the family business, decided he wanted out. It was first-team football or bust.

'I'd have taken less money to be able to play in the first team every week. That's where the glory and the high profile and the crowds were,' he says. 'One man has to pick the team and it wasn't a bad position for Ron to be in, having two players for one position. But only eleven can play and you don't want to be the twelfth, hovering on the sidelines. There's nothing to talk about afterwards.'

8

THE QUIET ONE: Ronnie Boyce

Born: 6 January 1943; East Ham, London
Debut: v. Preston North End (h), 22 October 1960
Apps/Goals: 339/29
Final app.: v. Leicester City (a), 30 December 1972

IF AN UNLIKELY 1960s PARALLEL CAN BE DRAWN BETWEEN FOOTBALL'S Moore, Hurst and Peters and American rockers Crosby, Stills and Nash of the same era, then Ronnie Boyce deserves to be considered as the equivalent of guitarist Neil Young – the reserved occasional fourth member whose contribution to the formation at the time was never quite fully appreciated from outside. Yet the reality is that Boyce played an essential role – one fully acknowledged by his companions – while shunning the limelight and stepping to the side of the stage to allow the attention to focus on others.

Boyce's placid nature made him a reluctant hero, but his commitment to the cause could never be questioned. His Hammers career spanned 36 years as player, coach and scout and during a large part of that the man known as 'Ticker' really did pump life through the veins of West Ham United. He scored the last-minute winner in the 1964 FA Cup final, set up the opening goal in the 1965 European Cup Winners' Cup final and, as a member of John Lyall's backroom team, became as reliable a coach as he had been a player. He provided a stabilising force during the turbulent days of the late 1980s and early '90s, although his departure in 1995 engendered some bitterness with the way the club sought to sever its ties with its most loyal of servants. 'I've got some terrific memories and great affection for West Ham as a club, except for the people who were running it at the time of my leaving,' he says.

Those who've read Geoff Hurst's autobiography, *1966 and All That*, will have noted how Boyce repeatedly appears in the middle of group photographs – using sauce bottles to discuss tactics in Cassettari's café, clutching a glass in celebration during the train journey home following the 1964 FA Cup semi-final win against Manchester United, sitting happily in the dressing room with the same trophy a few months later. He appears the life and soul of the party, the centre of attention, self-assured and content. Yet he reveals: 'I've never been a confident sort of person. It was other people who had faith in me, such as chief scout Wally St Pier who took me to the club.'

Hammers fan Ronnie grew up within a crowd's cheer of the Boleyn Ground, attending Brampton Juniors and East Ham Grammar School while progressing through youth football in his natural midfield position. His father Bill, who ran a grocery provisions shop, had been a promising player himself and was invited to West Ham for trials before granddaddy Boyce 'put the block on it' because of the lack of security attached to such a profession.

Having had to be content with playing for former employers Tate & Lyle and the Army, Bill was happy to comply with St Pier's request for young teenager Ronnie to start training with the Hammers on Tuesday and Thursday evenings. 'Parents were never a problem for Wally because he was such a lovely man. He had a certain way about him and mothers would fall in love with him,' says Boyce.

Within six months of leaving school at the age of 16 – having stayed on an extra year to take (and fail) eight O-Levels – Boyce had made his first-team debut in a

Southern Junior Floodlit Cup match against Millwall and signed as a professional. He was just 17 when manager Ted Fenton handed him his league debut in October 1960, with his dad continuing to provide support. Says Ronnie: 'He'd be critical when he felt it was necessary, without being harsh. The main thing he used to have a go at me about was always giving the ball to Bobby Moore. He felt that if Bobby could do something then I could as well.'

Boyce's breakthrough came in 1962 following the sale of midfielder Phil Woosnam under new chief Ron Greenwood and he quickly established himself as an integral figure in the centre of midfield, a role he would perform for the next eight seasons. 'There were a hell of a lot of attacking players in the side during the mid-1960s and my job was to play more of a holding role. I wasn't blessed with a great amount of pace but I had the ability to read situations and put myself in the right position where I could make tackles.'

Boyce made the team run like clockwork and was the heartbeat of the side, hence his nickname. 'We called Ronnie "Ticker" because when he was ticking over well the whole team seemed to play well,' said John Lyall, youth coach at the time. 'He was a superb interceptor and a good and intelligent passer of the ball. As a player he epitomised all the good things Ron Greenwood stood for as a manager.'

Greenwood himself observed: 'In other people's eyes Ronnie was a most underrated player, but to us he was invaluable. The thing that impressed me most about his play was his ability to do the simple things quickly and efficiently.' Former team-mate Geoff Hurst claims that Boyce was 'a player's player', but the man himself believes the ever-knowledgeable Hammers crowd fully recognised his attributes. 'I like to think that the supporters appreciated the job I did and that was always good enough for me.'

Never would the fans be more appreciative than during 1964 and 1965 as the team won two trophies. Boyce scored twice in the 3–1 win against Manchester United in the FA Cup semi-final at Hillsborough – 'the pitch was a mud heap and with United's side including the likes of Charlton, Best and Law, it wasn't a game we were expected to win' – and then headed the dramatic last-gasp winner against Preston North End in the final. 'It seemed to take an eternity for the public to realise it was a goal. Because I knew the ball was going in, I ended up running around the goal and some say I was the first player to do that.'

Following the successful capture of the European Cup-Winners' Cup against

TSV Munich 1860, the West Ham triumvirate of Moore, Hurst and Peters experienced World Cup glory in 1966. For Ronnie, the full cap to add to his half dozen youth appearances for his country, never quite materialised. 'I suppose it all comes down to my nature. I was never an over-ambitious sort of person. So the fact that I wasn't chosen for England after being told that I was going well and so forth didn't upset me. I was just happy being in West Ham's first team and playing with three men who'd represented England and won the World Cup.'

Boyce continued to ply his trade for the Irons into the new decade, although first-team appearances dramatically tailed off during the 1971–72 and 1972–73 seasons in which he played just three times. Former Hammer Frank O'Farrell brought his Man Utd team down to Upton Park for Ronnie's testimonial game in November 1972 and Boyce's final First Division outing took place the following month in a 2–1 defeat at Leicester as a substitute for midfielder Trevor Brooking. Remarkably, he was still just 29 and yet he found himself banished to the reserves for another three years.

'I'd had a few injuries and in those days it just seemed right that your first-team career ended at around the age of 30,' says Boyce. 'I was always a sheepish sort of person so I wasn't going to upset the applecart. I was still enjoying playing in the reserves and genuinely felt that I could help the youngsters coming through.'

It is typical of the man's character that, although a busy midfielder, he avoided a single booking during his first-team years, collecting just one yellow card in a reserve game. 'I like to think I was the same person on the pitch as off it. I never really got involved in any trouble. The one booking I did get was for dissent.'

Boyce enjoyed instant success once appointed as youth-team coach, guiding the kids to the 1975 FA Youth Cup final. He moved up the ranks to share a first-team coaching partnership with former defender Mick McGiven under manager John Lyall during the 1980s. 'I got on well with Mick. He knew what he wanted and was very determined. One of us would assist John while the other took the reserves, then we'd swap roles. I got the best of both worlds because I was gaining experience of working with John while also managing my own side.'

When Lyall was sacked following relegation in 1989, both coaches remained to assist Lou Macari. McGiven bailed out shortly before the new boss – leaving Boyce to pick up the pieces for the trip to Swindon on 18 February 1990. Striker Jimmy Quinn scored twice to help the Hammers to a 2–2 draw and as speculation grew as to whom the next manager would be, caretaker Ronnie's name was thrown into the ring. 'My wife told me I was mad not to go for it,' he says. 'I might have had the opportunity but in my own mind I was adamant that I couldn't have taken the pressure. You've got to be of a certain make-up.'

Youth-team manager Billy Bonds was eventually named as Macari's successor and Boyce continued in his role as assistant boss – not that he'd ever really been officially awarded the title under the previous management. After two full seasons – during which the Hammers won promotion and were quickly relegated amid the Bond Scheme protests – Ronnie conceded that maybe the time was right for Bonds to appoint a new right-hand man. 'Bill wasn't the sort of character to have said anything but I just took it upon myself to say to him: "Do you want to bring somebody in?" When you've been at a club for a long time there comes a stage when you think your role is becoming a bit run-of-the-mill. So Bill eventually brought Harry Redknapp in and I became chief scout.' Boyce briefly worked alongside the outgoing Eddie Baily and he says: 'During the short period I worked with Eddie I picked up a great deal.'

Within two years Redknapp had replaced Bonds in the Hammers hotseat and the new boss was keen to make changes. Says Boyce: 'Harry knew what he wanted and also had his own network of people who could recommend players so there were times when deals were done and I wasn't involved. But football was changing and perhaps there were certain things happening that I couldn't get on with.'

Redknapp wasn't happy with aspects of the scouting and coaching set-up and towards the end of 1995 replaced Boyce and reserve-team manager Paul Hilton. 'I was offered a part-time scouting position but naturally wanted to know what sort of redundancy figure I'd be receiving having worked full-time for West Ham for my entire professional life. Managing director Peter Storrie gave me a figure that I thought was derisory so I went to see chairman Terence Brown. He hit me with questions like: "What have you done since you've been in the chief scout's position?" and went on about the average age of the side, when Harry had been the one who wanted defender Tony Gale to have another contract at the age of 34. If you've been at a club for 36 years you'd like to think you've done some good things in that time. You wouldn't leave someone feeling like that so I left the club and haven't been back since.'

Following his departure Boyce scouted at Queen's Park Rangers and Millwall –

broken up by a brief spell as a sheet metal worker – before being invited by chief scout Charlie Woods to work on a part-time basis for Tottenham Hotspur. He still has deep affection for the West Ham supporters but has no idea when he might return to Upton Park to watch a game. He says: 'Like a lot of people who have done a hell of a lot for the club, I've never been invited back.'

9

NATURAL BORN THRILLER: Martin Peters MBE

Born: 8 November 1943; Plaistow, London
Debut: v. Cardiff City (h), 20 April 1962
Apps/Goals: 364/100
Final app.: v. Ipswich Town (h), 14 March 1970

WITH RONNIE BOYCE THE LAST YOUTH PRODUCT TO MAKE A SERIOUS impression on the first team under manager Ted Fenton, the first under successor Ron Greenwood was Martin Peters. It turned out to be a record-book statistic of deafening resonance.

Peters embodied in a nutshell Greenwood's fresh ideas on how football should be played – he showed forethought, instinct, awareness and knew how to entertain. A natural sportsman, he had it all, yet ended up ruing his own versatility. While his West Ham and England colleagues Bobby Moore and Geoff Hurst were defined by their leadership qualities and goals respectively, Peters became saddled with a reputation as the ultimate 'utility player'. He despised the term, complaining in his autobiography, *Goals from Nowhere*: 'It is an old theatrical term that, my dictionary explains, means: "An actor employed to play unimportant parts when required." For a footballer to be called useful is to me almost as bad being called useless.'

His managers for both club and country thanked the heavens that they had a player of his quality who could slot effortlessly into any role. However, after Peters' frustrations boiled over in the mid-1960s and he complained to Greenwood that he was fed-up being 'a general dogsbody', a free role was created especially for him. 'Broadly, he filled the gap behind our strikers, playing wide when he chose to, pushing forward when he wanted to,' said Greenwood in his book, *Yours Sincerely.* 'It was a job which only a player of Peters' quality could have done. His understanding of space and timing was delightful.'

West Ham fended off intense interest from other London clubs – Arsenal in particular – before Peters joined on apprentice terms in 1959. Chief scout Wally St Pier had tracked him so hard that he ended up becoming a friend of the family. St Pier was a frequent visitor to the Peters' home in Dagenham, strolling over to the local park with Martin and his father to watch a game or indulge in an impromptu kick-about with his young find.

A London, Essex and England Schoolboys regular, Peters was too young to play in the 1959 FA Youth Cup final and too old to appear in the equivalent game in 1963 in which Martin Britt scored five goals in a sensational 6–5 aggregate win over Liverpool. By the time Britt was awarded his full debut at the end of that 1962–63 season, Peters had already been a first-team regular for a year, having held onto his place in the side after ironically ousting Geoff Hurst from the right-half position on his April 1962 debut at home to Cardiff City. Peters had scored eight goals and started games at left-back and up front as well as in midfield. He'd even played as an emergency goalkeeper after Brian Rhodes suffered an injury in an away game, again against Cardiff.

Says Britt: 'Martin was a good reader of the game and for quite a slim chap he was very strong as well. He was a good striker and volleyer of the ball and also very good in the air, so you would always want him around the box. But he was also a good defender. He could do everything.' Or almost everything. 'One observation, although not a criticism, was that he didn't have quite the pace. If he'd had that extra bit of pace – he became world class anyway – he'd have been mega-mega world class.'

In 1962–63, Peters made 36 league appearances as West Ham finished 12th. He also appeared for England U23s, scoring twice on his debut in a 6–1 thrashing of Belgium at Plymouth. The following campaign, although hampered by a knee injury, he was ever-present until December; then he suffered the biggest downer of his West Ham career. Greenwood sacrificed Peters after the Hammers were thrashed 8–2 at home against Blackburn on Boxing Day. His replacement – tough guy Eddie Bovington – came in, played well and took over at right-half for the rest of the campaign. Peters played just 12 more times that season, but the real sickener was missing out on the 3–2 FA Cup final glory against Preston.

Recalls Britt: 'I think we all felt very sorry for Martin, because really he was good enough to be there and he should have been there. Circumstances were such that he had a little bit of a rough time and Eddie came in. Eddie was a very good tackler and a dynamic sort of midfield player; Martin was a creator. But it did the job and they got the result, so you can't criticise.'

In *Yours Sincerely*, Greenwood explained how he came to jettison Peters, whom he felt had been going through a lean patch, after the Rovers humiliation. 'The return game was only 48 hours later. I wrote down a team and there were nine changes. Then I wrote another and then another until I felt I got the team exactly right – and now there was just one change! Eddie Bovington for Martin Peters.'

Devastated but determined, Peters dug deep to return the next season with all guns blazing. Cultured performances in defence, midfield and attack saw him scoop the Hammer of the Year award and he was ever-present in the run to glory in the 1964–65 European Cup-Winners' Cup. In one of the greatest Wembley games ever, West Ham beat TSV Munich 1860 2–0 and this time Peters, not the injured Bovington, got to climb the famous steps to claim a winners' medal.

For most of 1965–66, Greenwood relieved Martin of the utility tag and played him as an attacking midfielder. The 22-year-old's profile rocketed. He returned to Wembley to make his full England debut against Yugoslavia in May 1966. Just six England games later he was lining up alongside Moore and Hurst in a World Cup final, scoring the all-important second goal in the epic 4–2 victory.

England's performance that day had West Ham – and more specifically Ron Greenwood – written all over it and for the next few seasons the on-pitch understanding between the illustrious trio would make the Hammers addictive viewing. Greenwood wanted skill and expression and it culminated in plenty of goals at both ends, with Peters and Hurst grabbing the lion's share for West Ham as their interchanges took on a telepathic brilliance.

Recalls winger John Sissons: 'For one game we'd worked all week on me playing balls to the near post. Beforehand, Ron told me that Geoff was going to make runs to the near post, Martin was going to be at the back post and that I should keep crossing to the far post. Martin got two goals within about five minutes because all the defenders were flying in to mark Geoff and Martin was ghosting in on the far post. In that way, Ron was so tactically brilliant.'

In 1966–67, Peters scored 16 goals in all competitions. He scored 18 the following season and 23 the one after that. There were Peters goals in stupendous wins: a 7–2 home rout of Fulham in February 1968. There were Peters goals in outrageous draws: a 5–5 thriller at Chelsea in December 1966. Somewhat surprisingly there was just the one Peters hat-trick, notched up in a 4–0 win over West Brom in 1968–69. That was sweet revenge for Martin, who had been West Ham's sole scorer in a telling 4–1 League Cup final second-leg defeat to the Baggies in 1965–66, the Hammers losing 5–3 on aggregate.

Despite all the sizzling action in the mid-to-late-1960s, West Ham made little impression in the league and began to falter in the early rounds of the cups too. Peters claimed it was this reason and not, as has been suggested by so many observers, his type-casting as 'the other one' of the World Cup winners, which led to his departure for Spurs in a British record £200,000 deal (Jimmy Greaves joining West Ham in exchange) in 1970. 'Why should I be number one in the side led by the captain of England and the man who scored three goals in a World Cup Final?' Peters questioned in *Goals from Nowhere.*

'It was okay playing in such great games for West Ham, but I wanted more than that.'

Thus he became the only one of the threesome to leave Upton Park while still at his peak. Martin got his wishes at Tottenham, inspiring the side to UEFA and League Cup victories. Stints with Norwich City and Sheffield United would take his league appearances tally to 722, while 67 caps were earned for England.

Peters dallied with a player-manager role at Sheffield United. But being (as ex-England manager Alf Ramsey asserted) 'ten years ahead of his time' as a top player counted for little in the scruffy dug-outs of the lower divisions. His reign lasted just a few months and left him at a low ebb, according to Martin Britt. 'He couldn't get back into the game and had a very difficult period in his life. He had a very tough time until he suddenly found out there was a life after football.'

His reincarnation would include working alongside Geoff Hurst for a motor insurance company, making 1966-themed after-dinner speeches, becoming a non-executive director at Tottenham and working in hospitality back at West Ham. The Mr Versatile tag he disliked so much during his playing days would, it seems, be the making of him as a highly successful entrepreneur.

10

MOORE, HURST, PETERS . . . AND ME: Jack Burkett

Born: 21 August 1942; Edmonton, London
Debut: v. Fulham (h), 30 April 1962
Apps/Goals: 181/4
Final app.: v. Sheffield Wednesday (a), 16 December 1968

JACK BURKETT'S SIX-YEAR FIRST-TEAM RUN AT WEST HAM NEATLY enveloped the most successful period in the club's history. The good things he learned about football on the Hammers groundstaff in the 1950s helped him enormously during the halcyon days of the mid-'60s, but knowing how to hold a three-pronged gardening implement wasn't necessarily one of them.

'There's a lot of stuff we did which would come to be regarded as too dangerous, with all kinds of health and safety issues,' says Burkett, who became an authority on such matters as a regional co-ordinator for the Footballers' Further Education & Vocational Training Society. 'I remember 15 of us had to dig up the pitch with forks, walking from one end to the other. Then we had to train on that surface later in the day. And we had to clean out the old Chicken Run, which was smelly with rats running around. But we made a lot of money from that because, where people used to throw coins for peanuts and programmes, the sellers would throw change back and they used to drop it.

'They were fun times, growing up. There was a groundsman who'd been there a long while who always used to wear a cap because he'd lost his hair through a disease when he was younger. We didn't realise that. One day our striker Brian Dear rigged up a bucket filled with paint. The groundsman knocked it over and, of course, it went all over him, but he never took his cap off. Naturally we all scarpered, but we were always laughing about that.'

Although a true Cockney, born in Bow Hospital, Burkett was raised in Tottenham. As a fan he'd visit Arsenal and Spurs on alternate Saturdays. He briefly trained with the latter, but Hammers chief scout Wally St Pier worked his magic once more to tempt Jack east after seeing him shine for Tottenham Schoolboys.

As a left-back, Burkett idolised West Ham's Noel Cantwell, noted for his swashbuckling style and eagerness to join the attack. 'That first night made up my mind that West Ham was for me. Taking the training session on the pitch at Upton Park were Noel, captain Malcolm Allison and right-back John Bond. No disrespect to Tottenham, who tried to buy me back later in my career, but all we used to do in training there was run round the track, whereas West Ham used the ball.'

Having joined the groundstaff in 1958, Jack appeared for West Ham in the 2–1 aggregate defeat against Blackburn Rovers in the 1959 FA Youth Cup final. Two years later Ron Greenwood replaced Ted Fenton as manager. Even as a teenager Burkett could tell there was something special about the new gaffer's ideas on coaching. 'He was the best coach in England, probably the best there's ever been,' he says.

Greenwood wanted to broaden his players' horizons in every way. If that meant taking them to the other side of the world, then so be it. Foreign pre-season tours became part of the West Ham experience.

'My first with the first team was to Africa in 1961,' Burkett says, 'but I'd been due to go to Switzerland on a youth-team tour. I had to have all the jabs at once, whereas the rest of the squad had them over a period of time. My left arm inflated so much I couldn't get my shirt on properly. Later on we toured Europe and America. It made you grow up and developed you, having to play against different nationalities with different ideas. I think it made us more of a continental team than a British team.'

In for the perennially injured John Lyall, Burkett made his debut in a 4–2 home win over Fulham in the final game of 1961–62. In an era when West Ham's playing staff might number as many as 50 professionals, competition was fierce – except on the looks front. With his square jaw and flaxen hair it was Burkett, not golden boy Bobby Moore, who was the local heart-throb. Up west, four mop-topped Liverpudlians were about to send the girls wild. Out east, it was Jack. 'It was a bit embarrassing, but I was the favourite. When I ran out they used to scream. As it would later become the Beckhams, back then it was the Burketts!'

Early into the 1962–63 season, Lyall was laid up with a knee injury that eventually ended his career. Burkett seized the moment. The new No. 3's Cantwellesque style of running on the balls of his feet with his arms in the air would become a familiar sight over the next half-decade. Greenwood's emphasis on flowing, attractive football suited Jack down to the ground – not that he was averse to using less aesthetic techniques when required.

He proved that to almost suicidal effect in the 1964 FA Cup final win over Preston. 'If that game had been played in later years I would have been sent off,' he says. 'Their winger, David Wilson, was a decent player and the first tackle I did on him, I caught him. Next one, I touched the ball and him at the same time, he turned and went over. The third time, I won the ball but I went through him and it looked as though I'd kicked him. The referee ran past me and said: "You don't want to be the first person sent off in a cup final, do you?" It didn't hit me what he'd said until a few minutes later. After that I settled down.'

Burkett did, in fact, make the record books in 1965–66 when he became the first person ever to be substituted for West Ham, midfielder Peter Bennett replacing him in a 2–1 home win over Leeds United. By then he'd picked up his second winners' medal as one of nine home-grown Hammers in the glorious 2–0 victory against TSV Munich 1860 in the 1965 European Cup Winners' Cup final. Striker Geoff Hurst rated Jack as one of West Ham's best performers on the night, along with Moore, goalkeeper Jim Standen and two-goal hero Alan Sealey.

Three members of that side would return to Wembley to win football's ultimate prize in July 1966 and Burkett harboured serious regret that he didn't also appear in England's 4–2 World Cup final win over West Germany. 'I felt at the time that I was a better player than Ray Wilson, the left-back, because I'd had the success in the previous two years and was at the peak of my career. You have to be confident in your own ability, but he got selected and good luck to him.'

Jack believes he did his England chances no favours prior to the World Cup when he and colleagues Ronnie Boyce and John Sissons opted out of an Under-23 game in favour of touring America with West Ham. 'The club came first and none of us got selected after that.'

With an appearance in the 5–3 aggregate League Cup final defeat against West Bromwich Albion in March 1966, plus losing semi-finals in the same competition against Leicester City in 1963–64 and WBA again in 1966–67, the defender had packed in more drama than most players see in a lifetime. He'd hardly had time to pause for breath – and his body knew it.

Burkett's back started to play up not long after his World Cup disappointment. Sidelined through injury and lack of form for much of 1966–67 and the following season, he found it tough getting his place back in the side and, somewhat rashly, asked Greenwood for a transfer. It was the impetuous action of a successful young man with a sore back and a bruised ego – and one he regretted making. 'I made a mistake. I was feeling bad about being left out, so I asked to be put on the list. Ron Greenwood said: "Okay then, if you want to go."

'Ron let me go (to Charlton Athletic, for £10,000) but that opened the door at left-back for John Charles, then Frank Lampard, just as it had opened up for me when John Lyall got injured. You live and learn, but it was nice to be associated with a West Ham side that won things.'

11

(COCKNEY) REBEL WITH A CAUSE: Brian Dear

Born: 18 September 1943; Plaistow, London
Debut: v. Wolves (a), 29 August 1962
Apps/Goals: 85/39
Final app.: v. Chelsea (a), 19 December 1970

FORMER WEST HAM BOSS JOHN LYALL ONCE REFERRED TO AN OLD expression that 'there aren't too many 28-year-old teddy boys' when emphasising that players eventually grow up. If ever a West Ham player defiantly personified that rock 'n' roll spirit of rebellion then it was Brian Dear. But while he'd flick through the Bill Haley and Elvis 45s with young team-mate John Charles at his local record shop, Dear's style was less hotrods and hotdogs and more Cortinas and chips as he resisted the demands of the establishment and conformed to nobody's rules but his own.

Dear did his rebel-rousing in a burst of fury during a few short, hedonistic years before imploding from view. By the time he did get to 28 years of age, his professional career was over and he strutted headlong into the pub trade. Installed behind the bar, his longstanding taste for alcohol dragged him into a whirlpool of self-indulgence that eventually required him to show a determination in recovery that most felt he never illustrated during his playing years.

Dear played his football – as he lived his life – his own way. 'I had a mind of my own and I've not changed,' he insists. 'When we trained I used to lump people. And I played as I trained. I didn't take any shit from people. Nobody ever kicked me around because I wouldn't allow anyone to.

'I once had a row with Harry Redknapp, then our winger. He hit me on the chin and I just stood there, so Harry went: "Shit, that was my best punch!" I just laughed and said: "Fuck off, Harry, leave me alone." Then there was the time I knocked out Liverpool defender Tommy Smith. Believe me, he never got up.'

As a youngster Dear scored goals for fun – despite playing as a left-winger – and after impressing at schoolboy level with East Ham (alongside future Hammer Ronnie Boyce), Essex (with Martin Peters), London and England, he learned his trade the hard way as a groundstaff boy in West Ham's Metropolitan League side under the stewardship of Ernie Gregory. 'It was a good upbringing,' he says. 'You'd play against sides such as the Metropolitan Police and they'd kick lumps out of you. We were just 15 or 16 years old but they took no prisoners. A bloke called Gus Simmons played for Tonbridge and after I went by him one day he said: "Oi, do you want to be a footballer? Because if you go past me again I'll break your fucking legs." It was hard.' Except the scoring goals bit.

Brian may not have registered goals in his first six full appearances during the 1962–63 and 1963–64 seasons, but his career took off when deployed up front during the 1964–65 campaign. Up until that point he'd had to show patience and he admits: 'I used to watch from the sidelines hoping the team wouldn't win. I was sitting there at Wembley in 1964 hoping they wouldn't win the FA Cup final – it was just professional jealousy.'

Having been told by manager Ron Greenwood that he had one more season to prove himself as he lagged behind strikers Geoff Hurst and Johnny Byrne in the pecking order, the turning point in Dear's career came when asked to fill in for the injured Byrne in a league game against Sunderland in March 1965. 'Ernie Gregory told me that Ron wanted to see me. I thought I was going to get a bollocking because it was only a few days after my row with Redknapp. But Ron told me I was playing against Sunderland and I scored both our goals in a 3–2 defeat. I was in the bath after the game when Ron came in and said: "Have you got a passport?" I told him I did and he said: "You're coming to Lausanne with us." I told him I wasn't going to Europe unless I was playing but I did and scored the first goal in our 2–1 win. I couldn't stop scoring after that.'

Another two goals a week later in the return leg against Lausanne helped take the Hammers through to the semi-finals of the European Cup Winners' Cup and confirmed Dear's graduation. In all, he scored 14 times in 15 games that season

– a phenomenal return during his first proper run in the team. 'Anyone will tell you I was the greediest fucker around – shoot on sight. I either scored funny goals or spectacular goals. You see, I wasn't manufactured like Geoff Hurst. Ron Greenwood turned him into a centre-forward and did an unbelievable job. But I was a natural and didn't have to work at things because they weren't hard for me.'

A combination of taking his talent for granted and enjoying the good life was never going to help Dear in the long run. But in 1965 he could do no wrong. His five goals in 20 minutes in the 6–1 win against West Bromwich Albion in April is still a record while a month later he played a starring role in the European Cup Winners' Cup final. Brian – just 21 at the time – was earning £30 a week but bagged £800 for playing in the Wembley win over TSV Munich 1860. 'I loved it even more because I was a local lad,' he says. 'But that night was amazing when you consider all the big nights when we used to go out and enjoy ourselves – we just had a small function at Wembley and then went home.'

Dear is the first to admit that he celebrated success more than most of his colleagues. He says: 'Martin Peters, Geoff Hurst and I were all good mates but they did different things. I was a roughneck from the area. Some of us used to go to the pub after training because there was nothing else to do. If you had a few drinks you could run it off in training the next day. I wouldn't say I'd regularly go in with a hangover but if I did I wouldn't have been the only one. There weren't many days when we didn't go out for a beer. And after games we'd go to the Black Lion in Plaistow. We celebrated after every game – win or lose, go on the booze.

'In those days there'd be celebrities such as Jimmy Tarbuck, Kenny Lynch, Max Bygraves and Eric Sykes hanging round the local pub. And there was a little clique, including 'Budgie' Byrne, Eddie Bovington, Johnny Charles, Bobby Moore and me who used to get invited to various dos in the West End. We always knew how to behave, although there was one night when I went to see the singer Tom Jones and my trousers ended up around my ankles.'

Brian believed that everything was going to fall into place after his initial burst of success, but he failed to maintain momentum. The fact that he still wasn't guaranteed a starting place in the Hammers line-up only served to demotivate him but he maintains that he had a decent relationship with Ron Greenwood.

'Ron could handle me – the only one who could. He could be hard if he wanted to be. But he never came into the dressing room shouting and hollering at people, he'd come and talk to you. All I used to say to him was that you've got to have different characters in your side. I played one week, then turned up for the next match with my gear for an overnight stay and wasn't on the team sheet. I kicked the door and bashed the table but Ron just said: "Listen, Stag, you're still playing in the reserves." He was a fine and tender man. He got hurt easily. He didn't like the hangers on and if people took liberties with his players he used to get upset.'

After two poor years Dear returned to form with 16 goals in 30 games during the 1967–68 season. However, with Hurst and Peters topping the Hammers' goal charts for the fourth successive year in 1968–69, his opportunities remained limited. Fittingly, he scored in his first farewell game for West Ham in a 1–1 draw at Leicester on 1 February 1969 before making a £25,000 move to Fulham.

Thirteen games and seven goals later, Brian was on the move again, this time to West Ham's south-east London rivals Millwall. 'I hated it at Millwall. I used to turn up every day, have a mouthful of hot water, go and see the doctor and be told to go home because of my temperature.'

Released by Millwall in the summer of 1970, Dear – at just 26 – was on the dole and playing his football at non-league Woodford Town. But Ron Greenwood slung his former pupil one last lifeline. 'I was over at the West Ham training ground one day and Ernie Gregory said: "Ron wants you." I thought he was going to tell me not to keep hanging around but he said: "We miss a character here, somebody to make us laugh. How would you like to come back?"'

The overweight Dear got himself fit and impressed enough in the reserves to win himself a recall for the home game against Tottenham on 17 October. But he failed to score in four games and he admits: 'The spark seemed to have gone then. Before I'd have ripped the net out with the few chances I was getting. And then we had the Blackpool nightclub incident and that finished me.'

Dear's well-publicised late-night drink with good friends Bobby Moore, Jimmy Greaves and Clyde Best – the day before an FA Cup tie in January 1971 – was one too many for somebody sitting in the last-chance saloon. But Brian's nose had already been put out of joint. 'We had a team meeting the day before the game and Ron had the cheek to say he was playing Clyde Best up front because he needed someone to show a bit of strength. I thought: "You make me die. I've knocked people out for this club."'

After leaving the club in 1971, Dear became a publican and continued to exploit his larger-than-life character. 'When all you've ever done is play in front of a crowd, you like an audience – whether it's big or small. And I had an excellent constitution for taking a drink. At its very worst I was doing a bottle of brandy and a bottle of port before having anything else in the day.

'When you're an alcoholic, you don't realise what you're doing to yourself. But you also don't realise what you're doing to other people. You don't realise that your kids are frightened of you or that your wife won't go out with you in case you suddenly turn and start wanting to fight people. It went on for a long time.'

On Boxing Day in 1992 Dear realised that a radical change of lifestyle was needed. He quit the booze, ignoring Alcoholics Anonymous to rely purely on his own iron will. 'It's been easy,' he insists. 'Everything comes easily to me.'

In 2001 he sold his European Cup Winners' Cup shirt and the ball from his five-goal game against West Brom to West Ham for their planned museum. His European medal, meanwhile, disappeared during a burglary on his home but Dear has never been sentimental about trinkets – although he loves the fact that he was nominated for and received the title of Freeman of the City of London. 'Geoff Hurst ain't got one of those,' he beams.

PART TWO

Greenwood's Influence

12

THE FRUIT OF WALLY'S LABOUR:
The 1963 FA Youth Cup final

AT THE THIRD ATTEMPT, WEST HAM'S YOUTH TEAM HAD DONE IT.
Manchester United in 1957, then Blackburn Rovers in 1959, had twice broken the
hearts of Hammers' kids in the FA Youth Cup final. But in 1963 all the effort that
had gone into the development of talent at Upton Park paid off. Liverpool were
beaten 6–5 over two legs by a West Ham side featuring a future manager in Harry
Redknapp, a true boy wonder in John Sissons and one of the first black players to
make his mark in the English game, skipper John Charles.

All three played their part in a dramatic victory in which a 3–1 deficit from the
first leg at Anfield was sensationally overturned under the lights in east London.
The undisputed star of the moment was rampant striker Martin Britt, who bagged
five goals, four with his head. Says Sissons: 'I've never seen manager Ron
Greenwood smile or laugh so much. He was overjoyed after the second leg.
Liverpool's boss Bill Shankly called us a bunch of animals afterwards. I don't think
any London team had ever been called that – all the animals were in the north. It
was an incredible, incredible game.'

Keen to ensure his doctrines were being adopted at all levels, Greenwood
tended to take over the running of the youth side for cup games. At all other times
Jim Barrett Jnr – son of 1930s Hammers legend 'Big Jim' Barrett and a former
player himself – ran the side. Yet if the credit for the 1963 victory lay anywhere, it
was surely with Wally St Pier.

Arguably, the legendary chief scout was more crucial to the development of
youth products at West Ham in the 1950s, '60s and early '70s than anyone at the
club. Without his magical eye for potential and the hours of work he dedicated to
establishing a no-stone-unturned scouting network, there would have been no FA

Youth Cup victory in 1963. In fact, West Ham fans might never have come to regard Bobby Moore, Geoff Hurst and Martin Peters as their own had it not been for St Pier.

Born in Beacontree Heath, Essex, Wally was a centre-half for West Ham for six seasons in the 1930s. Manager Charlie Paynter appointed him as chief scout soon after he quit playing and over the next four decades his sixth sense would ensure that the club benefited from a remarkably consistent stream of talent. Not every boy made it; some would jump ship to other clubs' youth schemes. But the hit-rate of this universally loved man was quite incredible.

So what motivated St Pier? Jim Barrett Jnr wonders if his tireless devotion to fulfilling the dreams of East End schoolboys might have had something to do with a tragedy he was affected by from his pre-scouting days. 'I remember my father saying that Wally had told him about a very sad accident. These two boys were playing at the bottom of a garden and one of them drowned in a ditch.'

Barrett continues: 'He was a fantastic man, a gentleman. Wally had his ear to the ground in the local area and knew all the kids coming through. We even had a couple of schoolteachers working with the boys. They would know what he wanted.'

St Pier's work went way beyond watching schoolboy football. If he thought a lad showed promise he'd keep constant tabs on him and get to know him personally. 'He would always talk to you as if you were a friend,' says Barrett. 'And he'd spend hours trying to sell the club to people. Other clubs had scouts, but West Ham were way ahead of everybody else.'

Interviewed in the 1960s, St Pier was asked what it was he looked for in a young player. 'Football intelligence and the ability of the boy to read a game,' he said. 'If the character of the boy is not right, you don't pursue it.' In the same article he cited not Bobby Moore as the find who'd excited him most on first viewing ('he was none too impressive, but I felt there was something to work on'), but Trevor Dawkins. Wing-half Dawkins – 'a real cracker' – was also rated extremely highly by Barrett, his A-team manager. Although he would shine in the 1963 Youth Cup final, the Essex youngster would go on to make just six appearances for the first team.

Dawkins' career suffered in part from intense competition for places during the club's golden era. Yet seven other members of that Youth Cup-winning side would go on to make more than 25 appearances for West Ham, so upholding the incredible star-spotting reputation of Wally St Pier, who died in 1989.

13

THE TRAILBLAZER: John Charles

Born: 20 September 1944; Canning Town, London
Debut: v. Blackburn (h), 4 May 1963
Apps/Goals: 142/2
Final app.: v. Leeds United (h), 2 April 1970

FOR A SUN-KISSED TROPICAL ISLAND, SEE THE GREY CONCRETE OF Canning Town. For laid-back striker, see aggressive defender. For West Ham's first black player (mixed race to be precise), see not Clyde Best, but Cockney John Charles.

Unquestionably, Best was the first truly high-profile black footballer in the British game. But as captain of the Hammers' 1963 FA Youth Cup-winning side – six years before Best arrived from the Bermudan league and took up lodgings at the Charles residence – it was John who was the real trailblazer.

Charles' earliest football memory was of kicking a ball higher and harder than any of his school pals as they ran amuck through the post-war dereliction of the East End. It was the same propensity for giving it some welly that so impressed West Ham manager Ted Fenton once 'Charlo' had made the dream jump from Hammers-supporting London and Essex Schoolboy star to groundstaff in December 1959. Says Charles: 'Ted called me into his office and said: "Hello John, glad you're with the club. You'll get a lot of name calling in this game. I like the way you play, so just keep kicking 'em and you'll be alright."'

Racial abuse was a harsh inevitability of the times, as Martin Britt, Charles' youth-team colleague, recalls. 'I can remember playing for the reserves at Ipswich when somebody in the crowd made a remark like "You nigger!" to John. Right-back Johnny Bond went into the stand, got hold of this bloke and said: "If I ever hear you say that again . . ." There weren't many black players in the game but we never saw John as being black.'

Woe betide anyone who shouted insults within earshot of Charles' mum, either. Says John: 'When she heard people call me a black bastard she used to say: "Oi, don't you call him a black bastard. I'm the only one here who can call him a black bastard." She was great, my mum.' Her son's skin was thick, as well as black. 'When I was a kid at school I was pretty fucking hard. If you're the only black kid in the school someone's always going to start on you, but they soon left me alone.'

Charles took to life on the groundstaff like a duck to water. Covered in paint and hands full of splinters, football sometimes seemed the last thing West Ham wanted to teach him. Yet he must have been learning something in Ernie Gregory's Metropolitan League side because, a little over three years after joining the club, he was skippering West Ham to their first FA Youth Cup final victory in three attempts. Suitably impressed with the centre-half's development, Fenton's successor Ron Greenwood awarded John and youth team colleagues Britt and John Sissons their first-team debuts (Charles stepping in for Ken Brown) in a 1–0 home defeat by Blackburn at the tail-end of that 1962–63 season.

So began seven years of stop-start first-team involvement, John playing in many classic games but always facing quality competition whether at half-back, centre-back or full-back. Highlights included appearing in all but the third round as West Ham reached the semi-final of the European Cup Winners' Cup in 1965–66, succumbing to Borussia Dortmund, and being in the side which notched the club's record First Division victory, an 8–0 rout of Sunderland in October 1968. Although highlight is probably the wrong word, he also scored West Ham's consolation goal in a breathless 6–1 home defeat by Manchester United in May 1967, which sealed the league championship for the Reds.

Charles' uncompromising style was rarely less than wholehearted, but as the seasons passed a troublesome hamstring proved an increasing bind. He was hampered too by an eagerness to play as hard off the pitch – often as part of Bobby Moore's social crew – as he could on it. 'I've spilt more booze down my tie than most people drink in their entire lives,' he says. It was during one post-match soirée that *our* John Charles met *the* John Charles – and possibly even saved the legendary Leeds, Juventus and Wales striker's life. 'We used to go to the Black Lion near the ground after games. That's where I first met him. We shook hands, had a good drink, then I took him to a party in a block of flats in Canning Town.

'I didn't fancy this party after a while, so I said: "Come on, let's piss off." We did and a short while later the flats fell down. One side of the block just collapsed.' The two Johns had narrowly escaped what became known as the Ronan Point disaster, a tragic incident which claimed three lives.

After Jack Burkett's form fell away dramatically in 1966–67, Charles slotted in at left-back. He played 35 games that season, 23 the next and a personal best 39 times in 1968–69. Regular involvement was what he craved, even if that meant concealing misgivings about aspects of Greenwood's coaching. 'He used to confuse me a bit with his tactics. He'd talk and talk and talk and I'd be thinking: "What's he fucking talking about?"

'We played a friendly in Germany one time and they had a bloody good player running rings round us. John Cushley, our new centre-half from Celtic, put him right out the game. Greenwood said to him at half-time: "John, you're playing well, but leave the rough stuff out." After the game Mooro and I were pissing ourselves at this. Bobby says: "He's bought this geezer Cushley to stop people. Now he's stopped one, he doesn't want him to." Cushley was a tough guy, but Greenwood wanted him to play it pretty and he couldn't do it. He never made another tackle for West Ham.'

As a new decade dawned, first-team tackles by Charles were becoming collectors items too, due largely to hamstring stress. It was the same problem that eventually ended the career of his brother Clive, a full-back who had also joined West Ham by then. Clive's injury woe wasn't exactly helped by his elder sibling. Recalls John: 'I played with him in the reserves against Chelsea once. There was me, Cushley, Brian Dear – all the boys in there sweating booze. Everyone was having a right old tear up in the penalty area. There was a big heap of players – legs, arms and everything all trying to get the ball. After a while I got up and just went "Bang!" and kicked this leg. Everyone stood up and there's my brother. I'd kicked Clive's fucking leg. He was rolling on the floor in agony and I'm thinking: "Christ almighty. All those legs and I kick his."'

After the 1969–70 season, Greenwood attempted to trade John and midfielder Peter Bennett for Orient's Tommy Taylor. John agreed on the premise that Orient's boss, ex-Hammer Jimmy Bloomfield, would make it worth his while and asked for a £4,000 signing-on fee. After Bloomfield retorted with words to the effect that: 'The fucking club ain't got £4,000,' a crestfallen Charles made the shock decision to quit the game altogether, at the age of just 26.

Instead he was going to work for his in-laws' greengrocery business. Colleagues and supporters were dismayed by his decision, but injuries were becoming a nightmare and anyway, market traders drove flashier cars than many footballers in the early 1970s. 'My first week's wages was £200 in my hand,' he says. 'My wage at West Ham was £65 a week. I thought: "Aye aye, this is lovely."'

Charles made an effortless transition from dressing room to Spitalfields market in the City of London. The thing he missed most about football – the banter – was every bit as good and generally life for John and wife Carol was sweet. At least it was until the 1980s, when the big supermarkets started to put the squeeze on small traders. 'From having bundles of dough, being a flash bastard in the pub, all of a sudden I was sitting in the corner wondering where my mates had gone. It just went to my head. I became frightened, wouldn't go out and eventually ended up in the cracker factory.'

One night John escaped from the psychiatric hospital, walked home and hid in his bedroom. An ambulance arrived to take him back, but when the paramedic scurried back down the stairs and announced that John had a pick-axe handle beside him, events turned farcical. 'I had it beside the bed because before I'd been sent away I'd become frightened of monsters and just wanted a tool beside me. Anyway, my mate said he'd come up and talk to me. He started chatting and asking me where I got the pick-axe handle from because he really needed one. I said: "Why?" He said: "Because if I shape it a little bit I can use it as an extension on me paint roller." I'm thinking to myself: "Is it him who's fucking mad or me?"'

Charles eventually came to terms with his psychiatric problems but, in a dramatic life of ups and downs, the biggest blow of all came in 2000 when he was diagnosed with lung cancer. He would tackle the condition with great courage and without ever losing his sense of humour – which is more or less the way this unique youth product approached the game during a patchy but hugely significant West Ham career.

14

TRIUMPH AND TRAGEDY: Martin Britt

Born: 17 January 1946; Leigh-on-Sea, Essex
Debut: v. Blackburn Rovers (h), 4 May 1963
Apps/Goals: 26/7
Final app.: v. Leeds United (a), 5 February 1966

NOT TOO MANY WEST HAM PLAYERS CAN CLAIM TO HAVE SCORED the winning goal at Manchester United. Or scored four goals in a cup final to stick a pot in the Hammers' trophy cabinet. Or played football for nearly three years with a broken knee. But such is the case with Martin Britt.

The striker played just 26 first-team games for West Ham but his contribution and commitment to the club's cause should not be overlooked – especially with his legs carrying the damage to this very day.

Having shared his debut with John Charles and John Sissons in a 1–0 home defeat by Blackburn in May 1963, Martin was making just his third appearance when asked to face the likes of Bobby Charlton, Denis Law and former Hammer Noel Cantwell at Old Trafford on 26 October later that year. Manchester United were top of the league, having won every home game that season, but Britt struck in the 36th minute after a well-rehearsed move involving midfielder Ronnie Boyce to claim a famous victory.

Remembers Martin: 'It was fantastic that we'd scored a goal through something manager Ron Greenwood had had us practising that week. We never got a kick after that but we managed to hold out despite Alan Sealey getting carried off and leaving us down to ten men for over half an hour.'

Scoring goals came naturally to Britt. Being brought up in Leigh-on-Sea, he started to make a name for himself with Essex and London Schoolboys before attracting the eye of West Ham's chief scout Wally St Pier. Says Martin: 'Wally was the reason I signed for West Ham United. He was like a father figure to me. I could have signed for most of the London clubs – including Arsenal and Tottenham. Spurs used to take on 30 or 40 boys a year, Arsenal 14 or 15, while West Ham only signed five of us. That made me feel that they'd look after us and give us time to develop.'

Former manager Ted Fenton was so keen on Britt that he tried to sign him for his next club, Southend United, after being sacked by West Ham. 'I think he made an offer to my parents that would have helped them out. But my mum and dad were happy to let me sign for whatever club I wanted to, which was still West Ham.'

Britt quickly established himself, winning three England youth caps and more or less going straight into the Hammers' reserves because of his height. 'I was called "The Guv'nor",' he says. 'As groundstaff boys we used to clean up after the senior pros had gone home and I had to allocate the work. We used to have a lot of fun. Johnny Sissons, John Charles, Trevor Dawkins, Johnny Dryden, Bill Kitchener and I were all good friends.'

All six played in both legs of the FA Youth Cup final against Liverpool in 1963. The 3–1 first-leg defeat at Anfield left West Ham with an uphill battle but the side were left with an almost impossible task after going 2–1 down in the return match at Upton Park. Against the odds, Britt claimed centre-stage with four goals – all headers – to secure an unlikely 6–5 victory. 'West Ham's hero in a match full of valour, courage and ruthless ruggedness was chunky chappy Britt who took this game by the scruff of its neck,' declared the *Stratford Express*.

It was Britt's hat-trick header – which levelled the aggregate score at 5–5 – which caused a storm of protest. 'Harry Redknapp sent the cross over, I went up to head the ball and took their keeper at the same time. He finished up – along with the ball – in the back of the net. Tommy Smith was my room-mate for England youth games and he never spoke to me again. When I got the winner with three minutes left the crowd went absolutely crazy.'

Such delirium was to be in short supply during Britt's career, however. Having absorbed the influence of manager Greenwood who took a close interest in the development of youngsters – 'I used to listen to everything Ron said. It was all about timing and laying the ball off properly,' he remembers – Martin's potential was to be ruined after collecting an injury at just 18 years of age.

First-team opportunities were always going to be limited with strikers Geoff Hurst and record-signing Johnny Byrne ahead of him in the pecking order but Britt still managed four goals in 11 outings during the 1963–64 season. Then disaster struck. Remembers Martin: 'During training I got pulled down and sat on my right knee. I went to get up but I couldn't straighten my leg. I was carried off and every time I bent my knee I had a terrible pain.

'A Harley Street specialist told me that I'd damaged my cruciate ligaments and gave me a series of exercises to do but didn't suggest an operation. It took me about six weeks to play again but from that point on the leg never felt right. I had treatment virtually every day because the knee used to swell up like a balloon. And I used to drive home from games with my left foot on the accelerator because I couldn't bear to have my right leg touching it. There was obviously something wrong but I carried on like that until I got transferred to Blackburn.'

Britt failed to play a single first-team game during the 1964–65 season but somehow managed to make 14 appearances the following campaign, scoring three times. 'Because I was left-footed I got away with it, but it got to the point where I couldn't jump with my right leg,' he says.

Suddenly, a move to Blackburn materialised. 'Greenwood got a bit peculiar with me. He said he just wanted to give me a rest but it went on for a few weeks and he wouldn't say anything to me. Ron went down in my estimation. I said: "If you're not happy with me, would it be better if I moved on?" But he said: "There's no way you're going anywhere." Suddenly I got told that a club had made an offer for me – would I be interested in talking to them? I realised that, although Ron was a wonderful coach, he wasn't the greatest man-manager. He did hurt me a little bit.'

Britt initially rejected Rovers' overtures but said: 'If you give me X amount I'll consider it.' The Lancashire club acquiesced to the player's demands and, with a transfer fee of £25,000 agreed, the 20-year-old Britt signed on the dotted line.

Martin may have moved north with both his nose and right knee out of joint, but hopes of a fresh start were dashed when he broke down after just a handful of appearances. 'Unfortunately, they didn't have a full-time physio, just somebody who came along on match days. So suddenly I wasn't getting daily treatment.'

Britt was sent for an exploratory operation and recalls: 'The specialist came to see me afterwards and said: "You've broken your right knee." He told me he'd removed a chunk of bone and that it looked like it had been there for three or four years. I had chronic arthritis in the knee and was told never to do anything on my legs again.'

Not surprisingly, Blackburn felt that the Hammers had ripped them off. Says Britt: 'The clubs had a terrible row about it because Rovers wanted their money back. Brian Dear recently told me that he could remember West Ham having to give some of the money back.'

Without an insurance scheme in place, the PFA took up Martin's claim for retirement and he received an ex-gratia payment of £250. 'Because of my disability it went to the industrial injuries court and I had to attend a hearing in Westminster as West Ham refused to pass on my medical records. In the end they were produced and they proved that I'd been injured for three years,' he says.

Britt was awarded a lifelong pension but he subsequently refused the payments because 'I didn't think it morally right to take the money when the injury wasn't affecting my business'.

Martin's Upton Park apprenticeship initially stood him in good stead and he remained at Blackburn for a further 18 months in a coaching capacity. 'Rovers were 20 years behind the times and with my FA coaching badge I was able to come up with all these new ideas.'

Having been encouraged by Greenwood to study, Britt used his education to good effect by establishing his own textile business. Since the late 1980s he's organised golf events for charity – inviting a whole host of former West Ham stars to participate – although his troublesome legs (which required four further operations) prevent him from playing more than 11 holes himself.

He explains: 'I was told that my left leg had been protecting my damaged right leg and now my left is worse than my right. It's in a terrible state.' Rather than think of what might have been, however, Martin has always adopted a positive philosophy. 'People say: "Weren't you unlucky?" but I played for a great club in West Ham, represented my country, got accepted for university and ended up running my own business. I consider myself a lucky man.'

15

'GREATNESS IS HIS FOR THE TAKING': John Sissons

Born: 30 September 1945; Hayes, Middlesex
Debut: v. Blackburn (h), 4 May 1963
Apps/Goals: 265/53
Final app.: v. Arsenal (a), 4 April 1970

JOHN SISSONS' PLACE AT THE TOP TABLE AMONG WEST HAM'S
greatest wingers cannot be questioned. Neither, however, can the fact that he lost
his edge just when he should have been reaching for the stars. He wasn't the first
West Ham player whose powers mysteriously fizzled away and doubtless he won't
be the last.

John puts his fall from grace down to a woeful lack of self-belief. 'I was shy and
immature,' he says. 'Possibly it was the way I was brought up, in the sense that I
didn't have to fight too hard for things. I had natural talent, but character-wise I
wasn't an angry player who would kick back if someone kicked me. I shouldn't
have taken the nonsense I stood for.'

Club scouts virtually camped outside the Sissons residence in suburban
Middlesex in the late-1950s. Cheetah-fast, John excelled for his county side and
became the first lad from his area to play for England Schoolboys, scoring four
goals on his debut. Manchester United, Wolves and his favourites Chelsea were all
on his trail but, for such a shy kid, kindness and trust were going to prove far more
important as a means of getting him to sign up than any bullish ego-flattering.

Charlie Faulkner, a west London foot soldier for West Ham chief scout Wally St
Pier, had the necessary warmth in abundance. 'It was my allegiance to Charlie that

made me go to West Ham. He lived in Hayes and used to pick me up from school and drive me over to east London for training sessions. He'd buy me fish and chips on the way home, put five shillings in my pocket, things like that. He made it easy for me to go to West Ham.'

Within a year of joining as an apprentice professional in 1962, Sissons became integral to the success of the youth side and also starred in England's 1963 Little World Cup victory. He would eventually represent his country at every level except full international, although he came tantalisingly close during the 1964–65 season. 'England boss Alf Ramsey had rung our manager Ron Greenwood to say he wanted me to play in a game, but Ron in his wisdom said he thought I was a bit young and not ready for it.' Geoff Hurst, who owed so many of his vintage West Ham goals to Sissons' pinpoint near-post crosses, firmly believed the winger deserved to play for England. In his autobiography, *1966 and All That*, Hurst wrote: 'John was one of the truly outstanding young talents of that generation. He had a wonderful left foot and the sort of pace that Ron Greenwood believed put him in the same class as George Best.'

In May 1963, Sissons played in the thrilling FA Youth Cup final against Liverpool, his crosses helping Martin Britt's forehead knock the life out of the Merseysiders in the 6–5 aggregate victory. He would go on to play more senior games than any other member of that side. 'I climbed so fast,' Sissons says. 'I only had a short period of washing dressing rooms and cleaning boots. Then all of a sudden I was a first-team player and people were cleaning my boots.'

Aged 17, he debuted in a 1–0 home defeat to Blackburn Rovers prior to the Youth Cup final. In May 1964, with just 23 games under his belt, Sissons would enter the history books in the 3–2 FA Cup final win over Preston as the youngest player ever to score in the great Wembley showcase. That feat made him the centre of attention as West Ham's open-topped bus crawled through the East End streets the following day. His left-sided colleague Bobby Moore had become one of his biggest fans. In *Bobby Moore: The Life and Times of a Sporting Hero*, Moore observed: 'John Sissons kept threatening to be the best left-winger on Earth. When he came into the league side as a teenager Johnny was pure gold.'

Like so many of his colleagues, Sissons regarded the 1964 FA Cup victory as a disjointed affair, which paled against the side's performance in the European Cup Winners' Cup final the following year. 'I had a particularly good season in 1964–65 and scored some vital goals in that cup run,' says John. 'One of them was away against Spain's Real Zaragoza in the semi-final. We'd won the first leg 2–1, but we were 1–0 down in the second game when I got a breakaway from the halfway line. I got to the edge of the 18-yard box and just hit it with my right foot. It was very unusual for me to strike a ball with my right, but it flew into the bottom corner. That goal got us the draw, so we were through to the final.'

The stunning 2–0 win over TSV Munich 1860 at Wembley earned John his fourth winners' medal for England and West Ham in two years. It would be his last as a Hammer, but there'd be plenty more classic games in the pipeline as Greenwood's attacking entertainers went about cornering the market in extravagant scorelines. 'It was wonderful free-flowing football to play,' says Sissons, who played 51 times in both 1964–65 and 1965–66. 'Against Leicester City (in a 1–0 home win in 1968) they took a corner, our goalie claimed it and threw it out to me. I moved 40 to 50 yards down the line, crossed and Martin Peters headed it into the back of the net. Two moves and the ball was in. When Leeds United were absolutely unbeatable I scored a hat-trick against them in 30 minutes in a League Cup game in 1966 at Upton Park and we beat them 7–0. That was West Ham.'

Being slightly built, Sissons got his fair share of clobberings from opponents who were fast enough, or cunning enough, to catch him. But he had two things other than his speed to fall back on against bloodthirsty defenders: one-touch intuition and Bobby Moore. 'Bobby used to say: "John, if you're in trouble, just give it to me. Don't worry about it." It was just give and go. You never held onto it. We worked week-in, week-out on one-touch football. 'Budgie' Byrne, our striker, was always there; Bobby was always there.

'As the game wore on the full-back would realise I wasn't going to hold the ball so they'd have no opportunity to clatter me. Then I'd find myself with a little bit of extra space, an extra two or three yards to hold it and have a go at them.'

Astonishingly, John admits that even when he was an automatic choice, when comparisons were being made between him and legendary left-footed Hungarian Ferenc Puskas, he would stand and stare in incredulity at seeing his name on the team sheet. He desperately needed someone at the club to tell him he was worthy, especially when West Ham's mid-1960s golden era gave way to season after season of under-achievement. 'As time went on, Saturdays became a little bit of a trauma for me. I loved training and the midweek practice matches, but come Saturday the pressure had become so great that I ended up not wanting to make mistakes.' Bobby Moore cited John's 'boy wonder' emergence as part of the problem. 'Ron Greenwood was still calling him young John when he was 25.'

By the end of the decade – just six seasons after a pre-1964 FA Cup final publication had declared that 'greatness is his for the taking' – Sissons' confidence was shot. 'I wasn't very happy at all. We'd been having a tough time and I'd personally been having a terrible time.' In the spring of 1970, after a miserable team meeting following another lacklustre performance, he went up to Greenwood's office and overcame his shyness to express his discontent. In principle both parties agreed that a move was probably the right way forward. A move away from London, that was. 'The end of the 1969–70 season arrived and I believe that Bill Nicholson, the Tottenham manager, came in for me. I honestly thought Ron did not want me to stay in London in case I suddenly hit form. Then Sheffield Wednesday came in for me. Ron said: "That's fine, John, you can go."'

After three happy seasons in Yorkshire, he had a disappointing spell at Norwich City. 'Ted MacDougall (who'd recently failed to fit in at West Ham) and myself never saw eye to eye.' A fleeting moment of joy came when he made a return to Upton Park on New Year's Day, 1974. 'Norwich lost 4–2 but I had an absolute blinder. Ron came up to me after the game and said: "You still haven't lost it. You could open a tin of peas with that left foot."'

Fittingly, Sissons ended his career in English football in 1974–75 at Chelsea, the team he'd supported as a lad. Then it was off to build his fortune in South Africa, a path earlier trodden by his good pal Johnny Byrne. The Sissons business empire, with motor products at its core, would eventually grow to include a guesthouse run by his wife a couple of hours outside Cape Town. John built a bar festooned with Hammers memorabilia to remind him of the best days of his football career. One year a West Ham fan holidayed at the guesthouse and he would always remember the look on the man's face as it dawned on him that his lager was being poured by an Upton Park icon.

If only the shy Sisso of the '60s had tapped into the awe in which fans and colleagues held him, West Ham might have seen many more years of vintage wing-play from one of the club's most naturally-gifted players ever.

16

THE YOUNG AT HEART: Dave Bickles

Born: 6 April 1944; West Ham, London
Debut: v. Liverpool (a), 14 September 1963
Apps/Goals: 28/0
Final app.: v. Manchester City (h), 13 May 1967

MOMENTS BEFORE WEST HAM'S UEFA CUP TIE AGAINST STEAUA Bucharest on 4 November 1999, nearly 25,000 people in Upton Park stood in silence in memory of former Hammers Johnny Byrne and Dave Bickles who'd both recently passed away. Each had last kicked a ball for the club 32 years earlier but while Byrne's goalscoring exploits will be remembered far more than the 28 appearances made by Bickles, it was the latter who remained involved with the Hammers until cancer claimed his life.

As a part-time coach with the club's academy programme, Dave helped in the footballing development of nine-to-twelve-year-olds – as he also did in running the Newham Schoolboys side and as full-time sports master at Brampton Manor school in East Ham.

As a player Bickles gained youth honours with England and rose through West Ham's ranks to make his first-team debut during the club's participation in the American Soccer League tournament in the summer of 1963. A central defender, Dave made his league debut alongside Bobby Moore in the 2–1 win at Liverpool in September of that year – a victory the Hammers would fail to repeat in his lifetime – but the form of Ken Brown initially kept his first-team opportunities at a premium.

'It meant a lot to him to play for West Ham,' says Linda Bickles, who married Dave in 1964 after a four-year courtship. 'He was West Ham through and through. He'd have loved to have played more games for the club but it was a shame he was so unfortunate with injury.'

Bickles made 13 appearances during the 1965–66 season, during which he partnered Moore in successive wins against Arsenal (2–1), Tottenham (2–0) and Manchester United (3–2) at the tail-end of the campaign. But his long-term prospects were damaged following a clash with Liverpool's Ian St John during a 1–1 draw at Upton Park at the beginning of the following season. Says Linda: 'Dave fell and dislocated his shoulder but it wasn't properly diagnosed. It turned out that a piece of bone had actually broken off. It should have been looked at straightaway but West Ham were very neglectful. It was only when Dave moved to Crystal Palace that he was sent to a specialist and ended up with a steel plate being inserted.'

Bickles returned to action to play just nine more games before joining Palace in October 1967, aged only 23. 'He was choked at leaving West Ham,' says Linda. 'They said Dave wasn't putting enough effort into games but it was literally because of his damaged shoulder. It looked as if he was afraid to tackle but he just couldn't. Palace sorted out the injury but I think it may have restricted his movement because nothing really happened for him after that.'

Dave moved from Palace to Colchester United before later becoming player/manager of Romford in the Southern League and then boss of Collier Row in the Spartan League in the early 1980s. At the same time he became a PE teacher and started work at Brampton Manor. Says Linda: 'West Ham used to send their players into local schools to coach children and Dave just never stopped. He absolutely adored kids.

'He was an excellent coach. If he'd have pushed himself a bit more I think he'd have achieved a lot more as a coach. I kept telling him and others did too, but he was too easy going. He was a very quiet and laid-back person and I think he just became content with what he was doing.'

Hammers youth-team boss Tony Carr, who had known Bickles since they were on West Ham's books together and had invited him to start coaching at the club in the early 1990s, agrees with Linda's sentiments. 'Dave was always content with his lot,' he says. 'He never struck anybody as having any great ambition; he was always happy and comfortable with what he did. But he was a larger-than-life character, always had a smile on his face and was very approachable. I brought him back into the club so that he could put a little bit back into the professional game and the kids loved working with him because he was a nice guy.'

Health concerns first surfaced in 1997 when Dave started to feel unwell. Says Linda: 'We got him to go to the doctor and it turned out that he had cancer in one of his kidneys, which they said wasn't life-threatening because they could take the kidney out and he could live with just one. But when Dave went under the knife the doctors discovered it was too late and that the cancer had spread. They told me he only had three months to live but because he was so fit he lasted another two years.'

Following discussions between the Bickles family and their doctors, it was decided to spare Dave the anguish of knowing how serious the problem really was and how little time he'd actually been given. 'He knew he'd got the cancer in his kidney but I stipulated that he wasn't to know anything else,' says Linda. 'I knew it had spread but the doctors agreed that it was probably best not to tell him too much and ultimately it helped him live longer. Having said that, I often think Dave didn't do himself any favours by lasting those two years because by the end the cancer was everywhere.'

Dave Bickles died on 1 November 1999 and the headmaster of Brampton Manor paid tribute to his service by closing the school for a day. A few days later the Upton Park crowd had the opportunity to show its respect prior to the kick-off against Bucharest. 'I didn't go to the game,' admits Linda. 'I didn't feel up to it because it was too soon after his death. But I insisted that our three sons – Gary, Craig and Glen – went along. And they were glad they did.'

17

BETTER LEYTON THAN NEVER: Peter Bennett

Born: 24 June 1946; Hillingdon, Middlesex
Debut: v. Bolton Wanderers (h), 4 April 1964
Apps/Goals: 47/3
Final app.: v. Arsenal (a), 4 April 1970

PETER BENNETT'S SPIRITUAL HOME MAY BE IN THE EAST END BUT, despite spending nearly ten years at West Ham, he only really found professional contentment after switching to Second Division neighbours Orient.

Bennett left Upton Park as part of the player-plus-cash deal that brought defender Tommy Taylor to the Hammers in October 1970, and he admits: 'From the very first day at Orient I felt more at home. I loved it there and thought it was a fantastic club. Perhaps I just found my level there.'

Peter certainly had a difficult time at West Ham, playing just 47 first-team games across a period of seven seasons after making his debut in April 1964. Having been discovered – along with Middlesex Schoolboys team-mate John Sissons – by scout Charlie Faulkner, Bennett spent his early days at the club as an inside-forward and was part of the team that won the FA Youth Cup in 1963 just before he turned professional. 'They were the best times of my Hammers career,' he says. 'We had some fantastic experiences and they were a great bunch of guys – people like Harry Redknapp, Bill Kitchener, Colin Mackleworth and Johnny Sissons. We were all good mates. A-team boss Jimmy Barrett was a big influence, as was manager Ron Greenwood. But after my youth days were over I didn't really enjoy my time at the club. It wasn't just a case of not getting into the first team; it was also down to personality. I didn't really fit into the scheme of things.'

With the likes of Geoff Hurst, 'Budgie' Byrne, Martin Peters and Brian Dear blocking the attacking positions in the side, it was fortunate that Peter – or 'Les', as he was nicknamed by coach Ernie Gregory, after the former Spurs and West Ham player – could play in a number of roles. 'My preferred position was midfield or at the back, where I eventually ended up playing at Orient after replacing Tommy Taylor.'

His breakthrough came during the 1965–66 season, when he made ten appearances and scored his first goal – in a 6–2 defeat at Chelsea in April. But Peter had written himself into the Hammers' history books when he became the club's first ever substitute during the 2–1 home win against Leeds United on 28 August 1965. After replacing full-back Jack Burkett in the 53rd minute, with the score at 1–1, Bennett made an instant impact when linking up with Hurst to set up the winner. His next appearance came a month later as a starter for the game at Liverpool, in which another substitute made his presence felt. 'In those days you had to be injured to be substituted,' he says. 'We were winning 1–0 at Anfield when their manager Bill Shankly wanted to change things. I can remember him shouting to one of his players: "Oi, you, you're injured!" Geoff Strong came on as a substitute for Chris Lawler and he headed the equaliser!'

Despite his versatility, Bennett still found games hard to come by during the mid-1960s. 'It was a very successful period for the club and there were some fantastic players in the team. We won the Youth Cup in 1963, the FA Cup in 1964, the European Cup Winners' Cup in 1965 and Bobby Moore, Martin Peters and Geoff Hurst won the World Cup with England in 1966. The first day back at pre-season training for those three after the World Cup finals was absolutely amazing with the amount of photographers that turned up. It was an incredible period to be at the place, but after that the team started to break up and it was a difficult time.'

Between the summers of 1966 and 1969 Peter made just 15 appearances as he struggled to gain a foothold in the side. 'I think I lacked confidence,' he admits. 'And the Upton Park crowd could sometimes get on your back. As a player coming into the team you can get unfairly compared to the more established players and some liked to compare me with midfielder Ronnie Boyce – which I didn't think was right because I was a different sort of player. But it's difficult when you're not getting a run of games. When you're just covering for injuries it's much harder to make a long-term impression.'

Peter was also of the view that being a product of the club's youth scheme was not necessarily an advantage. 'I think you're treated a little differently as a homegrown player. Players that have been bought seemed to enjoy a slightly different status, with the carpet being rolled out for them a bit more. I was never content with the situation but there wasn't much that I could do.'

Bennett's best run of games ironically came during his final full season, 1969–70, when he made a dozen appearances – mostly in midfield. He roomed with Trevor Brooking – also struggling to get a regular place in the side at the time – and coincidentally played his last first-team game on the same day of the year as his debut, on the fourth of April. And at the beginning of the following season the move a couple of miles across east London to Orient's Brisbane Road was offered to him. 'The deal was done very quickly,' he recalls. 'I was told that the opportunity to go to Orient was there and within a few days it was done and dusted. At the time I was thinking: "Yeah, this is what I need." From a playing point of view it was the right thing to do.'

Peter spent eight years at the Os until a broken leg ended his playing career in 1978. Since then he's established his own carpentry business, while the family's sporting links continue very successfully in the shape of son Warren, a professional golfer on the European Tour.

18

THE GAMBLER: Harry Redknapp

Born: 2 March 1947; Poplar, London
Debut: v. Sunderland (h), 23 August 1965
Apps/Goals: 175/8
Final app.: v. Liverpool (h), 15 April 1972

FOR MANY, HARRY REDKNAPP EMBODIES THE SPIRIT OF THE EAST END entrepreneur made good through his own instinct and initiative. His first-team appearances as a West Ham player spanned seven years and following his return to Upton Park in the 1990s he spent the same length of time as manager, relying on his ability to duck and dive in difficult circumstances to consolidate the club's position in the Premiership.

He moved into the Hammers hotseat in controversial circumstances, losing the friendship of predecessor Billy Bonds in the process. 'I've got no time for the man,' Bonds concluded. And Redknapp's critics felt it somewhat appropriate that he should lose his job amid similar acrimony at the end of the disappointing 2000–01 campaign in which the team finished 15th in the table.

West Ham's official website may have issued a statement on 9 May 2001 declaring that Harry and the club had 'agreed to part company' but the reality was that he was sacked during a meeting with chairman Terence Brown. 'I was pushed,' confirms Harry. 'I went in to see him and he was upset that I'd told the press that we needed to spend £16m in the transfer market if we were going to get back into the top six or seven of the table the following season. I knew we needed to improve the team and it was a realistic assessment. But he felt I was putting him under pressure and he got the hump about it.'

Money was always going to be at the centre of the dispute. Redknapp had worked a minor miracle during his period in charge, securing three successive top ten finishes (between 1998 and 2000) for only the second time in the club's history and taking them into the UEFA Cup (via the Intertoto Cup) after a second-best-ever fifth placing in 1999. Those achievements came while appearing to make a healthy profit in the transfer market, with Redknapp gambling on bargain-basement deals and operating on a basis of selling one player to recruit three as the club invested heavily in the redevelopment of Upton Park.

Huge profits had been made on the sale of players such as Eyal Berkovic, Slaven Bilic and John Hartson and when the club cashed in on youth product Rio Ferdinand in November 2000 to the tune of £18m – a world record fee for a defender – Redknapp hoped that most of the money would be available for team strengthening. Six players were recruited for just £6.5m as the manager sought to fill out a shallow squad, but with most of the new arrivals failing to impress, chairman Brown felt sufficiently justified in denying Redknapp the chance to spend any further.

The club's official press release following Redknapp's sacking expressed its 'sincere appreciation of all Harry has done' but Brown's tune had changed by the time the official chairman's statement was published in November. Not only did it somehow manage to show losses on transfer dealings over a seven-year period (claiming gross expenditure of £79m compared to a figure of around £55m calculated by supporters) but additionally, in an undisguised attack on the former manager, the report spotlighted some of his flop signings as it attempted to justify Harry's dismissal.

Speaking for the first time about his reaction to Brown's statement, Redknapp says: 'I thought it was disgusting. This was the same man who, just a few days before I left, was offering me a new four-year contract and saying he wanted me to stay at the club for the next ten years. Only he knows what his motives were but whatever they were they were wrong. He can say what he wants but at the end of the day we balanced the books. Having known the man it didn't surprise me, but it did disappoint me and it's soured any relationship I'll ever have with the club again.'

Just a month after Redknapp's departure, West Ham announced the appointment of former player Trevor Brooking as a non-executive director, who wasted little time in being critical of recent signings. 'The club has the seventh or eighth highest wage bill in the Premiership and my view is that we were well short when it came to seeing that reflected in the quality of the squad,' said Brooking. With Redknapp's successor Glenn Roeder also making comments about the squad's lack of talent in depth, it's no surprise to learn that Harry was dismayed that little acknowledgement was made of the restricted circumstances in which he had to work. 'I've been disappointed with lots of people at the club,' he says. 'I guess you find people out in these situations. The fact is that I was forced to take gambles in the transfer market and it's a punt – some come off, some don't. When we finished fifth I felt we could have continued to improve but we didn't have the money to push on.'

Redknapp was never likely to receive much support from Brooking, a close friend of Billy Bonds who stands by the belief that his former assistant cynically manipulated circumstances to push him out of the manager's chair in 1994. With Harry playing a major role in coaching and negotiating transfers, the West Ham board responded to apparent interest from his former club Bournemouth by initiating a reshuffle that would see Bonds move into a director of football role to accommodate Redknapp taking over first-team affairs.

Nose put well out of joint, Billy decided to leave the club and refused to speak to Redknapp – who he had taken on in 1992 as his right-hand man – from that point onwards. The rift has obviously been a talking point among ex-Hammers, among them '70s defender Kevin Lock, who says: 'Billy still speaks about what happened and he regrets not taking Trevor's advice. He asked Brooking about bringing Harry into the club and was told he shouldn't. But he did and Trevor says that Billy keeps telling him he should have listened to him.'

Redknapp insists his conscience is clear. 'When I went to see the chairman and managing director Peter Storrie that day in 1994 there were just two options in my mind – either going to Bournemouth or staying as Billy's No. 2. The fact that Bill decided to resign was his decision. I spent three hours begging him not to do it. If I'd done something wrong I'd be the first to hold my hands up. But people like to mix things, saying that Harry said this or Harry did that. I don't suppose I ever will talk to Billy again but I know I've got a clear conscience.'

Harry may have spent much of his life with claret and blue blood pumping through his veins, but as a child it was just plain red as he followed his father's instincts and supported Arsenal. He attended the Sir Humphrey Gilbert secondary modern school in Canning Town – 'probably the worst school in the East End at that time, a real nuthouse' – but his enthusiasm for football saw him study hard as a winger for East London Schoolboys. 'That was my saviour,' he confesses.

Former West Ham centre-half Dickie Walker, then scouting for Tottenham, invited Harry over to White Hart Lane. There was also interest from Chelsea, but Redknapp eventually decided to plump for the Hammers. 'My mate Colin Mackleworth, a goalkeeper who played for East London Schools, was signing for West Ham. The manager, Ron Greenwood, used to invite us along to watch youth games in midweek and that was a big selling point. They'd open up the boardroom afterwards and he'd come and talk to the parents for an hour after the game. It was a family club, one where you felt you were going to get an opportunity to play.'

Redknapp attended the FA's national football school at Lilleshall and played in the 1963 FA Youth Cup final, the victorious second leg of which he remembers for Greenwood 'saying it was the best night of his management career at that point'. Ron and A-team boss Jimmy Barrett were huge influences on the young Redknapp. Harry vividly recalls the time when, during England youth trials, he collected a ball on the flank and beckoned the midfielder who'd just passed to him to make an overlapping run. 'The coach stopped us and asked what I was doing. I told him that I was waiting for the player to come by me on the outside so that we'd have two men against the one full-back. He didn't have a clue, but it was something we'd do every day in training at West Ham.'

Redknapp made his debut in the first home game of the 1965–66 season and played 175 times before leaving in 1972. 'I don't think I ever achieved what I should have as a player,' he admits. 'As a 16 or 17-year-old I was probably as good as anybody around. I had pace, was quick and a good crosser of the ball. But the game started to change and it became harder for wingers to play. Suddenly there was no space and to be a consistent winger was an impossibility.'

With Johnny Ayris coming through the ranks, Redknapp was sold to Third Division Bournemouth – managed by former Hammer John Bond – for a fee of £32,000 and, after coaching stints in the United States and at Oxford City, he returned to his former club on the south coast to establish his managerial credentials during a decade-long stay in the 1980s. When West Ham released manager John Lyall in 1989, director Martin Cearns even approached Redknapp to see if he'd be interested in applying for the position. 'I told him I was interested and so he told me to go and see my chairman, who then said: "Oh, you've been approached, have you?" He then rang up Martin Cearns and threatened to report him to the Football Association. So that was that.'

Harry's return to Upton Park eventually took place three years later when manager Bonds decided to recruit help in the wake of relegation during the 1991–92 campaign. It was a season marred by protests against the Bond Scheme, which asked supporters to advance the club a minimum of £500 before being allowed to purchase a season-ticket. Remembers Redknapp: 'We went to Hornchurch for a pre-season game and I'd never heard players get so much abuse from their own fans. The players were even too scared to go out for a warm-up before games. That's how low they were on confidence. But we gradually got to grips with things and we got promoted to the Premiership the following season.'

With his intuitive scouting instincts, Redknapp also found it strange on his arrival that a midfielder such as Southend United's Peter Butler had been playing just down the road without anybody at Upton Park being aware of his potential. 'I thought he was just the type of player we needed so I got involved in bringing him to the club.' Nearly ten years later, as Harry planned to spend the money remaining from the sale of Rio Ferdinand to Leeds United, he was working on deals of a somewhat more substantial nature. Republic of Ireland striker Robbie Keane and France winger Laurent Robert were both being lined up to join West Ham, although Keane went to Leeds and Robert eventually ended up at Newcastle after Redknapp was dismissed.

Harry reflects: 'I was fortunate to manage such a good club for that length of time and I know I did a good job, keeping them in the Premier League and producing great players. We gave the fans great entertainment. But life goes on. I may be disappointed in people but I won't let it screw up my life. There are more important things to worry about than what's happening at West Ham.'

19

RUNNING INTO TROUBLE: Dennis Burnett

Born: 27 September 1944; Bermondsey, London
Debut: v. Fulham (a), 2 October 1965
Apps/Goals: 66/3
Final app.: v. Tottenham Hotspur (h), 9 May 1967

THE PROMISING BUT SHORT-LIVED FIRST-TEAM CAREER OF DENNIS Burnett finished on a sour note after a bizarre fall-out with manager Ron Greenwood. The right-back's frustration over the incident – the true facts of which he never shared with his colleagues – was compounded by the fact that few homegrown Hammers had to work as hard as he did to get noticed in the first place.

Raised in what he terms the 'footballing backwater' of Orpington, Kent – an area not patrolled by starfinder Wally St Pier's army of scouts – Burnett was tiny until well into his teens. 'When I was 15 I was 5ft 1in. I was a midget,' he says. 'I went for trials with the Kent county team, but being small I got kicked around and never got selected.'

On leaving school he took a job making contact lenses, but the desire to prove he was good enough – and tall enough – to make it in football ran deeper than his passion for optical equipment. Letters were fired off to various clubs asking for a trial. Most told him to forget it but, just as he was about to give up, West Ham replied in the positive.

The trial went well, even though Burnett was overshadowed by a flashy young entertainer. 'I was stuck in the team as an inside-forward and played alongside

Rodney Marsh (later of QPR and England). He was a celebrity even then. I think West Ham offered him an apprenticeship, but Rodney turned them down because Fulham were prepared to offer him a full-time professional contract immediately.'

Burnett originally joined on amateur terms in 1962 – one of the last players to do so – but after he helped West Ham beat Liverpool in the 1963 FA Youth Cup final, he was offered apprentice professional terms by Greenwood. Dennis accepted, even though his £12 per week contract was less than what he was earning making contact lenses. In October 1965, aged 21, he finally got a first-team run-out in a 3–0 defeat at Fulham. In 1965–66 and 1966–67, helped by the departures of experienced right-backs Joe Kirkup and John Bond, Burnett became a regular in Greenwood's plans, playing 36 and 30 times respectively. The high spot was an appearance in the League Cup final side that lost 5–3 over two legs to West Bromwich Albion in March 1966.

Two months earlier he scored in a 2–2 FA Cup third round draw against Oldham. It was a goal that would come to be regarded by the few shivering Hammers supporters who witnessed it as an absolute classic – not least because it was from about 80 yards out! 'If it had been caught on TV I'd have made a fortune,' says Dennis. 'The pitch was a skating rink. We were 1–0 down, kicking downhill in the second half with the wind behind us. Dennis Violet, the ex-Manchester United star, was dribbling towards our penalty area when he just over-ran the ball.

'I left the man I was marking and hit it as hard as I could. It went like a rocket. It bounced about four yards outside their penalty area and skidded off a solid lump of ice. The goalie dived, the ball beat him and went in the goal. Incredible!'

Burnett's view of the failed defence of the European Cup-Winners' Cup in the same 1965–66 campaign was not so sweet. He played in all the games leading up to the semi-final, then found himself the victim of a reshuffle to accommodate new signing Jimmy Bloomfield. If that decision left the Kentish lad feeling insecure, it was nothing compared to the chain of events in the spring of 1967 that led to his eventual departure from the club. 'We had this particular training session with coach Ernie Gregory at Chadwell Heath. It was a running session around the pitch. I was one of the quickest at the club. Some of the first-team players were moaning and lagging behind, but it wasn't a problem for me.

'After 25 minutes or so we assembled behind the goal and Ernie says: "What's the effin problem?" He went round everyone and they all said: "Nothing Ernie, no problem." He came to me and I said: "Well Ernie, we find it hard because we don't run like that enough. It's probably the first hard running session we've had for six weeks." I wasn't talking behind his back. He asked me what I thought and I told him.'

Dennis didn't think any more of it, then a day or two later he was summoned to Ron Greenwood's office. 'I went in and his face was as red as anything. He was in a rage. He gave me the biggest bollocking you've ever heard. It went along the lines of: "Who do you think you are telling our coaching staff what we should be doing in training? What makes you think you know best?"

'I was so naive. I didn't say a word or give him my reasons; I didn't do anything. I walked out of the office and never played again.

'I always wished I'd said something like: "Look Ron, somebody asked me the question. How would you want me to react? Be man enough to give my opinion or be a coward and say nothing?" He regarded me as a rebel who disagreed with his coaching methods.'

Banished to the reserves, he was called into the manager's office prior to taking his seat for a first-team game, only to be asked for his thoughts on being offered in exchange for a raw Charlton defender called Billy Bonds. 'I told Greenwood I'd have to think about it. He said: "Well, you've got until the end of the game." He told me to go home and talk to my wife, but to be back at his office at 5 p.m.'

Greenwood had gained special dispensation from the Football League to register Bonds by 5 p.m. on the Saturday rather than the usual Friday so that he could play in defender Ken Brown's testimonial game – not that this meant much to the now speechless Burnett. 'I was dumbstruck. I had a young kid, I'd just got married and moved to a new house. My wife didn't know what to do, so I went back and told Ron that I couldn't get my head round it. I got another huge bollocking. Again, he took it personally that I had an opinion and didn't want to go where he wanted to send me.'

Burnett lingered on in the shadows at West Ham after Greenwood signed Bonds anyway, for £49,500. John Charles had also jumped ahead of Dennis in the right-back queue. When Millwall came in for him early in 1967–68, both club and reluctant player accepted.

The signing of Bonds would turn out to be a huge coup for West Ham, but pure finances do not explain why the man he replaced, Burnett, was apparently treated so coldly by a 'family club'. 'Until I got forced out,' says Burnett, 'Ron Greenwood commanded my respect. He was a brilliant coach. Ron used to live in Brighton (where Dennis settled after quitting football and entering the building trade). We'd always talk when we saw each other, but I never mentioned it. I've never told anybody. I wish we had been in a situation where I could have brought it up, but there you go.'

20

FROM OCKENDON TO OREGON: Bobby Howe

> Born: 22 December 1945; Chadwell St. Mary, Essex
> Debut: v. Southampton (h), 24 September 1966
> Apps/Goals: 82/4
> Final app.: v. Sheffield United (h), 17 November 1971

WHEN HARRY REDKNAPP JOINED SEATTLE SOUNDERS IN THE LATE 1970s to begin his coaching career, fellow ex-Hammer Bobby Howe went with him. But while Harry returned to Britain after four years, thoroughly disillusioned after falling victim to a fraudulent scam while with Phoenix Fire, Howe remained in Seattle in pursuit of his American dream.

And boy did it come true. After seven years as assistant to several managers at the Sounders, Bobby became director of coaching for the state of Washington when the club folded amid the termination of the North American Soccer League in 1984. He remained in that position for 12 years, while at the same time becoming the assistant coach to the Under-17 national side (1986–89) and then head coach of the American Under-20 side (1989–93). In 1996 he was appointed director of coaching for the whole of the United States – becoming the Bill Clinton of the soccer world at that time – until his desire to remain involved in the 'nuts and bolts' of the game saw him become manager of Oregon's Portland Timbers in the A-League. Not bad for a kid whose West Ham ambitions were never fully realised as a player.

An Essex and London Schoolboys star raised just up the road from Ockendon, Howe attracted interest from Tottenham, Arsenal and Chelsea, but after being pursued by scout Tom Russell he decided to opt for the Hammers – despite being a Manchester United fan. 'West Ham was the closest club to my home and made the greatest approach towards the time I was going to sign apprentice forms. I also looked at some of the other players they were signing and thought it would be a wonderful opportunity. As it turned out, it was an excellent beginning because in 1963 I was in the side that won the FA Youth Cup.'

Bobby was a natural left-half but after making his first-team debut in 1966 and playing a handful of games, he eventually got a little run at left-back during the 1968–69 season after Frank Lampard had broken his leg. When Lampard returned he moved into midfield, making 34 appearances during the 1969–70 campaign. He says: 'I was known more for my work ethic and my ability to get up and down the field. As a midfielder my endurance level was pretty good, but as I developed as a player I became a better defender.'

Howe had to show endurance off the Upton Park pitch, too, as that's where he spent much of his early Hammers career. 'I felt I deserved an opportunity to get into the team earlier than I did,' he says. 'For a couple of years I was playing very well in the reserves and there were a few occasions when I had to go knocking on manager Ron Greenwood's door to tell him that I needed to get a look-in. If I'd had my chance earlier I think I would have played a lot more games for the club.'

Bobby played in the infamous 4–0 FA Cup defeat at Blackpool in January 1971, a game he understandably describes as 'a nightmare'. Bobby Moore was dropped for the following three league games but returned in the 4–1 home defeat by Derby as a substitute for Howe. 'I didn't start many games after that because the team started to play quite well and I just wasn't part of that. It was a very disappointing feeling but the reality was that I probably didn't deserve to be in the team at that time. I was working very hard to get back into the side but the longer you're out the more your confidence goes.'

Having the greatest of respect for Greenwood, he refused to allow his lack of games to undermine his relationship with his manager. Indeed it was Ron who was behind the initiative to send West Ham players into local schools to coach youngsters, something that provided Howe with the appetite to pursue coaching on a serious basis. After gaining a preliminary badge (his evaluation being conducted by future England manager Bobby Robson), he became, at 22, one of the youngest men to gain a full coaching badge at Lilleshall.

Says Howe: 'Ron had a saying: "Simplicity is genius." It was all about doing the simple things well. Ron urged people to play to their strengths. One of his assets was to get you to expand your horizons from a tactical and technical point of view in training. But within a game he'd urge you not to do anything that was beyond your capabilities.'

As a defensive player, Howe could recognise how the emphasis on attack was disproportionate to the amount of time spent working on shutting up shop. 'You have to concentrate on forward play to a degree because it's much more difficult to create than destroy. But I still felt we could have defended much better as a unit and if we had we'd have been more successful.'

For Bobby, the major frustration was the amount of time he spent watching action from the substitute's bench – particularly during the 1971–72 season, his last at West Ham. He says: 'There was a lot of competition for places and once you've tasted the first team you can't go back into the reserves.' In 1972, former Hammer John Bond paid £30,000 to recruit Howe for Bournemouth – who were chasing promotion from Division Three – and Bobby jumped at the chance to gain regular first-team football (followed months later by Redknapp).

Retiring at the age of 28 due to wear and tear in the wake of earlier cartilage operations, Howe coached at Bournemouth and Plymouth before taking the giant leap across the pond to the States. 'I spent ten years at West Ham and that period was a huge influence on me as a coach. I would like to think the style we tried to portray at that time has been injected into my own teams.'

21

THE BEAUTIFUL GAME: Trevor Brooking CBE

Born: 2 December 1948; Barking, London
Debut: v. Burnley (a), 29 August 1967
Apps/Goals: 635/102
Final app.: v. Everton (h), 14 May 1984

AS ONE OF THE MOST EXTRAVAGANTLY GIFTED PLAYERS EVER TO grace Upton Park, Trevor Brooking represented the perfect link between midfield and attack. He would rekindle his role as a linkman on returning to the club as a non-executive director in June 2001 in the wake of manager Harry Redknapp's departure, with a remit of bridging the apparently yawning gap between the board and the training ground.

Diplomacy became the Brooking trademark during many years as a BBC pundit, but the circumstances of his homecoming to West Ham were not without a hint of intrigue. Like chairman Terence Brown, he was critical of Redknapp's transfer dealings. Then there was the fact that he remained such good friends with former playing colleague Billy Bonds – 'I trust him more than anyone else in my life' – with whom Redknapp suffered an acrimonious fall out in 1994 after a managerial reshuffle which Bonds (then manager) felt Harry (his assistant) had worked in his own favour.

Brooking maintains that he always tried to 'keep out' of the feud. 'Harry knew I was very matey with Bill and I didn't agree with what happened. Unfortunately they haven't spoken since and that's sad. I used to call in at the training ground a lot when Bill was around, but I didn't do that afterwards because there was always that little bit of sensitivity there.' He also believes that playing the role of middle-man while Redknapp was in charge would have been a non-starter. 'I don't think Harry would have liked someone like myself at West Ham, because he very much controlled the playing area. It's something I spoke to Glenn Roeder (Redknapp's replacement) about before taking the job. I didn't want Glenn to think I was hovering over him.'

Trevor's appointment suggested that Brown felt a degree of reparation was required following Harry's reign, especially in the area of contracts and transfer dealings. And Brooking's opinions about investments following the £18m sale of defender Rio Ferdinand in November 2000 echoed criticism of Harry in the Chairman's Statement of 2000–01. Says Trevor, an astute businessman in his own right: '[The board] were concerned and the purchases were being questioned, although naturally Harry would have challenged that. If any questions were asked Harry used to say: "Well, there's no-one in the boardroom that knows anything about football; you've got to leave that to me." It was not even a discussion point.

'Harry did some really good things. He developed the youth system again, the style of football was maintained and we got into the top half of the table for a few seasons. The query area is if you sell Rio, you want to try and get some quality players in as a result. Unless you are spending that on people who are going to be competitive in the first team, you've got dead wood.'

No-one could dispute the fact that West Ham got terrific value for money when they offered Brooking apprentice professional terms of £7 a week in 1965. Not that manager Ron Greenwood or chief scout Wally St Pier had seemed particularly enthusiastic about the slightly bulky lad from Barking. Brooking trained with Spurs and Chelsea juniors before the club on his doorstep – who he watched from the West Stand – belatedly approached him. 'It was Ron who spotted me,' says Trevor. 'Ilford Boys got to the quarter-finals of the English Schools Trophy and we had a lad called Barry Simmons, captain of England Schoolboys, who Ron had come to see. We lost 2–1, but I played well on the night.

'The next morning Wally knocked on my door and said: "I didn't want you to think that we weren't interested, the fact that we haven't been round." Afterwards my mum said: "What a stupid thing to say! Of course they weren't interested otherwise they'd have come round before." Mum was very forthright with her comments.'

Laden with O and A-levels, Trevor excelled at Ilford County High, but the inspirational effect of some simple words from Greenwood fired his imagination about a footballing future. 'Ron said two things to me at the Tuesday and Thursday training sessions – "pictures in your mind" and "always receive the ball sideways on".

'The first meant that wherever you were when the ball came to you, you should be able to shut your eyes and say: "Right, the No. 4 is there, I've got a fella closing me down here, I've got a defender up there, but there's no-one here." So the secret was that you took the ball there and bought yourself a few extra seconds. With receiving the ball sideways you either stopped it and carried it, or if the pass was weighted nicely you just let it run.'

Within little over a decade, both traits would be crucial to his world-class reputation, yet his climb to those giddy heights was not without its frustrations. 'In my early days I was a wing-half. There was a lad called Keith Miller in our A-team, he was the wing-forward. One day, little Jimmy Barrett, a former Hammer and the A-team manager, swapped us over. I started playing a little bit further forward and suddenly I was creating goals and everyone was thinking I should play there more regularly.' Unfortunately for Brooking, with Martin Peters and Ronnie Boyce in their midfield pomp, it was only as a striker where the opportunities came.

In the August of 1967–68, the England youth international came in for Brian Dear to make his first-team debut up front in a 3–3 draw at Burnley. 'At that stage I wasn't sharp enough or confident enough. I'd wear the No. 9 shirt and that's when people used to say: "He's a bit slow." I scored a hat-trick (in a 5–0 home win over Newcastle in April 1968) but it was during a period when I probably wasn't at my happiest.'

Scoring nine goals, Brooking came runner-up in the Hammer of the Year in that first season, but by the turn of the decade his dissatisfaction with being played out of position, or dropped altogether, was making him feel distinctly unsettled. Having played 28 times in 1967–68, he had regressed to becoming a fringe player by 1970–71. 'Ron never liked to drop a senior player, so there was Bobby Howe, Jimmy Lindsay, myself, Peter Bennett and Harry Redknapp who used to vie for two places. If we lost a match and Ron wanted to change the team, it would be one of us who got dropped.'

A dismal start to the 1971–72 campaign saw emergency midfielder Tommy

Taylor pushed back into defence. Brooking, on the transfer list at the time, seized the moment. Back in the side in central midfield, he inspired Hammers to a 13-game league run during which they were beaten just twice. 'Who knows what would have happened if we hadn't lost the first three games of that season?' he says. 'I got in, did really well and from then on was never dropped.'

There was a real poignancy to Trevor's rising profile during the next couple of seasons and the start of his inextricable link with the No. 10 shirt. At the same time, Bobby Moore, with whom the No. 6 jersey would be forever associated, was on his way out at both club and international level. Fears abounded about whether West Ham could ever come even close to replacing the World Cup-winning trio of which Moore was the star, but once again the East End (and Woolwich) came up trumps. 'After Bobby, Geoff Hurst and Martin Peters left in the early '70s it was always going to be a problem for the club,' says Brooking, 'so it was a bit of fortune that myself, Billy Bonds and Frank Lampard came along. We did almost replicate the lifeblood of the club. We were able to carry on that little dynasty, that little nucleus of home-produced players. Well, Frank and myself were home-produced, while Bonzo wore his heart on his sleeve so much and stayed so long that people forgot that we bought him.'

Between 1975–81, the three appeared together in the finals of two FA Cups, a League Cup and a European Cup Winners' Cup. Brooking scored a famous FA Cup-winning goal with his head in the 1–0 victory over Arsenal in 1980 and scooped three of his record five Hammer of the Year awards during this period. His sublime balance and control with either foot enabled him to out-play the very best defenders, a facet never better exemplified than in a pulsating 3–1 home win against Eintracht Frankfurt in the European Cup-Winners' Cup semi-final of 1976. His reputation was further boosted by many audacious goals, including two against Frankfurt and a brilliant effort at Derby County in November 1975 that earned him ITV's Goal of the Season.

The fact that West Ham so often struggled in the league in the 1970s made his standard of football all the more remarkable. Another breathtaking performance came in the final game of 1976–77, when West Ham needed to beat Manchester United at home to stay up. 'I played out of my skin and it was just one of those fantastic occasions, although you have to ask what the hell we were doing at the bottom of the table if we could beat Man Utd 4–2!'

Showing great loyalty after relegation in 1978, his quality stood out like a sore thumb during the three-year Second Division hiatus, to the extent that he came runner-up in the Football Writers' Footballer of the Year awards in 1980. He came to be widely regarded as the elite creative force in the England side too, aided partly by Greenwood's elevation to the top job in 1977 and also by his uncanny understanding with star striker Kevin Keegan. While with FC Hamburg, Keegan even tried to entice Brooking to join him in the Bundesliga. 'I think my style of play would have been ideally suited to playing abroad,' says Trevor, 'and Kevin tried to get me to Germany. But I was 33 and it was a bit late by then.'

Keegan's former side, Liverpool, then arguably the top club in Europe, also had designs on Brooking. 'Their England lads were asked to talk to me. It would be unfair to say I wasn't tempted. The appeal was the possibility of a league championship and the chance of regular European football. But the fact is that West Ham's style of football played to my strengths. Neither Ron or John Lyall, his successor, restricted me in a defensive role in midfield.'

It was Brooking's understanding with wide-left dribbler Alan Devonshire that caught the imagination at club level in the latter part of his career. Says Trevor: 'Why he didn't get more England caps I'll never know. He was a much better player than Peter Barnes of Manchester City, who Ron picked, because he tackled. Then Ron took Arsenal's Graham Rix to the 1982 World Cup. I just think Dev was much better.'

Suffering with a groin injury, the 27 minutes of play Brooking saw in Spain '82 (in a 0–0 draw against the host nation) proved a disappointing international swansong after 47 games for his country. He still had enough quality to win another Hammer of the Year poll in 1983–84 but, at the end of that season, his decision influenced by a long-term injury to Devonshire, Trevor called it quits.

Seventeen years on from being cheered off the pitch after his farewell game (a 1–0 home defeat versus Everton), Brooking – made a CBE in 1999 – was able to take up the option of returning to West Ham in the boardroom. One could only hope that his affinity with the club would never be tarnished through working for it, as had happened with a growing list of his former colleagues.

22

DREAMING OF A: Frank Lampard

Born: 20 September 1948; East Ham, London
Debut: v. Manchester City (h), 18 November 1967
Apps/Goals: 665/22
Final app.: v. Liverpool (h), 20 May 1985

'FRANK TYPIFIED EXACTLY WHAT WEST HAM WAS ABOUT – GREAT commitment, great loyalty and great intelligence.'

Claret and blue acclaim doesn't really come much greater than that, especially when long-serving manager John Lyall is the man behind the words. Described by Lyall as 'a cornerstone' of his team for 15 years, Lampard is the club's second-highest all-time appearance holder behind Billy Bonds and the homegrown Hammer with the most games under his belt.

'Hatchet men' are perhaps not so representative of the West Ham way, but fans who remember Frank's legendary clashes with Orient and Notts County winger John Chiedozie in the early 1980s will easily relate to the tough-tackling full-back's comment that he 'could put it about a bit'. Says Lampard, who perfected the art of scything down anything within range with a right leg that seemed to swivel 360 degrees at the knee: 'People still talk about those incidents in front of the Chicken Run. Chiedozie had tremendous pace and I wasn't the quickest around – but I let him know I was there, let's put it that way.'

While bearded bandit Lampard provided the perfect partner-in-grime for skipper Bonds when it came to a thoroughly filthy battle in the trenches – and the Hammers certainly found themselves in a few sticky holes during his 18 years of service – he rarely got credit for using his brain. Said Lyall: 'Frank was a full-back who thought about the game. Whichever player he marked, he made sure he knew all about their strengths and weaknesses. He was totally dedicated and we instilled in boys like him a sense of loyalty that survives to this day.'

And so it does. After leaving the club as a 37-year-old in 1985 – having made 665 appearances and collected two FA Cup winners' medals, a Second Division Championship medal and two England caps – Frank returned in 1994 as assistant manager to Harry Redknapp, with whom he shared a rollercoaster seven-year partnership until pushed out of Upton Park in 2001. 'West Ham are still my team,' he says. 'That's something that nobody can take away from you. Even now, all my mates are West Ham men. If I hadn't have been playing for the Hammers I'd have been going to watch the games as I had done as a kid. You're just claret and blue and that's how it is.'

Initially a goalscoring inside-left, Lampard was spotted by chief scout Wally St Pier playing for West Ham Schoolboys having 'sneaked in at left-back despite being right-footed' and he signed professional forms in 1965. 'When I got involved with the first team at West Ham Ron Greenwood was always on at me to try and use my left foot more often. And then he said: "Well, try using the outside of your right foot." So I used to run with the ball and curl it down the line with the outside of my right foot. That got me out of a lot of trouble over the years. And when balls were delivered from the far side of the field, it was much easier for me to volley them away. People used to ask me what a good left-back needs and my answer was always: "A good right foot!"'

Drawing heavily on the influences of fellow full-backs Noel Cantwell, John Bond and Jackie Burkett, as well as coaches Greenwood and Lyall, Frank emerged through the ranks as a tenacious defender who could play a bit. And striking the right balance between defending and playing was the key to his success. 'I had a good mentor in Bobby Moore,' he says. 'Of course, there are times when you've got to smash the ball away but you've got to learn that for yourself. I can remember Ron stopping a training game when defender Alan Stephenson booted the ball up the pitch on his first day at the club. He said: "I don't want you to do that, I want you to get the ball down and play football."

'I found Ron a very interesting man when talking about football. He simply commanded respect. He could lose his rag at times but generally he was more concerned with trying to work things out and putting them right. He encouraged young players to visit local schools for coaching and I went back to my old place – Pretoria in Canning Town – initially with Johnny Bond and later with Harry Redknapp and Dave Bickles during afternoons. We used to get £12 a week for doing four sessions – Monday to Thursday. That was how I got to know Harry really.'

John Lyall pays tribute to Lampard's spirit of determination by saying: 'Frank was a very special player, a great club man and a manager's dream. He would play for you with a broken leg.' The defender had the opportunity to prove the latter remark after sustaining a leg-break in a 2–1 win at Sheffield United in April 1968, just six months and 19 games after making his first-team debut. 'I went to Sheffield Royal Infirmary for an operation immediately after the game and next day our physio Rob Jenkins took me back home by train. When we pulled in at London I had to hobble up the platform and Rob went and got one of the luggage trolleys and stuck me on that. I was in plaster for 27 weeks and it was a nightmare.'

Frank missed a year's football but overcame any initial psychological barriers – including that of using shin pads for the first time – to cement himself into the Hammers' defence, mostly at left-back but occasionally on the right. Having won England youth and U23 honours, he collected his first full cap against Yugoslavia in 1972 (under Sir Alf Ramsey) and returned to Wembley three years later with the Hammers for the 2–0 FA Cup final victory against Fulham. 'That game meant a lot to me because it brought me up against Bobby Moore, with whom I'd roomed for eight years. What pleased me years later was that Bobby said in his book that, when playing against me, he knew I was thinking just like he was.'

Sadly, Frank's next appearance in a final – against Anderlecht in the European Cup-Winners' Cup the following year – brought not triumph but despair as one fatal moment turned the game. He'd been taking painkillers for most of the season to combat a pelvic injury but the matter came to a head in Brussels with a wayward back-pass that cost the Hammers their early lead. 'As I went to kick the ball it was like a cricket ball dropping out of my stomach. The pain was horrendous. If that pass hadn't gone astray we'd have won that game.'

The pain of torn stomach muscles may have subsided relatively quickly but the hurt of that 4–2 defeat was only really erased four years later. That was in 1980, when Lampard unexpectedly soared through the air to head a dramatic extra-time winner in the FA Cup semi-final replay against Everton at Elland Road. 'It was just one of those things – I was in the right place at the right time,' he says with incredible understatement about the defining memory of a cup run that culminated in a 1–0 Wembley success against Arsenal. Rousing verses of 'I'm dreaming of a Frank Lampard', as fans recall the vision of him dancing manically around a corner flag, have floated like bubbles into the East End air ever since.

Along with a surprise second full England cap, against Australia in May 1980 (thanks to national boss Greenwood), further success was enjoyed when the 1980–81 team steamrollered the Second Division and reached the final of the League Cup. How grateful he was that he'd resisted the opportunity to join Norwich – managed by his old mate John Bond – while feeling depressed after the Hammers were relegated in 1978. 'All I'd ever really known was the East End and, as I was driving into East Anglia to talk to Norwich, I realised it wasn't me. I went through the motions and told them I'd think about it, but knew it didn't feel right.'

Just as former team-mate Ronnie Boyce did before him, Frank spent his final playing days at Upton Park in the reserves, passing on his wealth of experience to the crop of youngsters coming through before moving to Southend United on a free transfer in 1985. 'I got a lot of pleasure from helping the young lads during that last year,' he says. 'But there comes a time when you know in your own mind that it's right to go. Deep down I knew that I couldn't do it at the top level any more.'

Following his one-year stint as player/coach under the Bobby Moore-managed Southend, Lampard concentrated on his property business affairs before taking up an offer to coach West Ham's youngsters a couple of times a week. When Harry Redknapp – a brother-in-law, as well as a friend – rejoined the club as assistant to manager Billy Bonds in 1992, Frank got involved in some scouting and two years later he was asked to become Redknapp's right-hand man. 'From the day Harry returned to the club I think he was possibly earmarked to be manager one day. So when he did take the job I had a feeling that he would come to me. It wasn't a big surprise.'

With his amiable personality, Lampard was an ideal choice to bridge the gap that inevitably exists between a boss and his players. 'The assistant manager's job is to get amongst the players and win their confidence. I found I could do that quite easily. It's not about having a high profile; it's about keeping things ticking over behind the scenes.

'Harry and I also spent a lot of time with the kids – travelling down to Kent to watch Rio Ferdinand play and having him over at my place where he got on well with my son Frank. I remember having a cup of coffee with Joe Cole in his parents' flat in Camden, just to make sure we signed him up. It was all part of the job.'

He adds: 'I guess Harry and I were more like brothers than manager and assistant. There wasn't much that either of us could do without the other knowing. We used to discuss everything and to his credit he made decisions that some people might have shied away from.'

Lampard is proud of what his partnership with Redknapp achieved in terms of consolidating the club's place in the Premiership during the latter part of the 1990s. He says: 'We had to build a decent squad and while waiting for the kids to come through we had to put square pegs in round holes just to keep us going. The crucial thing was bringing in strikers John Hartson and Paul Kitson during the early part of 1997. We went to great pains to convince the chairman to go for it and to the club's credit they put their hand in their pocket to get them both. That kept us in the Premiership that year. Our record stands up quite well and I think we left the club on a good footing.'

That enforced departure took place before the final game of the 2000–01 season following a meeting between Redknapp and West Ham chairman Terence Brown. 'Harry phoned me after it had finished and just said: "He sacked me." I said: "I suppose I'd better come with you then." I took it as a formality that we'd leave together, despite having two years left on my contract – not that I was asked to stay.'

23

A SCOT'S TALE: Jimmy Lindsay

Born: 12 July 1949; Hamilton, Scotland
Debut: v. Sunderland (a), 21 December 1968
Apps/Goals: 45/2
Final app.: v. Nottingham Forest (a), 10 April 1971

WEST HAM'S SCOTTISH CONTINGENT IN THE LATE 1960s AND EARLY '70s never experienced the best of times. The signing of Bobby Ferguson in 1967 for £65,000 – a British record for a goalkeeper – from Kilmarnock was seen by some as one of manager Ron Greenwood's more questionable purchases, not least because he turned down an option on Leicester City's brilliant England keeper Gordon Banks in the process. Long-serving Fergie was popular and a fine shot-stopper, but not so hot on crosses. Similarly John Cushley, a centre-half signed from Celtic also in 1967, never looked entirely comfortable as the commanding Ken Brown's successor.

Perhaps boosted by the good omen of a J. Lindsay having reportedly played in the very first Thames Ironworks fixture in 1895, right midfielder Jimmy Lindsay looked like having enough about his game to be able to buck the unfortunate tartan trend. Sadly, the colossal blow of breaking both legs in quick succession put paid to his Hammers career after just three seasons of first-team involvement.

If that was unfortunate, so too was West Ham's inability to sign the future Scottish superstar striker that Lindsay shared a bedsit with in Barking. 'The year after I joined the groundstaff, Kenny Dalglish came down from Glasgow and Ron put him in digs with me,' says Jimmy. 'He had no intentions of signing for West

Ham; he just wanted to have a look. He went to everybody, including Manchester United and Liverpool (a decade before they signed him from Celtic), but Kenny was a Rangers fanatic. You couldn't believe they missed him.

'I don't think he said more than 12 words to me all the time he was down here. All he wanted to do was eat and go to the pictures. I was put in charge of getting him to training. I remember one of his first practice matches. We used to do a lot of one- and two-touch football, which did my head in when I first came down. Anyway, the game started and you'd think he'd played it all his life. You didn't have to be a genius to see he could play a wee bit.'

As for Lindsay, he was all set to sign for Arsenal before West Ham's chief scout Wally St Pier heard through the grapevine about the potential of a hardworking schemer shining for Glasgow Schoolboys. Ron Greenwood travelled up to East Kilbride to meet Jimmy and his parents and that swung it. 'The main reason I went down to West Ham was that Ron impressed my mother,' says Lindsay. 'She thought he'd look after me.'

Lindsay joined the groundstaff in the summer of 1966 and linked up with a group of trainees that included Trevor Brooking and Frank Lampard. He even found himself marking Brooking in an England v. Scotland youth international – 'I used to try and kick him up in the air and he'd never even swear.'

Having shared digs with one great Scot, in December 1968 Lindsay was all set to make his first-team debut against another – his all-time idol, ex-Rangers and Scotland maverick Jimmy Baxter. Unfortunately, Baxter's affection for the bottle ruined the script. 'I was so looking forward to that game. Baxter, my hero, was playing for Sunderland at the time. To me that was unbelievable. But he never played. I spoke to someone after the game and they'd found him in the gutter at 3 a.m. that morning. He'd been out drinking and the police had to take him to the cells.' To add to Lindsay's disappointment, West Ham lost at Roker Park by a 2–1 scoreline.

On a close-season tour of the USA, Jimmy would realise that a legend closer to home could handle his drink rather better than Baxter. 'I roomed with Bobby Moore and the first thing he did was fill the bath with ice. Then he went down to the supermarket, bought a load of Budweiser and put it in the bath. I said to him: "Are we not going to have any baths then?" He said: "Just use the shower." Nobody could drink like Mooro.'

Defender John Charles was another of Jimmy's drinking partners, as well as being a pain in the neck in training. 'The stick I took for being a Scot was terrible and it was Charlo mainly. He was an aggressive full-back who used to kick a lot. I said to him in training one day: "Have a kick again, Charlo, it's free." That's all I ever got from him from then on.'

Lindsay's industrious approach impressed Greenwood enough to keep the 19-year-old in the side for four more league games after the Sunderland match. Then, on 26 February 1969, disaster struck on two fronts in the FA Cup fifth round. West Ham were the victims of a famous giant-killing by Third Division Mansfield Town and Lindsay broke a leg. 'It was 0–0 when I went off and we lost 3–0. Somewhere like Mansfield you needed one or two players who could tackle a bit and we had too many faint hearts at times. Ron said afterwards we would have won if I'd stayed on.'

Rehabilitated by the start of the 1969–70 campaign, Lindsay scored his first goal for the club in a 2–1 defeat at Stoke City in the August. He made 18 starts that season and by the time season 1970–71 came around he had established himself as one of the young midfielders most likely to prosper in the new decade. His understanding with fellow youth product Harry Redknapp down the right side was looking particularly promising. 'He was a joy to play with,' Lindsay says. 'I always knew what Harry was going to do. He'd sprint down the wing and if the full-back went with him I'd know I could roll it in behind him and he'd come back for it. Then, if he came towards me wanting it, that would mean he'd want it over the top. It was so simple.'

Making 18 more appearances that season, Lindsay was piling the pressure on the experienced Ronnie Boyce for a regular berth in the midfield engine room before another calamity effectively ended Jimmy's West Ham career. 'I fell through a roof. I was at my digs and I went up to get a ball for some kids off this corrugated roof. I fell through and broke my other leg.

'I never really made it back from that. I didn't apply myself very well. I didn't seem to be getting anywhere and too many people in the pubs down in London would be telling me what a good player I was and how I should be in the team. Once you start to believe that you end up getting nowhere.'

Nowhere for injury-prone Lindsay meant Fourth Division Watford. A damaged knee finally ended his playing days at Shrewsbury Town, where he settled and took up work for the county council. His demise at West Ham was sudden and disappointing, but at least the Scottish hoodoo hadn't affected him as much as it did Edinburgh-born winger Doug Eadie. Brought south of the border at around the same time as Lindsay, Eadie was shown the door after just two first-team showings in 1966–67.

24

KEEPING WITHOUT CONFIDENCE: Peter Grotier

Born: 18 October 1950; Stratford, London
Debut: v. Tottenham Hotspur (a), 19 April 1969
Apps: 54
Final app.: v. Derby County (a), 21 April 1973

WEST HAM GOALKEEPERS HAVE GENERALLY BEEN EITHER REVERED OR reviled by Hammers fans. By his own admission, Peter Grotier leans more towards the latter – despite it being announced by manager Ron Greenwood in 1970 that he'd found 'our keeper for the next ten years' (an accolade more famously associated with Grotier's successor Mervyn Day).

'I got a better reception at Upton Park when I returned as a player with Cardiff City (six years after his 1974 departure) than I did when actually playing for West Ham,' admits Peter. 'I felt I got some unfair criticism from the supporters and it was hard to get accepted by them. I found it very difficult at times.'

Never more so than after a 4–1 home defeat by Derby County in February 1971. 'I had an absolute shocker. I stubby k'd a goal kick and the ball struggled to make it out of the penalty area. Their striker Kevin Hector was on the edge of the box and even though I blocked the first shot he put the ball back past me. It was a real low point.'

Confidence is an essential commodity for all goalkeepers but Peter rarely got the boost he so obviously needed at times from West Ham's management – or the affection from the supporters usually reserved for homegrown Hammers. It was only when he eventually left the club that he finally found his feet. He says: 'Ron Greenwood was a lovely man and a fantastic coach, but he was never one who would sit you down in his office and tell you what he felt. I didn't think he could handle people face to face and you never really knew where you stood with him.'

Grotier grew up in London's Stratford as an Orient fan, idolising striker Dave Dunmore who'd left West Ham in an exchange deal that brought midfielder Alan Sealey to Upton Park. He'd already played in goal at primary school level but when he moved to West Ham Tech in Canning Town it turned out that the West Ham Schoolboys goalkeeper was in the same year – an opportunity between the sticks only opening up when the other lad got injured. Peter was then spotted by Clapton's youth-team boss and played in Sunday leagues around Walthamstow and Leytonstone. 'I played at Hackney Marshes one week and a guy called Arthur Lamb who worked for West Ham under chief scout Wally St Pier was over there watching a game. I wasn't aware of it but apparently the club had followed my progress during my early teenage years.'

An offer from Portsmouth was ignored for the sake of Peter's education. But two months before his 16th birthday, Wally paid a visit to the Grotier household to persuade him to play a game for West Ham's South East Counties side. 'We beat Watford 2–1 and on the following Tuesday I was asked to go and see Ron Greenwood at Upton Park. It was a dream come true. Within 48 hours I'd left school and it was actually on the day of my birthday in October 1966 that I signed for the club.'

Following a one-year apprenticeship in the youth team under the guidance of coach John Lyall – which saw him included on tours of Zambia, Switzerland and Italy – Grotier turned professional. 'All my winnings at West Ham were at youth and reserve-team level,' he declares, with honours including the Southern Junior Floodlit Cup (1967, 1969), the South East Counties League Cup (1969) and Metropolitan League trophies with the A-team. At 18, however, Peter found himself making a first-team debut after first-choice goalkeeper Bobby Ferguson had blundered in a 3–1 defeat at West Bromwich four games from the end of the 1968–69 season.

Suddenly he was to face legendary goalscorer Jimmy Greaves in a visit to Tottenham Hotspur. 'Prior to the game the papers referred to it as "the pupil versus the professor". But one of the most memorable things was coming out before kick-off and seeing a monkey show on the pitch. All these monkeys were leaping around and I was thinking: "What the hell's going on here?"'

It wasn't the greatest of starts for the youngster, with Greaves scoring the only goal of the game by appearing to poke the ball through Peter's legs. A second appearance followed just two days later in a 2–1 home defeat by Arsenal, but he then had to wait until the final 12 games of the 1969–70 season for another opportunity as the Hammers struggled and finished in 17th position. 'Ferguson was going through a bad time so I was brought in again and I also played 21 games in the first half of the following season. I thought I was doing quite well, but obviously Ron Greenwood didn't agree because I was then dropped.'

Even though he admits that he received criticism for his ability in the air, Grotier had always considered that feature to be one of his strengths. That was until Alan Stephenson – a very tall centre-half – started to unwittingly influence his approach. 'Alan was very commanding and I stopped coming for balls,' says Peter, 'so I did start to lose quite a lot of my game.'

He made just six appearances during the 1971–72 campaign – once again kept out of the side by Ferguson – and a further 13 the following season. 'I just got the impression that Ron Greenwood used to sit in his office with a dice in his hand and whoever's name came up with No. 1 against it used to go in goal.' But like many homegrown products, Peter often found himself acquiescent of the situation. 'When you're a young local lad, you always accept things more than if you were signed from another team. Initially I was just happy to be playing for my home club.'

Although he often had to rely on feedback from reserve-team boss and goalkeeping coach Ernie Gregory as much as Greenwood – even when playing first-team games – Grotier was left in no doubt as to the manager's feelings after one particular defeat in October 1972. 'We'd got beaten 4–3 up at Manchester City and I can remember Ron telling me that was probably the last game I'd ever play for West Ham. He actually said that to me in front of all the players in the dressing room.'

Ferguson was recalled the very next match, leaving Grotier convinced that his

Hammers career was over. Two final appearances were made in April 1973 – in a 4–3 win against Southampton and a 1–1 draw with Derby – as West Ham equalled their best placing of sixth in the top flight.

Things came to a head in August that year when Grotier was asked to fill in for the unavailable Ferguson for a home game against Ipswich. 'I went down with a virus and saw physio Rob Jenkins, who said he didn't think I'd be well enough to play. He called Ron who said: "Well, we've only got young Mervyn Day; if he comes in and does well you never know what might happen." That was that – Mervyn played (in a 3–3 draw) and I never appeared for the first team ever again.'

Peter spent a month on loan at Second Division Cardiff City and the rest of 1973–74 in the reserves. 'My last year at Upton Park was a total waste of time. I should have been putting pressure on the manager to get away but I was just a homegrown lad, still only 23 years of age.'

Thoroughly demotivated, Grotier admits he let his condition go a little. 'I wasn't looking after myself, I'd started to put on a bit of weight and West Ham were the type of club who, if you didn't look after yourself, they didn't look after you,' he says.

Grotier's saviour came in the form of future England manager Graham Taylor, then boss of Fourth Division Lincoln City, who set up a loan deal that ran over a couple of months. Says Peter: 'I lost at least half a stone, because I suddenly had somebody taking an interest in me. Then Graham called me into his office after trying to negotiate a permanent deal and said: "Will you be honest and tell me if you've been a bad boy at Upton Park?" I asked why and he told me that he'd found out that West Ham only wanted £15,000 for me. I said: "If you think that's a bargain, don't knock it!" I took Lincoln to my heart and decided to make a clean break.'

Grotier signed for the Imps in October 1974 and says: 'It was the best thing I ever did. I had so much more confidence and within six months I was a totally different person. People had total belief in me and I suddenly realised there were other things in life besides West Ham United.'

PART THREE

Flair in the '70s

25

A POPLAR KIND OF GUY: Pat Holland

Born: 13 September 1950; Poplar, London
Debut: v. Arsenal (h), 21 April 1969
Apps/Goals: 296/32
Final app.: v. Notts County (a), 17 January 1981

THROUGHOUT A WEST HAM CAREER THAT BOOK-ENDED THE 1970s, Pat Holland's wicked sense of humour kept everyone laughing in the dressing room. Yet underneath the comic skin, there was just a tinge of sadness that as a loyal, hardworking right midfielder, his football too rarely mirrored the idiosyncrasy of his wit. 'John Lyall said I was always a good runner with the ball,' says Holland. 'True, but I think: "Why didn't I do a little bit more than that?" I had my moments, flashes where I could beat people. But I never did myself justice. It's a shame really – I ended up as a grafter and my regret is that I had a little more than people saw.'

Pat was an Arsenal fan despite being raised in deepest east London, but as a schoolboy footballer he had to content himself with being tracked by the rival mob from White Hart Lane. That is, until Wally St Pier, West Ham's chief scout, got wind of the gutsy 15-year-old making waves in the Hammers' heartland. 'Wally followed up a call from a chap called Arthur Lamb, who'd seen me playing in Poplar, and he came to watch me in a game for the East London district side at Enfield. Bill Nicholson, Tottenham's manager, was about to come and have a chat with me when Wally came up behind me and asked if I'd like to train with West Ham the following Tuesday. I was too scared to say no. Wally was the top scout at the time and I was frightened of him. I went home and said to my dad: "I don't like him. He's a big man with big hands." It turned out that he was a lovely man.

'West Ham invited about eight boys to be interviewed by manager Ron Greenwood. It was late in the day when I turned up and the groundsman – a little Irish fella – had turned all the lights off. It was pitch black in Ron's office and in the dark all I could hear was: "Paddy, put those lights back on!"'

Pat joined the groundstaff in 1967. Two years later he would make his first-team bow against his heroes Arsenal, but before that there was work to be done on fragile confidence levels that belied his mischievous façade. 'I was always a very determined person, but I was a very shy lad too. John Lyall, youth coach at the time, got me into coaching 12 and 13-year-olds when I was 17. I never asked him why but I think the reason was to bring something out in me. We set up a centre in Tilbury in Essex and I also coached at what was then Plaistow Grammar School.'

On his league debut in a brutal 2–1 home defeat by the Gunners in April 1969, Pat got two kicks – 'one of the ball and one from their left-back, Bob McNab'. The over-awed youngster was quickly dispatched to the reserves. He came back with a bang, however, the following January. At home against Manchester United in the second game of a three-match run in which he again deputised for Harry Redknapp, everything fell into place and Holland scooped his first Man of the Match award in a 0–0 draw. The 1970s had started well and they soon got even better.

His first goal for the club came in March 1970 at home to Liverpool. Bill Shankly's fearsome Reds were sunk 1–0 in front of 38,239 fans, not by home debutant Jimmy Greaves but by a lad who 24 hours earlier had been hobbling around his council estate virtually in tears. 'I was having a bit of tea at home when there was a knock at the door. It was a few of the local lads asking if I fancied coming down to the playground for a game. Anyway, I've only gone and turned my ankle over.'

In a panic Holland had limped over to club physiotherapist Rob Jenkins' clinic, where a pressure bandage was applied and an agreement struck not to say anything about the incident to boss Greenwood. Jenkins had told Pat he looked doubtful for the Liverpool game but, miraculously, the swelling healed and the first *Boys' Own* chapter in Holland's Hammers career got written. In truth, the next few chapters were largely forgettable. In 1971, the erratic youngster was loaned out to Bournemouth to see if Fourth Division football could instil in him that certain 'presence' that was lacking. Greenwood told him he was too much of a 'shrinking violet', yet the answer to his problems lay not on the south coast but back at West Ham in the formidable shape of Trojan midfielder Billy Bonds.

'We used to have a 40-minute man-for-man session on a Thursday,' says Holland. 'You'd be allocated someone and you had to stick with them wherever they went. Who did I get? Bonzo, of all people. There was only one winner. We were diving and sliding into each other; Bill would knock me to the ground, then pick me up and say: "Come on, Dutch, let's go again." It was brilliant and toughened me up a lot.'

By 1973–74, Holland's growing stature had been boosted by moments such as a wonderful goal against Hereford United in a home 1–1 draw in the FA Cup third round. From the halfway line, he jinked up the right wing and left four players floundering in the mud before sliding home from a tight angle. Unfortunately, he couldn't prevent the Third Division minnows inflicting another giant-killing with a 2–1 win in the replay.

There were to be no such banana skins in the same competition in 1974–75. It was Holland's quick-thinking, this time from the left flank, which contributed to both of striker Alan Taylor's goals in the 2–0 FA Cup final victory over Fulham in May 1975. Worried about being substituted after a poor first half, Holland had swapped wings in an effort to convince Lyall to keep him on the field. The rest – haircut-obsessed fans included – is history. 'At the end the supporters came over the top. I was running around celebrating but I'll always remember one bloke coming up to me and shouting: "My wife cuts your hair!"'

In the mêlée following the final whistle, Holland was mistaken for a supporter by a befuddled policeman who initially refused him permission to climb the Wembley steps to collect his medal. He claimed it in the end, although injury would cruelly rob him of another FA Cup final medal five years later, when West Ham beat his favourites Arsenal 1–0. In the meantime, there was agony and ecstasy to be had in the 1976 European Cup-Winners' Cup final.

Pat appeared in all but one European round as he made a career-best 49 appearances that season. He opened the scoring in the final against Anderlecht in Belgium's Heysel Stadium. 'Before the game I said to winger John Ayris, a substitute that night, that if I scored I was going to run over and do an impression of Ken Dodd. Unfortunately the cameras didn't follow me, but John said it was hilarious.' Anderlecht equalised before half-time and after the Belgians had taken a second-half lead forward Keith Robson squared things at 2–2. Then a dubious Holland foul on Anderlecht's brilliant Dutchman Robbie Rensenbrink earned the Belgians a penalty and enabled them to take the initiative. 'I tried to get underneath him and do the Bobby Moore scoop tackle,' says Holland, 'but he hit my foot and went over. There was no reaction at all from his players. I knew I'd got the ball first.' West Ham eventually lost 4–2.

The incident would for once cause Holland serious humour failure. So too would the stick he received from the Upton Park crowd in the early part of his career. 'There are certain people who react badly to players even before they've kicked a ball. You'd see them at presentations and they'd say: "Do you hear us?" I'd say: "Yes." And they'd say: "Really? How do you concentrate?" I'd say: "Well basically, I have to fuck off into my own mind."

'Jimmy Neighbour (an early-1980s colleague) came up to me once when we played Chelsea. He said: "Pat, can I have a word? Does the Chicken Run ever get on your back?" He'd only been at the club a few months. He didn't realise the stick you could take and he couldn't handle it. Then again the fans could be unbelievable, like they were against Eintracht Frankfurt in the 1976 Cup-Winners' Cup semifinal. I've never known anything like it.'

Even the least sensitive boo-boy had to have sympathy with Holland after a 1–1 draw at Notts County in the deep winter of 1980–81. Connecting with a pass from Trevor Brooking, Pat poked the ball home but in the process collided with County's goalkeeper and smashed his knee. It meant again missing out on the chance of appearing in a major cup event, this time in the 1981 League Cup final and replay against Liverpool. Despite several operations and three years of rehabilitation, Meadow Lane would be the scene of Holland's final Hammers contribution.

In subsequent years Pat managed, coached and scouted for clubs all over London, including stints as Leyton Orient manager, Millwall assistant manager (under Billy Bonds) and Tottenham's youth coach. As a boy he'd been a Gunner – as a man, however, he would always be West Ham. 'I went back to Upton Park once with Spurs manager Peter Shreeves,' Pat says. 'There was a great move from right-back all the way up the field. They scored and I told Shreevesy I'd known they were going to. He said: "How did you know?"'

Holland, usually such a conversational steam train, settled on two words that said it all. 'Instincts. Habits.'

26

WINGER NOT WHINGER: John Ayris

Born: 8 January 1953; Wapping, London
Debut: v. Burnley (h), 3 October 1970
Apps/Goals: 65/2
Final app.: v. Ipswich Town (h), 16 October 1976

DIMINUTIVE RIGHT-WINGER JOHNNY AYRIS HONED HIS SKILLS BY spending hours smacking a ball against the sheds outside his parents' council flat in Wapping. He'd aim for a particular drainpipe or kick it onto the roof, guessing where it would fall to be there and catch it on his right foot.

His addiction to practice never waned, even later in life as manager of a leisure centre in South Woodham Ferrers, Essex. In a curious way it helps explain why he made just 48 starts in seven seasons with West Ham. 'Training was a joy,' he says. 'It was touch, it was pace, it was skill and I was lucky enough to have those attributes. Acknowledging that I loved the training perhaps more than I did the matches, it might sound strange to say but maybe I wasn't cut out to be a footballer. I should have pushed my case a bit more.'

There were other mitigating circumstances too, not least a shocking respiratory injury and the fact that Ayris felt he was 'protected' by manager Ron Greenwood, who he believed would only pit his 5ft 5in., 9½ stone frame against selected opposition.

All in all, John says he was just happy to go with the flow. 'It was one big boys' club. I loved the banter and the feeling of being looked after. You were cosseted so much.' It was ironic, then, that on FA Cup final day in 1975, when his tiny frame would surely have puffed up to twice its size with the pride of just being involved, he was halfway around the world all on his own in a hotel room. 'Missing the cup win over Fulham may have been the worst decision I ever made.

'The previous summer I'd been contacted by Roy Bailey, the former Ipswich player. He was out in South Africa running Cape Town City and he asked me if I'd like to go over there. I had a word with West Ham and they were quite happy for me to go. The next summer (after just nine appearances in 1974–75) I signed a three-month contract. On the day of the cup final, I was in Cape Town listening to it on the radio. I probably wouldn't have played. I probably wouldn't even have been the one substitute. But the regret is I would've got the suit, been on the bus and travelled back through the East End streets.'

That the 22-year-old was allowed to take a sabbatical at all is an indication of how much he had slipped down the pecking order since causing a stir as a teenage debutant.

Ayris attended a Catholic school in west London and as a result he played neither for his local district nor county sides. After a brief flirtation with Fulham's juniors, he was spotted by West Ham scout Wally Wood playing eight-a-side football in Mile End. Ayris excelled in the Hammers' Metropolitan League side and made his senior debut as a 17-year-old at home to Burnley in October 1970. His crosses and corners helped Geoff Hurst bag a hat-trick in a 3–1 win. Suitably impressed, Greenwood offered him a professional contract the following Monday.

He pulled on the No. 7 shirt seven more times in 1970–71, including for the infamous FA Cup third round defeat at Blackpool. That shambolic 4–0 drubbing and subsequent furore over the pre-match drinking session involving Bobby Moore, Clyde Best and Brian Dear (who came on as a substitute for Ayris) was a sickener for all concerned. However, for John it was as nothing compared to events during a 2–1 home win over Chelsea in September 1971.

Tracked by Ron 'Chopper' Harris, Ayris was running rings around the hardman until the riled defender stood his ground as his tormentor challenged for a header. Says Ayris: 'I'd been having it off against him. He seemed to be getting a bit wound up by it and the crowd were on his back. I think he decided that where I would go, he would go.' John flipped over Harris's shoulder, landing with a sickening thud. Groggily lifting himself off the floor, he realised to his horror that he was struggling to breathe and was soon subbed. Hospital tests the following day showed the impact had caused an air bubble to form in his lung, a condition he later found out can be life-threatening.

The gravity of the situation – the breathlessness, confusion and panic – had a lasting effect on Ayris' confidence, but he held no grudge against Harris, one of the more notorious members of an over-subscribed 1970s hardman club. 'There were a couple of other instances where I got caught out. One was against Tommy Gemmill of Celtic, when they came down for Bobby Moore's testimonial in 1970 (John scoring with an audacious lob a month after his debut). We were having a little chat and I could feel a pain in my foot. I looked down and he was treading on it. I'm thinking: "He doesn't know." But as soon as the ball came flying forward he was off.'

Off the pitch, the jokes and pranks ran thick and fast among Ayris' crew of Tommy Taylor, John McDowell and Pat Holland. Frank Lampard pitched in by coining John's nickname of 'Rat' after spying an unflattering passport photo. One away trip in January 1972 saw the Ratpack tearing around Buxton, their hotel base, firing water pistols at anyone who crossed their path. On that occasion, Ayris could be forgiven his youthful exuberance – he was still on cloud nine after coming face to face with his idol, Manchester United's superstar winger George Best.

West Ham had been limbering up at United's training ground ahead of their epic League Cup semi-final defeat against Stoke City at Hillsborough – and Best had taken time out from bedding Miss Worlds to do some light exercise. Ayris was too shy to say 'Hi', just as he was too modest to accept that as a substitute in the 1976 European Cup-Winners' Cup final loss to Anderlecht, he deserved to breathe the same air as the Belgians' clutch of Dutch international stars. 'I felt it was nice for me to see people I'd only seen on TV. I didn't realise that I was there with them; I was one of them. I was still a fan sitting on the bench.'

As the seasons passed he did a lot of that. By 1976–77, injuries were an increasing annoyance, while former non-leaguer Alan Devonshire was making a name for himself on the right, prior to shifting to the opposite flank. After just one start and two substitute appearances that season, the inevitable happened. 'Ron (then general manager) told me my contract wasn't going to be renewed. They were going to give me a free transfer to non-league Wimbledon. I didn't make a fuss, although I was devastated. I had so much faith in him that I just accepted it.

'We all went to the Room at the Top nightclub in Ilford after one of my last games, when I already knew what was happening. I was teetotal, but that night I drank and ended up with my head down the toilet at my girlfriend's house.' The player the fans nicknamed Cyril Lord – after the carpet king, for his propensity for hitting the turf – had had the rug well and truly pulled from under him.

Throughout his West Ham career Ayris lived at home with his parents in Wapping. He saw no reason to adapt his lifestyle. He was just a normal East End lad living out a *Boys' Own* fantasy and he loved every minute of the journey. Literally. 'It was good just being on the coach with the little table lamps and West Ham written along the side,' he says, 'even if the people looking in through the windows didn't know who the hell I was. It was a great adventure.'

27

A QUESTION OF PRINCIPLES: John McDowell

Born: 7 September 1951; East Ham, London
Debut: v. Blackpool (h), 31 October 1970
Apps/Goals: 296/9
Final app.: v. Cardiff City (a), 11 May 1979

JOHN McDOWELL MAY HAVE BEEN BROUGHT UP THE WEST HAM way but, like most Hammers fans at some time or another, he occasionally questioned the strict adherence to the club's traditional principles. 'I'm certain I heard manager Ron Greenwood turn round one day and say: "I'd rather see us lose 4–3 and play well than win 1–0 and play badly." Personally, I'd have much rather had the win bonus,' he says.

'There was one game where I pulled an opponent back as he was running into the box and certain to score. The referee gave a penalty, the bloke missed it and we went on to win the match. Ron came into the dressing room afterwards and complained: "If I see you do that in another game you'll never play for West Ham again." I said: "What are you talking about? We won the match." And Ron replied: "It's not the way we play football at West Ham."'

McDowell collected plenty of win bonuses during his nine-year first-team career at Upton Park – not least in the mid-1970s when the Hammers won the FA Cup and reached the final of the European Cup-Winners' Cup. But there were also several seasons of struggle and right-back McDowell – whose versatility saw him play in every outfield shirt bar the No. ll – was well aware of the potential conflict between stylish and consistently successful football. He says: 'There were times when I felt we tried to pressurise teams too much away from home, when maybe we should have tried to consolidate and make sure we didn't concede. But Ron always wanted his teams to play beautiful football and that was his indoctrination.

'After Holland played West Germany in the 1974 World Cup final, we came back to the training ground and Ron said: "Total football – that's the way to play." Ron wanted us first-teamers to play against the reserves using a rotation system like the Dutch and after 20 minutes we were well behind. Ron asked what was going on and I said: "It's a great idea but Trevor Brooking isn't Johann Cruyff and I'm not Johann Neeskens." He wanted to see West Ham win the right way although some people just wanted us to win full stop.'

Locally born McDowell had been a Hammers fan ever since being pushchaired past the Upton Park gates as a three-year-old. He later stood with his father in the Chicken Run in the East Stand and then moved onto the North Bank, idolising the likes of Phil Woosnam, Johnny Byrne and the triumvirate of Bobby Moore, Geoff Hurst and Martin Peters. 'It was a dream come true to join West Ham a year after England won the World Cup and to find myself suddenly training with three of the greatest players in the world,' he says.

John had been spotted by chief scout Wally St Pier playing full-back for Newham Schoolboys against a Havering district side that included future team-mate Tommy Taylor. 'We slaughtered them 9–0 and I had virtually nothing to do, but I must have done something right because I was asked to start training with the club twice a week.' When a two-year apprenticeship was offered, John's father told him: 'It's your choice – but don't come crying to me if it doesn't work out.' That was all the encouragement he needed.

McDowell played for the junior, Metropolitan League and reserve sides – mainly at full-back, although the tradition would be for youngsters to be moved around to find their best positions – before making his first-team debut in October 1970 aged 19. The match against Blackpool saw McDowell start at right-back alongside right-sided centre-half and pal Tommy Taylor, but within a few minutes Bobby Moore had switched with Taylor to provide the novice with some assistance. 'Bobby guided me through the first part of the game, telling me where to go and talking me through everything.'

John's successful arrival at full-back as a replacement for the suspended Billy Bonds eventually resulted in the latter moving into midfield for several seasons. His first full campaign, 1971–72, saw him play 54 times as the Hammers came so close to League Cup glory, eventually bowing out of the semi-finals after four epic encounters with Stoke City. McDowell was guilty of conceding the famous penalty that emergency keeper Moore tried in vain to save during the eventual 3–2 defeat at Old Trafford.

Another penalty incident involving McDowell occurred in the same competition the following year, as he conceded the spot-kick that saw Stockport County gain an unlikely 2–1 win to become the first Fourth Division side ever to beat the Hammers. Says John: 'I got dropped after giving that penalty away. Ron and I did have our occasional bust-ups. But I was a very fiery character in those days and nobody could talk to me after a game. People used to wait until Monday to tell me what I'd done wrong on a Saturday because I'd just argue with them.'

That was still the case when John Lyall succeeded Ron Greenwood as first-team boss in 1974. McDowell had great respect for the man who first coached him as a junior but that didn't stop him feeling frustrated when he felt things could have been done differently. The 1974–75 season ended gloriously with an FA Cup final win and the team finishing a respectable 13th in the table. But John, who had by then amassed 13 England U23 caps, was disappointed that West Ham failed to build on the success. 'When we went into Europe during 1975–76 there were probably three positions in the side that were lacking. If one or two key players were injured their replacements weren't really up to scratch – and we didn't buy, which was the club's biggest mistake.'

The Hammers topped the table in November after 15 games of that season but won just one league match after Christmas to plummet to 18th. Yet they'd succeeded in battling their way to the final of the European Cup-Winners' Cup, with McDowell moving into midfield and Keith Coleman filling in at right-back. 'I suppose things all came to a head in the final against Anderlecht. We were on top until Frank Lampard injured his groin just before half-time and Robbie Rensenbrink scored to make it 1–1. We came in for the break and, for some obscure reason, John Lyall decided to change three positions instead of just bringing on Kevin Lock to replace Lampard at left-back. He brought Alan Taylor on up front, pushed Pat Holland back to right midfield and switched me to left-back. I said to John: "I'm not going to do it. You're wrong, bring Locky on." In the end I went along with it but I knew it was never going to work. I think John only did it to get Taylor back into the side for another cup final, but the whole thing went to pot and it really annoyed me.'

The eventual 4–2 defeat didn't exactly put McDowell in the best of moods for the summer of 1976 and his skies darkened even more after he seriously damaged knee ligaments on a pre-season visit to Majorca. A cartilage injury to the same knee saw him miss the entire 1976–77 season and the first half of the following campaign that ended in relegation. 'I got back into the side,' he says, 'but I'd lost a yard of pace. Not that it affected me too much, because I was 26 by then and could read the game much better.'

John was entitled to a testimonial in 1979 but with the club only allowing one benefit game to be staged per year there was a queue forming. 'Patsy Holland and Bobby Ferguson had both been at West Ham longer so it meant I'd have to wait a few more years before I could have my game. My contract was about to expire and I asked John Lyall to give me a three-year contract to see me through to my testimonial. He said the directors would only give me a year, adding that they were unsure about my knee. Since returning I hadn't missed a match because of it, so I asked him to fight for me in the boardroom.

'John made no progress so I said I'd have to leave. But instead of giving me a free transfer – to thank me for the service I'd given having cost the club nothing – they wanted something like £150,000 as a transfer fee. I told John that I could hardly be worth that much if they thought my legs weren't going to last. In the end I joined Norwich for £90,000, which I thought was still a ludicrous amount of money. I suppose that was John's way of getting back at me after our argument during the Anderlecht game in 1976 and I've not spoken to him since I left the club.'

28

JUST LIKE MY DREAMS: Kevin Lock

Born: 27 December 1953; Plaistow, London
Debut: v. Sheffield United (a), 29 February 1972
Apps/Goals: 161/2
Final app.: v. Bristol City (a), 17 September 1977

ONCE UPON A TIME, A STARRY-EYED CHILD WITH A HEAD FULL OF dreams would sit in his bedroom and gaze out of the open window at the balls of light illuminating the night sky, waiting for the much-anticipated explosion of sound to indicate that his beloved Hammers had scored a goal.

His hero was Bobby Moore – an icon of footballing perfection – and, like so many East End schoolboys, his fantasy was to one day pull on the claret and blue shirt and wear it with the same sort of pride and distinction.

For Kevin Lock, the dream came true – although he could never have imagined that he would find himself following the great man's footsteps on three occasions in a career that took him from West Ham to Fulham and then Southend United. 'I used to queue up for Bobby Moore's autograph,' says Lock. 'I was obsessed. I'd sit in my room during night games and listen for the roar when West Ham scored. On Saturdays my dad used to take me to Upton Park with my stool so that I could stand next to the tunnel in the West Stand. And at junior school I can remember being asked by a teacher what I was going to do when I grew up and I said I was going to play for West Ham. And all of a sudden I was there.'

The transition from fan to footballer may have seemed instant for Lock, who graduated through the Newham and Essex Schoolboys system before joining West

Ham's groundstaff at the age of 15 in 1969. But the awe he felt when suddenly finding himself in the company of Moore and other senior Hammers, combined with his naturally easy-going personality and the satisfaction of playing for the club he loved, contributed to Kevin never quite reaching the pinnacle of his profession in the way his undoubted talent suggested as a youngster.

'I played 14 or 15 games alongside Bobby during 1972–73 and for a lad who grew up dreaming of playing for West Ham it was a bit surreal. You're in the company of all these great players and it was like: "Should I be here?" Bobby was the greatest footballer who ever lived and I had the privilege of learning my trade by watching him. The man was just so immaculate in everything he did.'

Expectation and unfair comparisons weighed heavily on Lock's shoulders. As he emerged through the club's ranks, people started to talk of this cultured young central defender's bright future; after making his debut early in 1972 he was even dubbed by some as 'the new Moore'. It was a tag that never sat comfortably with Kevin. 'I suppose it was inevitable that people were going to try and make comparisons. I played in the same position as Bobby, was a local boy with blond hair, had played for the England youth and U21 sides and had been taught to play football the right way. I was flattered but I knew there could never be anyone else like him. Being groomed to take over from him put extra pressure on me and it was always in the back of my mind that, if I made a mistake, I was going to hear: "Oh, Bobby Moore wouldn't have done that."'

Like his father Tom, a winger who played for the Army during the war and nearly joined QPR, Kevin was left-footed and gravitated towards his natural defensive position. His West Ham Tech side were winning 'everything in sight' and attracted club scouts, with Pat Smythe of the Hammers keeping tabs on Lock's progress from the age of 13. 'Then I got a phone call from the chief scout Wally St Pier, asking if I'd like to go training two nights a week.' Kevin needed no persuading, especially as the club 'was known as having the best youth set-up in the country'. He adds: 'West Ham had a reputation for bringing players through, as well as encouraging them to play football. Manager Ron Greenwood was very technical and that's why he liked to get involved throughout the club, so that he could get young players to develop the habits he'd want to see if they made it to the first team. Everything was with a ball. I wasn't the most physical of defenders anyway but I could control and pass the ball and the club encouraged those strengths.'

Those attributes allowed Lock to feel comfortable in a number of positions and during his career he'd occasionally play in midfield – as he did on his debut appearance as a substitute in a 3–0 defeat at Sheffield United in February 1972. His first start came two months later, at Highbury against an Arsenal side featuring the likes of Frank McLintock, Alan Ball, George Graham and Ray Kennedy. 'Ernie Gregory, the reserve-team boss, told me I'd be playing so to get my hair cut. I did but Ernie said: "I told you to get your hair cut." I told him I had but he told me to get it cut again. And that happened three days running.'

Kevin made 19 appearances in his first full season, 1972–73, playing in a variety of positions but ending the campaign alongside his mentor Moore. A further 13 games came during 1973–74 – Moore's last at the club – before a hernia operation ruled him out for the rest of the season. It was also Greenwood's final campaign in direct charge of the first team and Lock reflects: 'I learned a lot from Ron. Everything was precise, although some may feel his ideas were perhaps too intricate at times. There were a couple of players who just couldn't grasp what he wanted them to do. But he had a specific idea of how he wanted the game played and he stuck to his guns. John Lyall was a disciple of Ron's anyway and when he took over it really was just a continuation of the same beliefs.'

Under the new Hammers boss and with Moore sold to Second Division Fulham, Lock was an ever-present during 1974–75, playing all 53 games in the centre of defence – mostly alongside Tommy Taylor – as the club reached the FA Cup final. Kevin remembers little of the game itself, which saw striker Alan Taylor score twice to defeat a Fulham side featuring Moore. Reflects Lock: 'The next day, after the homecoming tour, I was driving out of the West Ham car park as the police were holding people back. Suddenly there was a surge, a policeman fell forward and I ran over his foot. I drove up Green Street and a copper on a bike came tearing after me. It turned out that I'd broken the bloke's foot and I ended up paying his hospital bills.'

Injury struck Lock at the end of the 1975–76 season, costing him a place in the side for the European Cup-Winners' Cup semi-final games against Eintracht Frankfurt. Although fit in time for the final against Anderlecht at the Heysel Stadium in Brussels, Kevin was only named as a substitute. 'I was gutted. But what disappointed me most was when Frank Lampard got injured and striker

Alan Taylor was picked to go on at half-time. I thought I should have gone on because, as a left-sided defender, I was Frank's natural replacement.

'Some people would have been jumping up and down but I wasn't like that. I always felt I was fortunate to be at West Ham, was lucky to be in the team and I don't think I ever rocked the boat. Perhaps it was considered the easy option to leave me out, because I accepted things so much.'

That same year saw Kevin called into the full England squad for a European Championship game against Portugal – having already represented the U23s on three occasions – and he just failed to get on as a substitute. 'Kevin Beattie went down injured and I thought that was my chance, but he got up and carried on. My one regret is that I never got a full England cap.'

In many ways the summer of 1976 represented a turning point in Lock's career. The following season was a mediocre one by his standards as he suffered from niggling injuries and West Ham struggled in the league. A particular low point came during a 6–0 defeat at Sunderland when playing alongside Bill Green. 'I remember Johnny Lyall telling me afterwards that I needed glasses. He sent me to the opticians and, to be fair, it turned out that I did indeed need glasses!'

Then, in 1977, he was stunned to hear that the club had decided not to renew his contract which still had a year remaining. 'It really shocked and upset me, because they never told me to my face. I simply got posted a letter saying they weren't retaining my registration. I went to see (general manager) Ron Greenwood and he told me I shouldn't have got the letter before they'd spoken to me. He just told me that with other players coming into the side perhaps the time was right for me to go. I was gutted because I never wanted to leave West Ham. I felt very let down, having given everything for the eight years I'd been there at that point. I thought it was a shabby way to treat someone.'

With either Mick McGiven or Green being preferred alongside Tommy Taylor, Lock played just seven games during the relegation season of 1977–78 before joining Fulham for £60,000. 'It was a very difficult season, playing reserve-team football and wondering when and where I was going to go. I felt like I was in a daze a lot of the time because I'd never thought about the day I might leave the club.'

Lock's Fulham career lasted two years longer than his first-team span at West Ham, with Craven Cottage being his home until 1985, but he admits: 'I never had the same feeling for Fulham as I did for the Hammers. Playing for West Ham was the only thing I ever wanted to do and, for me, Upton Park was a holy ground.'

Such affection didn't prevent Lock from enjoying a successful career as a coach with other clubs. 'I always used the principles I learnt at West Ham when I was coaching,' he says. A free transfer to Southend United in 1985 saw Lock play and coach under manager Bobby Moore. Mooro's successor Dave Webb had Kevin as his assistant and together they guided the Shrimpers from the Fourth Division to the Second. In 1994 the pair spent a brief spell at Chelsea before linking up again for a four-year stint at Brentford. Having moved into the pub trade after deciding he'd had enough of the game, he acknowledges – as his contemporary John Ayris does – that perhaps he didn't quite fulfil his potential as a player: 'I could have stuck up for myself a bit more and been less accepting of certain situations. Maybe I was in awe of people and was just happy to play for the club. But people still come up to me and say: "Didn't you used to be famous?"'

29

'EVERYBODY'S LOOKING AT ME': Mervyn Day

> Born: 26 June 1955; Chelmsford
> Debut: v. Ipswich Town (h), 27 August 1973
> Apps: 233
> Final app.: v. Sunderland (h), 10 February 1979

MERVYN DAY WAS THE FIRST WEST HAM PLAYER TO HAVE HIS FORTUNE told by the press in a manner normally reserved for pop stars. Goalkeepers have rarely caught the imagination in the same way as outfield players, but for a couple of crazy seasons after his sparkling arrival in the big time, Day changed all that.

Sportswriters were convinced that West Ham and England's future was in safe young hands. The 18-year-old's reflexes and positional sense were out of this world and he was a photographer's dream with his carefully arranged feather-cut, so at odds with the scraggy Deep Purple roadie image favoured by an alarming number of his contemporaries. Day's pedestal was raised even higher by manager Ron Greenwood's well-meaning, if ill-advised quote that West Ham had found their goalkeeper 'for the next ten years'. It was a statement that would ring decidedly hollow within half that time, but Mervyn bore no ill-feeling towards Greenwood. 'For me, he was a superb man, a very caring man,' Day says. 'My family were always looked after by the club and by Ron in particular.

'My first day as an associate schoolboy I got taken by goalkeeping coach Ernie Gregory into the little gym behind the Upton Park dressing room and he had Martin Peters, an England World Cup winner, firing shots at me. As a 15-year-old, that was incredible.

'The bond got even closer when my father died when I was 17. I was an apprentice but Ron signed me as a full pro within a very short space of time to enable me to earn a little bit of money to help out at home. A short while later he signed me again and gave me an increase. He was almost a surrogate father to me.'

Day first came to Greenwood's attention playing for Chelmsford Schools, who reached the quarter-final of the English Schoolboys Trophy in 1970. 'My local paper took a picture of Ron standing on the terracing at Chelmsford City's ground, on his own, watching my performance. A top manager going to an under-15 game of another team to check on a player.

'I had the opportunity to go to quite a few clubs. It boiled down to a choice between Ipswich and West Ham. My family all originally came from Ipswich, but I ended up signing for West Ham because of Ron Greenwood.'

By coincidence, his first-team debut came at home against Ipswich in a 3–3 thriller in the second game of 1973–74. Bobby Ferguson's request to be left out for personal reasons and a virus affecting second-string goalkeeper Peter Grotier opened the door. The experienced Fergie would play just nine times in the next three and a half seasons as his young colleague's gymnastic agility rocketed him to an FA Cup winners' medal, England Under-23 recognition and the 1975 Professional Footballers Association's Young Player of the Year award. He came runner-up to skipper Billy Bonds in the Hammer of the Year polls of 1973–74 and 1974–75 – and also managed to squeeze a wedding in during that period too.

Although league form was poor in his first season (West Ham finishing 18th as

Day made 37 appearances), the Hammers were still recognised as one of the most attractive sides in the land. Part of Mervyn's instant appeal was the fact that he seemed to be involved in attack as much as he was in defence. 'I was always encouraged by both Ron and Ernie to throw the ball,' he says. 'In those first two to three years I threw it much more than I kicked it. If you push your back four up to the halfway line and kick it as high and as long as you can, that's not entertaining. But if you catch it and you throw it quickly and you get the full-backs moving, you contribute to the flow of the game and your side retains possession.'

With his thoughtful, diligent approach, Day was evidently from the mindful rather than madcap school of goalkeeping. Not that this stopped him from lowering his standards when the publicity machine was running full pelt. 'There was a horrible picture in *The Sun*, with the shirt off and all that sort of crap. I got into that stuff a little bit.'

'Crap' was one of the words that came to Day's mind during the victorious 1975 FA Cup run. 'We played Arsenal away in the sixth round. It was a horrible day and the rain was lashing down. It was 0–0 when John Radford came towards me and I threw myself at his feet. He knocked the ball past me but then trailed a leg to try and get a penalty. The referee didn't give anything and I got booed mercilessly by the Arsenal fans. We eventually won 2–0 (yelping BBC commentator David Coleman hailing Day's performance as: 'Goalkeeping SUPREME!') and in the next week's post I get some used toilet paper in a little envelope with the message: "We'll get you," signed by The Radford Boys.'

Day tactfully chose not to mention the incident to Radford when the striker signed for the Hammers two seasons later!

Mervyn subsequently wondered whether being a madcap type would have given him the front to cope with darker days ahead at Upton Park. Having earned such rave reviews and pocketed a winners' medal in the 2–0 FA Cup final win over Fulham and played in the 4–2 defeat by Anderlecht in the 1976 European Cup-Winners' Cup final – both before he was 21 – life seemed too good to be true. It was. He'd only ever experienced the smooth and was clueless as to how to handle the rough when it came. 'My West Ham career was peaks and troughs – and I didn't handle the troughs very well.

'My one criticism of the club was that perhaps they should have shielded me better. The older I got the more I accepted that troughs were part of the job. When

A 21-year-old Bobby Moore in action against Spurs in 1962. © John Helliar

Circa 1960 and on the threshold of good times (from left to right): coach Albert Walker, secretary Eddie Chapman, chief scout Wally St Pier, Brian Dear, John Charles, Mick Beesley, Eddie Presland, Ronnie Boyce, Dave Bickles,Derek Woodley, Roger Hugo, Martin Peters and Jack Burkett. © Steve Bacon

Wally St Pier, king of scouts and talent-spotter extraordinaire, gave West Ham nearly 50 years dedicated service. © Steve Bacon

Midfielder Trevor Brooking pictured on his testimonial evening in 1977 with Geoff Hurst, alongside whom he made his debut as a striker ten years earlier. © Steve Bacon

John Lyall and Ronnie Boyce served the club as players and coaches for a combined period of 70 years. © Steve Bacon

An unhappy Day: one-time 'wonder kid' keeper Mervyn endured a few of those in his last few seasons at Upton Park. © Steve Bacon

Hair apparent: Alvin Martin succeeded Billy Bonds as first-team captain. © Steve Bacon

The kids of 1981 with the FA Youth Cup: Paul Allen (front centre) and Bobby Barnes (front right) were already first-teamers; Alan Dickens (second in front) soon followed suit. © Steve Bacon

Pint-sized predator Tony Cottee beats England keeper Ray Clemence to score on his debut against Tottenham in 1983, © Steve Bacon

Hero turned villain: Paul Ince incurred the wrath of Hammers fans following his controversial departure.
© Steve Bacon

Former manager Ron Greenwood leads Martin Peters and Geoff Hurst onto the Upton Park pitch with a floral tribute to Hammers' ultimate homegrown hero, Bobby Moore, following his death in 1993. © Steve Bacon

Cheer up, Harry, anything could happen: Harry Redknapp and Frank Lampard enjoyed a rollercoaster seven years in charge in the Nineties. © Steve Bacon

Good pals Rio Ferdinand and Frank Lampard both had England recognition in their sights. © Steve Bacon

Joe Cole puts pen to paper in front of (clockwise from top) dad George, youth development boss Jimmy Hampson and youth manager Tony Carr. © Steve Bacon

Michael Carrick and Joe Cole (centre) lead the celebrations following the brilliant FA Youth Cup success in 1999.
© Steve Bacon

Jermain Defoe celebrates after scoring the winning goal at Manchester United in December 2001. © Steve Bacon

you're young you tend to think: "Oh Christ, everybody's looking at me, it's my fault." It was horrendous. I wasn't mentally tough enough at the time. Because I'd been given all the hype about how I was going to be this and be that, I'd never needed to fight through a few games.'

Although ever-present (as he was in 1974–75), he really started stumbling into the troughs in 1976–77. Two incidents in particular, within six days of each other in April 1977 and both in home 2–2 draws, precipitated a souring of relations with his once adoring fans. 'I had a couple of problems with being chipped,' he says. 'The famous one, which was on TV, was against Everton. After ten minutes, their attacker Ronnie Goodlass was just inside our half, I was wandering around on the edge of our box not concentrating and he chipped the ball over my head. Then Birmingham City's Trevor Francis chipped me from about 25 yards. I had this habit of wanting to be six yards out to narrow the angle, but got caught.' Day didn't do his popularity rating any favours by reportedly throwing a V-sign at jeering supporters.

'Eventually, in the December of the 1977–78 season, manager John Lyall left me out, although I didn't think I was playing that badly. Fergie came in and did a reasonably good job but we went down. I got back in when Fergie hurt his shoulder at home against Stoke City the following October. Then we got beaten 2–1 in the FA Cup third round at Fourth Division Newport on a very icy pitch. I got done over the top with a cross and someone headed in the winner at the back post.'

Ultimate humiliation came in the last of his 233 matches as a Hammer. 'We drew 3–3 at home with Sunderland in February 1979 and either I'd get booed every time I touched the ball or I'd get ironically cheered, which really got to me. As an outfield player I don't think it would bother you that much, but as a goalkeeper I had time to think, so it played on my mind. I thought: "Why am I bothering? I'm obviously not wanted here. What's the point?"'

His confidence shattered, Day discussed the situation with John Lyall. It had been an open secret that Lyall had been looking for a new goalkeeper and no amount of sympathy was going to change the fact that former QPR favourite Phil Parkes would be commandeering the green jersey from day one following his sensational arrival in February 1979 for £565,000 – a world record for a keeper. Day vowed to find another club, but to compound his problems he suffered a cartilage injury soon after Parkes arrived.

Once fit, Mervyn linked up with fellow outcasts, striker Billy Jennings and centre-half Tommy Taylor, at Orient for a cut-price £100,000 in the summer of 1979. He dug deep to rediscover his game, to the extent that he earned a move back to the top flight with Aston Villa, then went on to play a large chunk of his 700-plus career games with Leeds United.

Following the dismissal of Hammers manager Harry Redknapp in June 2001, many assumed that Charlton boss Alan Curbishley would defect across the Thames to his former club and bring Day – his assistant at The Valley – with him. In the event, Glenn Roeder stepped up to prove that old boys do not have a divine right to Upton Park's top jobs. Says Day: 'It had always crossed my mind that eventually it would be nice to go back to where I started. But the scenario that was purported in the press didn't happen and I was perfectly happy at Charlton.'

Despite his demise as a player at the club, Day always retained an emotional attachment that went beyond the fact that he was a homegrown Hammer. 'I'll always remember the way I was treated by Ron Greenwood when my father died. You can't put a price on things like that.

'Ron opened people's minds. It was no surprise to me that he was made England manager in 1977. The only surprise was that he wasn't in the job longer or perhaps even sooner.'

A bold statement. Some might say Day is entitled to one.

30

TOWN AND OUT: The 1975 FA Youth Cup final

A WEST HAM XI DESERVEDLY HAD ITS NAME INSCRIBED ON A MAJOR trophy in 1975, but for much of the season nobody could be quite sure which team it would be. For while the first team manoeuvred its way towards the FA Cup final – and eventual success against Second Division Fulham – the youth side was making the same progress towards lifting its own trophy.

Manager Ronnie Boyce had been running the youngsters for just a year by the time he'd guided them to the FA Youth Cup final and he was delighted with his instant fortune. 'I really enjoyed coaching the kids and it was a great feeling to get to the final in my first season in charge,' he says.

However, final adversaries Ipswich Town represented formidable opposition. With a team featuring many future first-teamers, the Suffolk side arrived at Upton Park for the first leg and disappointed the majority of the 10,227 home fans with a 3–1 victory. West Ham's goal came courtesy of Terry Sharpe.

The second leg at Portman Road was a formality, with Town securing a 2–0 win on the night and a 5–1 success on aggregate. Reflects Boyce: 'Ipswich had a hell of a side. They had quality players in the likes of John Wark, Russell Osman, Keith Bertschin and David Geddis among others and deserved to win.'

West Ham's side included just three future Boleyn regulars in defender Alvin Martin, midfielders Alan Curbishley and Geoff Pike, plus Paul Brush (then playing in attack), as well as midfielder Terry Hurlock who would establish a career for himself – not to mention a reputation as an X-rated hardman – with rivals Millwall. In spite of the cup final defeat, Martin has special memories of the 1974–75 season, having just said goodbye to his Merseyside roots to start a new life in London. 'We had a good group of players and a great team spirit in that side,' he remembers. 'It wasn't just down to Ronnie Boyce being a nice man; he was an excellent coach as well. He taught me things in the first three months at West Ham that I'd never been taught before.'

Boyce wasn't left to his own devices, however. Ron Greenwood, despite his promotion to the role of general manager a year earlier, continued to show great interest in the activities of West Ham's young players. It was something that Martin quickly became aware of. 'I'd play in youth-team games and Ron was so passionate in his support of us,' he says. 'He loved the game more than anybody, even at youth-team level. We knocked out Liverpool on the way to the Youth Cup final and I could see the joy in Ron's eyes. The satisfaction he got from that result was as if we'd won the World Cup.'

Alvin had failed to get the deal he was looking for at local club Everton as a youngster and was still adjusting to his new environment in the capital. But godfather Greenwood provided great encouragement to the kids coming through the West Ham ranks, following their progress all the way to the final during 1974–75. Martin remembers: 'Ron came up to me at one point and said: "We'll show Everton what they missed." Just that one thing lifted me unbelievably high during that period and made me realise what a great man he was.'

31

TALKIN' ABOUT MY GENERATION: Alan Curbishley

Born: 8 November 1957; Forest Gate, London
Debut: v. Chelsea (h), 29 March 1975
Apps/Goals: 96/5
Final app.: v. Leicester City (h), 26 March 1979

FEW EAST END FAMILIES HAVE CONTRIBUTED MORE TO THE TWIN pillars of Cockney youth culture – football and pop music – than the Curbishleys of Canning Town.

Picture the early 1960s scene. In one bedroom, its thin walls vibrating to the sounds of rock'n'roll, sits Bill Curbishley, destined to carve out a glittering career as manager of rock gods The Who. Out in the hallway kicking a tennis ball against an imaginary goal on the wall is Bill's younger brother Alan, set to become one of the top teenage footballers of his generation and later a respected Premiership boss mooted as a potential England manager. God only knows what Mrs Curbishley was putting on her sons' cornflakes!

Fast forward to 1969. While The Who are in America bringing aural anarchy to hippy festival Woodstock, back across the pond Alan is busy making serious noises in London junior football. A career with West Ham is what the ambitious 11-year-old has set his heart on, but he's still shrewd enough to exploit his music-business connections. 'Bill used to work for the Track record label, who had the early T-Rex and Thunderclap Newman as well as The Who,' says Alan. 'I'd go up to their offices in Wardour Street in the West End, take a few albums and sell them to the teachers at my school. I used to do quite well out of it.'

Grateful as his teachers were of their pupil's entrepreneurial skills, by the time Thunderclap Newman had disbanded in the early 1970s they would have been happy with any kind of communication from Alan. His mind was lost to football. A regular on Upton Park's North Bank, Curbishley was West Ham through and through. He was a friend of fellow Canning Town boy and Hammers first-teamer Frank Lampard, and lived a few doors away from the mother of West Ham defenders John and Clive Charles, who at the time had striker Clyde Best as a tenant.

'Because I knew Frank I was already mixing with people like Bobby Moore and Harry Redknapp, I knew them all. It was the natural thing for me to go to West Ham.' Even so, Alan was almost swiped from under the Hammers' nose by Chelsea. 'I was playing for Newham Schoolboys and quite a few clubs wanted me. One day my mum was round the Charles' house – they lived behind the old Memorial Ground that was West Ham's original home – and she told Mrs Charles that I was going to Chelsea.

'Wally St Pier, West Ham's chief scout, used to go round their house every Tuesday and Thursday for something to eat before training. He heard my mum and said: "Well get him to come down to us instead." She came back and told me I could go to West Ham, so I went on the Tuesday night and stayed.'

He came flying out of the blocks after signing apprentice forms in July 1974. Alan made such an impact in his first few appearances for Hammers' South East Counties League side that, at 16 years old, barely out of his school blazer, he arrived on the fringes of the big-time. 'After the pre-season they had an injury crisis and I found myself on the bench versus Everton at Upton Park in the August. At the time I was the youngest West Ham player ever to be named on the teamsheet. It was an amazing experience for me.'

Although he didn't get to play in that 3–2 defeat, West Ham fans managed to put a face to the name the following March. Curbishley made the starting line-up at home against Chelsea due to injury to skipper Billy Bonds. Undaunted by the responsibility, he was one of the Hammers' better performers in a 1–0 defeat. Early in 1975–76, Alan at last sampled the sweet taste of victory for the first time. And how. 'It was at home against Newcastle, with England striker Malcolm Macdonald and all that. Trevor Brooking was injured so I took his place in midfield. I scored after a few minutes, made another and we won 2–1.' *Match of the Day* presenter Jimmy Hill raved about Curbs' exciting contribution on TV later that evening. 'I became known as "Whizz" by people at West Ham,' adds Alan. 'My team-mate Pat Holland gave me that nickname after I burst on the scene like that.'

The previous summer Curbishley, by then an England Under-18 regular, had further augmented his boy wonder reputation with his exploits for West Ham's youngsters as they reached the final of the FA Youth Cup, only to go down to Ipswich Town 5–1 on aggregate.

Other than a little sideline selling badges at The Who concerts – including the band's famously ear-splitting 88,000 sell-out at The Valley, home of his future charges Charlton Athletic, in the summer of 1976 – Curbishley's career appeared to be set dead straight on many fruitful years with the Hammers. Aged 18 he appeared in both legs of the nail-biting European Cup-Winners' Cup third round tie against Dutch outfit Den Haag, a contest that finished 5–5 on aggregate and West Ham won on the away goals rule. Manager John Lyall included him as a substitute for the final in Belgium against Anderlecht, although he didn't play in that 4–2 defeat.

In November 1976 he further endeared himself to the fans with West Ham's fifth goal in a 5–3 thumping of Tottenham at home. Although by no means an automatic selection, he looked confident and comfortable whenever he was picked. Alan played just behind Trevor Brooking, mopping up loose balls and joining the master on forays upfield whenever possible. To Lyall, his fellow players and the soccer press it was patently obvious that here was an intuitively creative footballer in the best Boleyn traditions. That, in essence, was the problem.

By the late 1970s, Brooking was reaching his world-class peak and forging a wonderful partnership with left midfielder Alan Devonshire. Experienced striker Pop Robson could play deep to good effect, while for hard graft Lyall could turn to Pat Holland, Geoff Pike or skipper Billy Bonds, prior to his relocation into the back four.

Alan was getting games under his belt – 12 in 1976–77, 36 the following season – when people got injured or lost form, but he started to wonder whether in the long-term there were enough midfield berths to go round.

West Ham suffered relegation to the Second Division at the end of 1977–78 and as a difficult season of adjustment signalled the end for a clutch of underperforming Hammers, so it also coincided with a growing tension between Lyall and Curbishley, who moaned to the press: 'Trevor Brooking is a great playmaker, but everything seems to revolve around getting the ball to him.'

Says Alan: 'I was a bit hot-headed. If John had said something was black, I'd have said it was white. It was the stage I was at. All my family were West Ham fans and they wanted me in the side. I'd played 80-odd games but I felt I wasn't going anywhere. It was a difficult time.

'In the last six months of the 1978–79 season I wasn't very happy at all. I wasn't playing like I knew I could, I wasn't producing. Freedom of contract had just come in which meant you could leave. My contract ran out and I decided to go.'

With hindsight, Curbishley reckoned he exited too hastily to Birmingham City for £225,000 in the spring of 1979. He believed he would have made West Ham's 1980 FA Cup final side if he'd ridden out his youthful frustrations. Even so, his unexpected sale to the club's Second Division rivals saw him recapture his form and enter the England Under-21 frame.

'Whizz' had certainly arrived with a bang a few years earlier but, before Hammers fans could get cosily familiar with him, he'd upped and left. Curbishley the manager, however, would be a more patient individual altogether.

Following boss Harry Redknapp's sacking by West Ham in May 2001, Curbishley became the people's choice for his replacement. It wasn't just that he was a local lad who had played for the club, although for the more partisan supporters these would be perceived as the overriding qualities one should look for in a West Ham manager. It was also because Alan had worked wonders to develop unfashionable Charlton into a side capable of holding their own in the Premiership. The Addicks finished ninth in 2000–01, six places above West Ham.

'When the West Ham thing came up people were putting two and two together,' he says. 'I thought it was quite natural. I was as surprised as anyone when Harry left. It was a shock, but then I knew the next thing would be speculation about me. Obviously when it happens you start thinking about it, what could be or what would be. But I'd already committed myself to Charlton, all but signed the new contract. So it never really got off the ground in that respect. I'd agreed a contract a month before Harry got sacked.'

Many had assumed that, binding contracts or not, Curbishley would find the lure of working 'back home' irresistible and a deal would be struck. He still lived in deepest West Ham country, just a few miles from the Chadwell Heath training ground, while most of his family were Hammers nuts. Yet integrity, a characteristic he perhaps wishes he'd shown more of during his Upton Park years, won the day.

32

CRIKEY PIKEY: Geoff Pike

Born: 28 September 1956; Clapton, London
Debut: v. Birmingham City (h), 6 March 1976
Apps/Goals: 367/41
Final app.: v. Everton (a), 11 April 1987

AMONG THE MANY HOMEGROWN PLAYERS WHO HAVE LATER returned to West Ham in a coaching capacity – either for the club or as representatives of footballing associations – is Geoff Pike.

When the former midfield dynamo – one of the Hammers' top 20 appearance holders – worked part-time for the Football Association in the early 1990s he was a regular visitor, monitoring youth coaching to make sure everything was carried out in line with FA rules. Sadly, one such visit would have the most unfortunate of repercussions for both club and ex-player. After watching some junior trialists play in an 11-a-side match at Chadwell Heath – rather than in a regulation small-sided game – Geoff reported the fact to his employers. It was allegedly one of a number of infringements made by the club at junior level, ultimately leading to the suspension of West Ham's Centres of Excellence – the lifeblood of young talent – for an entire season.

Labelled as the whistleblower, Geoff was barred from the very training ground on which he'd honed his craft, as well as Upton Park. Six years would pass before youth boss Tony Carr and head of development Jimmy Hampson reconciled their differences with him and Pike admits it was an extremely difficult period in his life – being portrayed as the villain of the piece by the club he loved. 'I knew I hadn't done anything wrong,' he says. 'I just happened to drop in at Chadwell Heath when they were doing something that wasn't within the regulations. I felt it was my duty to report it and that was all. Apart from one or two very minor incidents, that was my sole contribution.

'The centres got closed down as the FA were investigating West Ham because of irregularities. I didn't close the centres down. My part in the saga involved one side of A4 paper which, later, I very willingly showed Tony and Jim.'

Geoff says the rift with Carr and Hampson lasted so long partly as a result of the failure of the FA to clarify his role. 'I felt aggrieved with the FA because they didn't back me up. And I couldn't go back into West Ham because I didn't think my words would be heard. It came to a head after I'd been working for the PFA for a couple of years and I was asked to do some coaching qualification assessments at Chadwell Heath. I felt it was time to bury the hatchet. To be fair to Tony and Jim, they were very willing to get together. We met on neutral ground, had a cup of coffee and it was all very civilised. They said: "Well, as far as we're concerned the matter is closed," and I agreed with that 100 per cent.'

This unfortunate episode was all a long way from Pike's first trip to the training ground in 1966, when youth development evidently had as much to do with spontaneity as it did regulations. One minute the ten-year-old was at home in front of the TV in Clapton, north-east London; the next he was taking the first step in a career that would see him become one of the few to play more than 350 games for the club. Says Geoff: 'One Tuesday evening my father said to me: "Hey, West Ham juniors train over at Chadwell Heath tonight. Why don't we go over and have a look?"' His dad was an Arsenal fan, but the influence of Hammers-supporting grandparents had filtered through.

'We jumped in the car and drove down. John Lyall – then youth coach – was there and he came over and said: "Can I help you?" My dad said: "Would it be possible for my son to join in?" John said: "Well he's a little bit young but as you're here he can have a go." I did and I must have impressed him because I was asked to come back.'

There was always a minority of fans who would have preferred it if the Pike family's car had broken down on that chance visit. Geoff wasn't always the fall guy

– he was, after all, voted runner-up in 1981's Hammer of the Year poll – but he had his moments of being yelled at for not having the finesse of other players. Naturally, his critics forgot their reservations whenever his hair-trigger shot bulged the back of the net.

Nobody celebrated a goal quite like him. If he scored it himself, he was ecstatic. If someone else had scored he'd be first on the scene to celebrate, jumping all over them like a playful puppy. Puppy love was much in evidence in a classic game during Pike's first full season in the first team in 1976–77. With typical theatrics, West Ham needed to beat Manchester United at home in the final match of the campaign to avoid relegation. 'We went 1–0 down after half a minute. Frank Lampard equalised from 30 yards, then a few minutes before half-time we got a penalty. I was pen-taker, but unfortunately I put it over United's crossbar. We came in and John Lyall, being the psychologist he was, said: "Just go out and do it for him," meaning me.

'The lads were terrific and within a few minutes of the second half I actually scored, which relieved some of the pressure. We eventually won 4–2 and managed to stave off relegation for another year.'

Due, he says, to complacency setting in, Pike had taken rather longer than he'd hoped to climb through the ranks after signing apprentice forms in 1973. 'I was taken on a first-team tour when I was 16 or 17. John tended to do that, try to blood you in a little bit. Possibly that might not have done me a favour because it made me too relaxed.'

In March 1976, ten months after experiencing FA Youth Cup final defeat against Ipswich, Pike made his first-team debut in a 2–1 home defeat by Birmingham City. 'It was between a lad called Yilmaz Orhan and myself as to who was going to play up front and who was going to be the substitute. Yilmaz had an injury but he swore blind that he was okay and for 45 minutes he limped around the field not doing himself any favours whatsoever. I never forgave him for that because I could have made my full debut, but I came on at half-time and was a little bit unfortunate not to score.'

Having initially joined the juniors as a striker, Pike would play as an emergency forward on several occasions. But it was as an industrious midfielder, firstly wide right then more centrally, that he made his name. He played the wide role in the 1–0 FA Cup final victory over Arsenal in 1980. 'For a two-week period I was very much on a high. My wife was nine months pregnant and my eldest son was born soon after the cup final.'

In 1980–81, Pike was ever-present as the Hammers romped to the Second Division title. 'There was a depth of quality about that team. The spirit came from the fact that when we crossed the white line we felt there was a 99 per cent chance we would win the game. I knew where Trevor Brooking was going to be, he knew where I was going to be and we both knew where strikers Paul Goddard and David Cross were. It was an absolute pleasure.'

Then there was the 1981 League Cup final against mighty Liverpool. West Ham lost 2–1 in a replay, but Pike rated the initial 1–1 draw at Wembley as his proudest Hammers moment. 'In most of the Sunday papers the next day I had top marks out of ten. That was extremely pleasing, knowing that I'd played on such a big stage.'

He kept racking up the appearances in the 1980s – 41 in 1981–82; 48, 35 and 38 in the following three seasons. Geoff tended to bounce back quickly from injury, which is why there was a cruel irony to his being sidelined with various problems for much of the 1985–86 campaign, in which West Ham finished third in the First Division. Although doing his bit to earn five crucial wins, Geoff played just ten league games. Consolation came in the FA Cup with another goal against Manchester United, a freak 18-yard looping header in a 2–0 fifth round replay win at Old Trafford. Most of the time, though, he found himself in Scot Neil Orr's shadow. 'Neil was the ideal man to take my place,' Geoff says, 'but because things were going so well it wasn't that easy to get it back. There was no rotation system – I had to fight my way back into the side again.'

It was a losing battle. In 1986–87, Orr left for Hibernian, but the arrival of Stewart Robson from Arsenal and emergence of Paul Ince from the youths ushered in a new era in central midfield. Pike again made just ten league starts and at the end of the season, aged 30, he was sold to Notts County for £35,000. 'I knew in my heart of hearts I could still play for the club,' he says. 'Given a fair crack of the whip the side could have benefited from me being around and vice versa.'

Both parties would eventually benefit from the relationship again once Pike's West Ham ban was lifted in 2001 and he reacquainted himself with his spiritual home as a regional coach for the PFA. Geoff says: 'I can now go back into an environment which I loved for so long and in which Tony Carr and I work closely together. It's an understatement to say I was a little bit disappointed that I wasn't able to go there – if you cut me I'll bleed claret and blue.

'Maybe in hindsight I should have said something a little earlier and not let the thing hang over me. But I was still employed at the FA so I couldn't really do that. It was a shame it came to that, but now I've gone back into the football club and hopefully things will be as good, if not better, than they were before.'

33

BENCHMARKS: Paul Brush

> Born: 22 February 1958; Plaistow, London
> Debut: v. Norwich City (h), 20 August 1977
> Apps/Goals: 185/1
> Final app.: v. Liverpool (h), 20 May 1985

'I ALWAYS FELT I HAD SOMETHING EXTRA TO PROVE. I WASN'T A bought player, so I generally had to do that bit extra to stay in the side. If something went wrong I felt that too often it was me who was left out and it affected my confidence.'

Paul Brush perhaps seemed a little too placid to be a defender. Coming into the side in the late 1970s, the left-back was always going to be compared to stalwart Frank Lampard, but his assurance on the pitch was often undermined by a lack of games in which he felt he should have been included. He says: 'When you've got the self-belief but you've not the opportunity to show what you can do, it plays on your mind that if you make a mistake it's going to be remembered more than if a senior player makes one.'

Despite having played in the six previous ties, Brush was the fall-guy as manager John Lyall opted for the experience of Lampard when selecting his line-up for the 1980 FA Cup final. Determined not to let the disappointment destroy his spirit, he trained throughout the summer with one thing in his sights – the Charity Shield game against Liverpool in August. He achieved his goal of playing at Wembley and started the 1980–81 promotion-winning season in the side, but lost out to Lampard after the Hammers failed to win any of their first three matches. 'The team then won five games on the trot and I knew I was only going to play when somebody was injured,' he says. 'And then perhaps you end up trying too hard when you do get a chance. But I always felt I was good enough to be in that side.'

Brush's frustration was all the more intense because of his emotional ties with the club, having cheered West Ham on from the South Bank as a boy. From the age of six he was playing football in the street with fellow Hammers wannabe Alan Curbishley near his home in Mafeking Road in Canning Town, where he lived until the age of 19. 'It was always my dream to be a footballer. And West Ham was where I wanted to play,' he says.

Having impressed in junior football, at the age of 11 a distinguished gentleman turned up on his doorstep. His name was St Pier – Wally St Pier – and he presented Paul with a licence to thrill by inviting him to train with his beloved Hammers as an associate schoolboy twice a week.

The left-footed Brush mostly played in midfield when representing Newham, London and Essex Schoolboys, but when he got taken onto the Hammers staff in 1974 it just so happened that eight of the 16 apprentices were midfielders. A scarcity of strikers therefore resulted in Paul being pushed into attack for a year and a half. 'I played up front in the side that reached the 1975 Youth Cup final and was actually the top goalscorer at the club that season with 18 goals,' he says. 'Later, after playing for the youth team at QPR one particular morning, I was a substitute for the reserves at Crystal Palace in the afternoon. A defender got injured after 25 minutes and reserve-team boss Bill Lansdowne (himself a former Hammer) said: "You're left-footed, go and play at left-back." I ended up playing in that position for virtually the rest of my career.

'I owe a huge debt to Bill because he played me at left-back in reserve games even though there were a couple of natural defenders ahead of me. I'd enjoyed scoring goals but at the age of 18 I realised I wanted to spend more time facing the play rather than mostly playing with my back to goal.'

Brush broke into the first team at the start of the 1977–78 season. A defensive reshuffle forced by injuries saw Lampard move across to the right to accommodate Paul, who retained the No. 3 shirt up until Christmas when right-back John McDowell returned to the side. The struggling Hammers won just five of the 24 league games Brush played in as they plummeted towards relegation, but he enjoyed the experience. 'Every chance to play was a bonus and it was just great to be involved.'

Paul fully established himself as the Hammers unsuccessfully attempted to bounce straight back to Division One, playing in every one of the side's 44 games during 1978–79. But the signing of talented Scottish teenager Ray Stewart increased competition for places in defence and a broken arm in late 1979 further restricted Paul's appearances before he experienced FA Cup final heartbreak. Then, with Stewart and Lampard holding down the full-back positions, West Ham steamrollered the rest of the Second Division during the promotion campaign of 1980–81.

Appearances became increasingly hard to come by and Brush says: 'When you've been an ever-present in your second season and it then takes you three more years to play the same number of games again, there's something not quite right. I'm not entirely blaming myself for that. I think I could have been a better player if I'd had a bit more encouragement.'

At least Paul could take some satisfaction on the coaching side, teaching youngsters the basics at the club's Chadwell Heath training HQ having gained his preliminary FA badge at the age of 21. And there were some happy times to reflect on despite his peripheral status.

The 1980 FA Cup semi-final replay, against Everton at Leeds United's Elland Road, saw him celebrating the 2–1 extra-time victory without knowing who'd actually scored with that last-gasp flying header. 'I asked why Frank Lampard was doing the TV interviews afterwards and was shocked to be told it was because he'd scored the winner!' Nine months later he was in the side that travelled to Russia and beat Dynamo Tbilisi 1–0 in the third round of the European Cup-Winners' Cup to restore some pride after losing the first leg 4–1. But he missed out on another cup final appearance the same year when the Hammers drew with Liverpool at Wembley in the League Cup and then lost the replay at Villa Park.

There was little evidence in Brush's first-team career of the predatory instinct he'd shown at youth level – in fact he scored just once, in a 3–1 home defeat by

QPR in his final season. But he says he enjoyed a decent relationship with the Upton Park crowd. 'I think they were appreciative of homegrown players. There was a definite affinity with people who came from the area, although there was always a handful of people in the Chicken Run who didn't like one or two players.'

The arrival of another left-back, Steve Walford, in the summer of 1983 suggested that Brush's days were numbered and even though he found himself back in the side when the former Arsenal man fell victim to injury during the 1984–85 season, Paul felt the time was right to make a fresh start elsewhere.

In August 1985 he was able to put the ups and downs of his football career in true perspective, when his wife Marilyn died from leukaemia. He'd known about her illness since the previous December – shortly before she was due to give birth to their son Peter – but had found the inner strength to play on. He says: 'John Lyall, the manager, was absolutely magnificent to me around that time. On a purely professional level I'm not going to remember him with great affection for leaving me out of the 1980 FA Cup final. But on a personal level he was brilliant when helping me deal with my problems.'

Lyall's support aided Paul's adjustment to life as a single parent, but when the Hammers boss offered him an escape from reserve football with a loan period to Second Division Crystal Palace, he willingly accepted the new challenge. He soon made a permanent £30,000 switch and a different environment did him the world of good. 'I grew up when I joined Palace and went from being a quiet, homegrown footballer to a senior player whose opinion was sought by everybody. It was the right move for me at that time. I had an hour alone in the car every day and that was important in terms of settling my mind after the problems I'd had.'

Injuries seriously blighted Brush's three years at Selhurst Park and he ended his professional career at Southend United. In 2001, having impressed as a coach (especially at youth level) at Leyton Orient under managers Pat Holland and Tommy Taylor, Paul became the third successive former Hammer to assume control of first-team affairs at the struggling Third Division club. His immediate aim was to fashion a side that 'plays football that's exciting, progressive and value for money to watch'. He was clearly determined to draw on his wealth of experience, insisting: 'The way you've been treated in your own playing career shapes how you want to do things when the opportunity to manage comes your way. I've learnt from the good and the bad.'

34

TWENTY-TWO-YEAR STRETCH: Alvin Martin

Born: 29 July 1958; Walton, Liverpool
Debut: v. Aston Villa (a), 18 March 1978
Apps/Goals: 580/33
Final app.: v. Sheffield Wednesday (h), 5 May 1996

IT WAS AROUND MIDDAY ON SATURDAY, 1 DECEMBER 1973, WHEN lanky 15-year-old Scouser Alvin Martin first met West Ham boss Ron Greenwood and his right-hand man John Lyall. He was with his father in the foyer of the Adelphi Hotel in Liverpool, where the Hammers were based prior to their First Division game at Anfield later that afternoon. 'The team came down for their pre-match meal and I can remember thinking: "Oh my God, it's Bobby Moore!" Ron and John then gave us passes for the game. My main interest was the free tickets but sitting down with the pair of them made a real impact on me.'

Predictably, Liverpool won the match (1–0) but if that brief meeting had anything to do with Alvin eventually deciding to sign for West Ham then it was still a pretty good day for the London club. As a fan of the victorious Reds the youngster would certainly have considered the afternoon a success, yet at the time he was close to committing himself to Merseyside rivals Everton, having signed schoolboy forms for the Goodison Park outfit.

'I'd been led to believe that I was going to be offered a full apprenticeship at Everton,' he explains. 'But in 1974 they had fewer places available for local kids than previously and only offered me semi-professional forms. I took it as an insult and told my parents: "I don't want this."'

At the time the young Alvin was playing for Netherton Boys, whose manager John McBride had contacts at QPR and West Ham and arranged trials for him at both London clubs. 'I was claiming my train fare expenses from both clubs so I was up on the deal straightaway,' he says. 'I arrived at Rangers in the middle of pre-season training and all they were doing was running. I wasn't really fit and although I did reasonably well in a trial game up against Stan Bowles I was told: "Thanks for coming down, you're a good lad but we don't think you're going to be good enough."

'Initially it knocked me back but I had another bite of the cherry at West Ham and also knew I was going to be fitter after two weeks' training. Then I got another call from QPR telling me there'd been a difference of opinion between the coaches and asking me if I could go back so that they could reassess me. I told them I was going on holiday but I was actually going to West Ham. If Rangers had offered me a deal I'd never have crossed London but as soon as I got to West Ham I realised it was a much better club. It had more tradition, players such as Billy Bonds and Trevor Brooking, while Ron Greenwood was more in touch with the kids. Everybody was so friendly and it was just a completely different environment.'

Until that point Martin had been playing as a centre-half for his school and right-back for Lancashire Schoolboys – yet at centre-forward for his Saturday and Sunday sides. Fortunately, he nominated defence as his best position when agreeing his two-year apprenticeship at West Ham, although Greenwood tried him out up front. Says Alvin: 'I wasn't the quickest and not the greatest of finishers, but I could hold the ball up and bring other people into play. Ron played me up front in a youth-team game with Bobby Moore watching. Ron called me in afterwards and told me that Bobby had said: "No, leave him at centre-half, he'll never be a centre-forward."'

Even as a defender Alvin still had much to learn in terms of using his natural ability to maximum effect. 'At that time I was very raw, aggressive and used to dribble with the ball a lot. I'd take the ball to the edge of the box and want to beat two or three players. I was full of confidence. But John Lyall would sit me down and tell me that I should try and play the easy ball and only use my skill if it was needed to get out of a tricky situation. I'd also want to win every first ball and end up giving lots of fouls away; now and then I'd get into aggressive situations where I'd want to fight somebody. But Ronnie Boyce, the youth-team boss, had the patience of a saint and always had one eye on me to see if I was getting homesick.'

Alvin showed commendable strength of character as he adjusted to life in digs in Plaistow and East Ham. He also drew comfort from the parallel that existed between his Merseyside homeland and the East End in terms of its sense of spirit and community. 'West Ham had some lovely people at the club at that time,' he says. 'Chief scout Wally St Pier didn't bring me to the club but he was synonymous with the way things were in terms of friendliness, honesty and integrity. From Ron, John and Ronnie downwards, the people were the salt of the earth. And it made me realise how lucky I was to be at the club. Everything was about tradition. The names of Bobby Moore, Geoff Hurst and Martin Peters were always being used as examples of the standards required and if you got anywhere near those you were going to be a success.'

Alvin did just that. If skipper Billy Bonds had already established himself as the Boleyn Buccaneer, then Martin – during the course of his 22-year stay at the club – became something of a West Ham Warrior. By the time of his departure in 1996, he'd played nearly 600 games (placing him fifth in the all-time appearances list) under four of the club's eight managers at that point; reached the final of the Youth Cup in 1975 and League Cup in 1981; won the FA Cup in 1980; experienced three relegations (1978, 1989 and 1992); enjoyed three promotions (1981, 1991 and 1993); captained the side to within a couple of games of the League Championship in 1986; won 17 England caps; had two testimonials and claimed three Hammer of the Year awards while overcoming numerous major injuries gained in the heat of the battle.

After signing professional forms in 1976, 'Stretch' – as dubbed by digs partner Keith Robson because of his long legs – might have felt he was being chucked in the deep end when making his first seven appearances during the relegation campaign of 1977–78. But he insists: 'As a kid the pressure wasn't on me, it was on the older players. I didn't let relegation affect me as I knew I might get more of a chance the following season.'

Alvin replaced Tommy Taylor as Billy Bonds' central defensive partner as the Hammers reinvented themselves to enter the 1980s as a team with huge potential. The 1980 FA Cup final success against Arsenal and 1981 League Cup final ties against European Champions Liverpool preceded the return of the club to the top flight on the back of a campaign that had seen the side amass a post-war Second Division record of 66 points (under the two points for a win system) after winning

28 of their 42 league games. 'I still look back at the 1980–81 side and think that was when I was at my best,' says Martin. 'I fancied myself and Billy Bonds to take anybody on. If we could have added the strikeforce of Tony Cottee and Frank McAvennie from the 1985–86 side to the rest of the 1981 team, we'd have won the title in the mid-'80s. That's how good the side was.'

Alvin's overall impression of the 1985–86 season, when the club finished third after challenging for the title (and he famously scored against three different goalkeepers in the 8–1 crushing of Newcastle in April 1986) definitely leans more towards achievement than disappointment. However, it was only his second year as skipper – after Bonds had stepped aside – and in retrospect he acknowledges the burden of such responsibility. 'The captaincy brings a pressure because when you're not playing well you've got to point the finger at other people knowing they can easily point the finger back. Looking back, I wish I'd lightened up more. I'd enjoy winning a game but then worry about winning the next one. And if I didn't play well it affected me. Later on I can remember having a bad game and the crowd chanting: "John Lyall out!" That really hurt because I felt responsible.'

Alvin's England career spanned a five-year period (1981–86) and although he played in the 1986 World Cup finals he'd surely have been a more dominant figure at international level had injury not intervened. A broken collarbone ruled him out of the 1982 finals while an instep injury drastically reduced his domestic appearances during 1987 and 1988 as West Ham laboured. 'I got a bang on my foot during my first year in the West Ham team and I think I must have fractured it. After a few weeks it seemed okay but about eight or nine years later I got arthritis in the joint. It was like playing with pebbles in my boot and I just couldn't run properly. But the team was struggling and John Lyall wanted me on the pitch.'

The late 1980s was a miserable time for Martin, with self-confidence mutating into self-criticism as the club slumped towards another relegation. 'I felt I was playing badly and told John that it might be the best for both of us if I moved on,' he says. Yet it was Lyall who was to depart after the club failed to renew his contract in 1989. 'I still believe the club should have stuck by him,' Alvin insists. 'Then Lou Macari took over and I told him I wanted to go – simply because I felt stale. But Lou told me to hang fire and see how things went. I then started to get closer to my usual form and agreed to stay.'

Although Martin suffered serious Achilles problems during the early years of

Billy Bonds' reign as manager in the 1990s, he persevered through difficult times to win not just respect but contracts that would keep him at the club until 1996. Fittingly, his final West Ham appearance – at the age of 37 – coincided with the debut of 17-year-old Rio Ferdinand, another great centre-half in the making. The Hammers drew 1–1 at home with Sheffield Wednesday and both men played as substitutes on a day that saw Alvin burst into tears – and not just because boss Harry Redknapp had failed to offer him a coaching post. 'I had the offer of another year's playing contract but felt that with the emergence of Rio I may as well let him come through. I couldn't have played at that level for another year and didn't want to be sitting in the reserves.'

With one eye on a management career – possibly back at Upton Park – Martin accepted ex-colleague Pat Holland's offer to join Orient on a player/coach basis. Sadly, an unsuccessful two-year period as boss of Southend United – 'possibly the wrong job at the wrong time' – undermined his long-term managerial ambitions, although he's very much of the view that what will be will be. 'I still can't explain what made me jump on a train to London as a 15-year-old when my parents wanted me to stay at Everton. Maybe it's fate but I'm an Essex boy now.'

35

CATCH-22: Nicky Morgan

Born: 30 October 1959; Plaistow, London
Debut: v. Luton Town (h), 9 April 1979
Apps/Goals: 25/2
Final app.: v. Stoke City (h), 19 March 1983

SINCE 1958, JUST SIX DEDICATED CENTRE-FORWARDS HAVE EMERGED through the ranks to play more than 25 first-team games for West Ham. Although that half dozen includes two undisputed Hammers icons in Geoff Hurst and Tony Cottee, it is a surprising statistic, somewhat at odds with the club's reputation for developing attack-minded players.

Nicky Morgan entered the category by the thinnest of whiskers in the early 1980s. East Ender Morgan was always confident in his own ability, but he felt he was in a classic Catch-22 situation for strikers: the goals never flowed, but then how could they if he wasn't given a decent run in the side?

Morgan's earliest coaching sessions were administered by his father, a decent amateur footballer, who worked on Nicky's potential on the streets of London's docklands. 'I'd have to kick a ball against a viaduct wall in Silvertown, with each foot, for half an hour every day,' says Morgan. 'At the time I found it a little overbearing, but I'm glad he did it. He was trying to make sure I was ready.'

Morgan was a Chelsea fan, but it was the cavalier Queen's Park Rangers side of the early 1970s that he and his dad would travel to watch. Nicky graduated from the terraces to the training field when QPR invited the striker to join their juniors, but the 25-stop tube ride in each direction soon had the youngster pining to train with a club closer to home. West Ham, impressed with his efforts for Newham's district side, duly obliged.

Morgan was offered full professional terms in 1977 and made his bow towards the end of the 1978–79 campaign. Having been relegated the previous season, West Ham's attempts to bounce straight back into the top flight were beginning to trail away in the second half of the campaign. Aged 19, he came in for the injured David Cross in a 1–0 home win against Luton Town in April, having only been named in the starting line-up an hour before kick-off. 'I played beside Pop Robson. I was slightly overawed but once I got into the game a bit and stopped worrying about it, it wasn't too bad.'

With Robson opting for a return to Sunderland in his native Northeast at the end of the season and strikers Alan Taylor and Billy Jennings both being shown the door, Morgan sensed he was in with a chance of regular action. It wasn't to be and, as the seasons rolled by, it became his head rather than a ball that he started hitting against brick walls. 'I spent a lot of time in the reserves and scored a lot of goals,' he says, 'but I didn't seem to get the break I wanted in the first team. For a long time I was hanging around waiting for that to happen.

'I wasn't injured or anything. The manager, John Lyall, just kept buying all these old strikers like John Radford and Stuart Pearson. Obviously he didn't think I was up to it and obviously I was a little bit pissed off with that, so I later took the opportunity when it arose to move on. I definitely felt I had the ability.'

Over the course of the next two seasons in Division Two, his anxieties increased as first Pearson and then record £800,000 signing Paul Goddard were paired with regular target-man Cross. Nicky would get occasional outings, scoring his first goal in a 4–1 thrashing of Charlton five days before West Ham beat Arsenal in the 1980 FA Cup final, coming on as a substitute and almost scoring in the resulting 1–0 Charity Shield defeat to Liverpool and appearing in two early rounds of the 1980–81 European Cup-Winners' Cup. A rare high was playing in place of the injured Goddard and scoring the last goal of that season, in a 1–0 win at Sheffield Wednesday, which secured the Hammers' record tally of 66 points in winning the Second Division championship.

But it wasn't until he was loaned out to Dutch First Division side Den Haag in 1981–82 that Morgan got the chance to show he could score consistently at the top level. 'I had a good spell there (seven goals in 16 appearances) and played against all the top teams like Ajax and PSV Eindhoven. I'd train mainly with West Ham during the week and fly over there at weekends, so I got the nickname "The Flying Dutchman". I was always coming back through Duty Free with Edam cheeses the size of footballs.'

When he returned to West Ham for the start of the 1982–83 season to find that his continental success cut little ice with Lyall, Morgan's confidence sank to a new low. By now in his early 20s, he was still very much a back-up player. Cross had gone but Scotsman Sandy Clark and Goddard were the first-choice strikers, while prodigious youth star Tony Cottee was steaming through the ranks. 'It was another season of doing not a lot,' Morgan says, 'messing about in the reserves, when I knew I was ready for first-team football.' After the grinding frustration of four substitute appearances, three starts and no goals, the forgotten forward was belatedly offloaded by Lyall. Negotiations were held with Portsmouth's chief scout in a service station on the M3 and Nicky duly took the southbound carriageway. He would later play for Bristol City, Stoke and Exeter and, after packing the game in he became a personal fitness instructor in Bristol.

Like many players from the days before agents were around to speak on their behalf, Morgan could never quite find it within himself to complain about his lot to his manager. Having been with the club since his mid-teens, he was more accepting of situations – at least on the surface. 'I never spoke to Lyall about it. I should have done. He wouldn't let me go, but wouldn't give me a real crack in the first team either. We never had a falling out or anything, I just couldn't understand it and nor could a lot of other people.'

PART FOUR

Loyalty to Lyall

36

ANGELIC UPSTART: Paul Allen

Born: 28 August 1962; Aveley, Essex
Debut: v. Southend (h), 25 September 1979
Apps/Goals: 192/11
Final app.: v. Everton (a), 8 May 1985

PAUL ALLEN'S £425,000 SALE IN 1985 SET A PRECEDENT THAT, WHILE of obvious benefit to himself and later the likes of Tony Cottee and Paul Ince, was a sickener for the fans he left behind. By the mid-1980s, it appeared that the ambitions, in their various guises, of outstanding youngsters could no longer be matched by West Ham. Equally frustrating for the supporters was the fact that the Upton Park board found the opportunity to cash in on its prize young assets increasingly difficult to resist. It was a chicken and egg situation – and both left a bad taste.

Although midfielder Alan Curbishley had left of his own accord in 1979, he was not considered a first-team certainty. Allen, on the other hand, had belatedly developed into the club's star attraction. Yet just weeks after being voted Hammer of the Year, he flew the nest. To compound the sense of outrage, he flew across Hackney Marshes to White Hart Lane. Paul says that his heart never wanted the move, but his career probably required it. 'I'd been in central midfield where it can get quite frantic. Then I got moved to the right-hand side. I had one or two games during 1984–85 where it went well and it just started to develop. I could see consistent progression when I'd only seen it in flashes before.

'I won the Hammer of the Year poll, but I didn't get a contract offer in writing until the end of that season. I felt that given how I'd developed it would have been nice to be offered something. It was never in my head to plan to get away.'

When the club did finally act to secure Allen's signature, it was too late – the midfielder's curiosity about the adventures that lay beyond Green Street had got the better of him. Boss John Lyall was to lose out on a second count when his £600,000-plus valuation of Allen was knocked down almost a third by a tribunal. 'By the end of the season I had Spurs and Liverpool to talk to – and there was mention of Arsenal too. There was also a lot of talk of John, who was hugely regarded and sought after, going somewhere else. I probably got caught up in that.

'An opportunity came around and I started to feel that maybe you can stay somewhere too long,' says Paul, whose cousins Martin and Clive would follow him in claret and blue. 'Perhaps it was time to push myself a little further. I'd had the honour of playing with the likes of Trevor Brooking, Alan Devonshire and Billy Bonds at West Ham and similarly knew I'd be competing against some incredible players at Spurs. It was an opportunity I had to take.'

Football was all-consuming as a member of the Allen clan growing up in Essex. The dads all played it (most notably Clive's father Les, who'd been part of Tottenham's 'Double' side of 1960–61) and the sons took to it instinctively. 'Clive and I used to play each other in the local district league. I was the ball boy for one of my uncle's Sunday sides. And then there was the opportunity to go to QPR when Les was the manager. Being around footballers in the players' lounge after the games gave me an incentive and got me thinking: "Yeah, I'd love to do this."'

After relegation from the First Division in 1978, Hammers manager John Lyall stepped up the recruitment process in the local area. Scout Len Hurford immediately struck gold by persuading Allen to train with West Ham as well as QPR. Paul also had trials with Arsenal, but as an Irons fan there was ultimately only one team for him. Soon after signing as an apprentice in 1978, he entered the exciting England youth team managed by innovative ex-Hammer Johnny Cartwright. Word started to get around that here was a focussed, energetic midfield player of exceptional quality. A part-work coaching publication, entitled *Football Handbook*, perceptively chose to follow 16-year-old Paul's progress during his apprenticeship. Its 'half-term' report concluded: 'You can't really ask for any more from a youngster in the first year of his apprenticeship. He knows there's still an awful lot to learn and work to do. Our job is to keep up with him!'

Allen would eventually smash Bobby Moore's record haul of youth caps, making most of his 23 appearances as captain. Another more widely recognised record would fall to the precocious teenager on 10 May 1980.

In September 1979, he returned from an England youth tour of Yugoslavia to a gloomy Chadwell Heath. Hammers' second season in Division Two had started badly, with four defeats in the first seven games. The League Cup provided a welcome distraction and Lyall saw it as a good time to gauge whether youngsters such as Dale Banton, Nicky Morgan, Billy Lansdowne Jnr and Paul were capable of providing some spark. Says Allen: 'John felt it was the ideal opportunity to put me in. It was against Southend in the third round. We beat them 5–1 in the second replay, Billy Lansdowne scoring a hat-trick. Thankfully for me things started to pick up for the team from there.'

Allen had been expecting to watch the Hammers with his mates in the South Bank that season, while picking up games in the youths and, if he was lucky, the reserves. But so impressed was Lyall with his teenage 'revelation' that he installed Paul in central midfield alongside Trevor Brooking – usually at the expense of either Geoff Pike or Pat Holland – for virtually the entire campaign, one that culminated in FA Cup final victory over Arsenal.

Allen and Brooking shared the lead role in one of the great chapters in West Ham's history – the former for being the youngest player ever, at 17 years and 256 days, to appear in an FA Cup final, the latter for scoring the only goal with a collector's item header. Says Paul: 'It was an incredible time. Within nine months I'd played in the South East Counties for West Ham's youth side, in the Combination and played pre-season fixtures at places like Walthamstow Avenue. Then, all of a sudden, I'm playing at Wembley.

'On the day, I had no nerves. Although we were in the Second Division I was quietly confident we could win because we had some outstanding players. Even the incident late on with Willie Young (the nation holding its breath as Paul beat the Gunners' offside trap and sped towards goal, only to be cynically up-ended by Arsenal defender Young) was not a problem with me. If Arsenal had earned a replay and then gone on to win I might have felt a bit different, but it didn't affect the result.' Nevertheless, Young's attempt to whack player rather than ball was the catalyst for the football authorities to implement new rules on tackling from behind.

Paul and cousin Clive, who became the first £1m teenager that summer when he left QPR for Arsenal, had made Allen the hottest surname in football. That didn't stop Paul taking his floppy fringe and dimples back to the youth team the following season to help Tony Carr's youngsters lift the 1981 FA Youth Cup. Says Carr: 'Paul had a tremendous attitude. Even though he'd won an FA Cup medal, he didn't look on the youth cup as anything less. He'd play exactly the same whether in the first team or the youths.'

It was another remarkable feat, but there was to be a heavy price for achieving so much success so soon. Allen's young body was struggling to keep pace with his career. 'I'd never want to take anything away,' he says, 'but the downside was that I couldn't get myself fit for two or three years. I was a young lad doing the training of grown men. I had terrible problems with injuries and it took a lot out of me.'

He made just one league start in 1980–81. 'I was fighting off little niggles the whole time. I wanted to train. I was ambitious and wanted to move forward. But by the age of 20 things had moved on and I just didn't feel I was playing how I knew I could. There were occasional highs, but then I'd get injured and I'd be stretching myself the whole time to come back and compete with people who were already fit. No discredit to West Ham, or John, who was always fair to me and rested me when he thought I needed it, but there was no structured rehabilitation in those days. If you were injured you were in the shadows until fit again.'

Hammers supporters had waited a long time to see an injury-free Paul Allen fulfil his potential and after four years of stop-start frustration, he appeared 47 times in a disappointing 1984–85 season (West Ham finishing 16th) in which his talent stood out like a beacon. And there was artistry as well as industry. In a 4–2 FA Cup quarter-final defeat against Manchester United at Old Trafford, he capped a superb performance with a brilliant run and strike from an acute angle. He also smashed valuable goals in home and away 1–1 draws against fellow strugglers Newcastle United. Meanwhile, his England career was back on track, Paul captaining the Under-21s against Romania. He would later be named in two 'B' squads, but the full cap for which he seemed destined never quite materialised.

Amid intense speculation about his future, Allen's last game for West Ham came in a 3–0 defeat at champions Everton in May 1985. Appearing for Spurs in the two games against West Ham the following season, he was given a torrid time by fans who felt utterly betrayed. It didn't help that in the first fixture, at a rain-lashed White Hart Lane on Boxing Day, Tottenham ended the Hammers' record 18-game unbeaten run in Division One.

Paul was naturally upset by the abuse, but serious health concerns over his baby daughter put the situation into stark context. As a result, Allen's first season with Spurs was a complete wash-out. In contrast, Mark Ward, his replacement at Upton Park, helped inspire West Ham to their best-ever First Division finish of third. Admits Paul: 'I'd be a liar if I said I wouldn't have liked to have been a part of that. Mark and Frank McAvennie really helped turn things around, because the year I left we'd been fighting relegation.'

After many seasons and two more FA Cup final appearances with Spurs, plus stints with Southampton, Swindon, Millwall and Bristol Rovers, Paul embarked on a career with the Professional Footballers' Association, organising the successful Masters' Six-a-Side veterans tournaments. Before his back started to play up, he appeared a few times himself – not for Tottenham, but for his first true love. 'It's a close run thing, but in terms of my allegiance it's West Ham. Hand on heart, that's the club I've always had a soft spot for.'

37

HAIR TODAY: Bobby Barnes

Born: 17 December 1962, Jamaica
Debut: v. Castilla (a), 17 September 1980
Apps/Goals: 54/6
Final app.: v. Sheffield Wednesday (a), 7 September 1985

HE WAS 17 YEARS OLD. HE'D JOINED HIS BOYHOOD HEROES AND made his first-team debut in Spain's legendary Bernabeu Stadium, scoring a cracker on his league debut at Upton Park three days later. He had teeny heartthrob looks and oozed confidence. Football being football, it was a recipe for disaster.

In the pre-'youth development' era when Bobby Barnes was being touted as one to watch, his destiny was pretty much in his own hands. He's the first to admit he let it slip through his hair-gel soaked fingers. 'It was attitude,' says Barnes. 'I got into the first team and was your typical Jack the Lad. I'd made it. I became far more occupied with the image of it rather than knuckling down to the hard work and pushing on.

'Without being arrogant, I was considered one of the brightest prospects of my generation. Although I went on and had a reasonable career in the Football League, I didn't achieve the things I'd like to have done for West Ham and I take the blame for that.'

His former youth coach Tony Carr had huge hopes for Bobby, but concedes that in the early 1980s talents like Barnes were still being left to their own devices once they had made the step up. 'It was a case of: "You're a first-team player now," which obviously shouldn't have been the way.'

Much of the expectation heaped on Bobby's young shoulders stemmed from the fact that he seemed, well, faintly exotic. Several years had passed since the last black player to hold down a regular place, Clyde Best, had left the club and Upton Park had an unfashionably Anglo-Saxon air, certainly in contrast to Latin-tinged White Hart Lane up the road. Suddenly, out of the imaginary dry ice, stepped an exciting attacker with a pop star's hairstyle and footwork to match. It soon transpired that Barnes – although born in Jamaica during a family holiday – was actually a Leytonstone boy rather than from the Copacabana or California. Not that he was in a hurry to blow the myth. 'The hair had an awful lot to do with the attention I got around the time of my debut,' he says. 'It was a showbizzy thing. I even did a couple of fashion shoots where they did me up as Michael Jackson.'

The media loved his shiny locks, but certain team-mates were not so impressed. 'I fell asleep on Paul Allen's shoulder on the coach once. He'd just bought a very expensive sheepskin coat. When we both woke up there was all this bloody grease over it. He wasn't best pleased. And Billy Bonds said he could never catch the ball after heading exercises because it was always covered in gel!'

It was Barnes' instinctive dribbling skills rather than his looks that had brought him to the attention of chief scout Eddie Baily. In 1979, just after he'd bagged seven O-levels, he was taken on as an apprentice after dalliances with two south London rivals. 'Eddie just turned to me one day and said: "Look, are you going to stop pissing about with Millwall and Palace and sign for us or what?"'

Bobby's dad had wanted him to follow the Barnes tradition and go to university, but his headstrong son insisted he could take a business studies course in the plentiful spare time his apprenticeship allowed.

So eye-catching were his performances for West Ham and England's youth sides that Barnes entered the first-team frame before returning to the kids to star in the 1981 FA Youth Cup victory over Tottenham.

In September 1980, at none other than Real Madrid's Bernabeu Stadium, he came on as a substitute for fellow youth product Nicky Morgan against Real's nursery side Castilla in the European Cup Winners' Cup first round first leg. West Ham lost 3–1, but won the second-leg 5–1 after extra-time to go through. Says Bobby: 'My game was overshadowed because there was an awful lot of crowd trouble, but not too many British players can say they made their first-team debut in the Bernabau. There were 40,000 there and running out to that after being used to playing reserve and youth football was tremendous.'

With Jimmy Neighbour and Pat Holland injured, Barnes kept his place for the following league game against Watford. In front of the *Match of the Day* cameras, the unknown winger (wearing a pair of boots lent to him by Holland) jinked his way in from the flank and smashed home one of the goals of the season in a 3–2 victory, setting tongues wagging in living rooms throughout the land.

It seemed that Lyall had produced yet another talent of Paul Allen-like precocity. Yet Barnes' debut proved to be the icing on a cake that never got properly baked. Failing miserably to capitalise on his dream start, he would appear just 29 times – often as substitute – during his first four seasons, with new signings, niggling injuries and a taste for the high life hindering his progress. New Romantics had made clubbing fun again and Barnes felt entitled to a few laughs himself. He says that while he wasn't quite ruling the roost at the Blitz club with Spandau Ballet, he wasn't far off it. 'I started getting involved in partying and going out with the older players when really I'd done nothing to justify it. There was the Stringfellows scene and we were going to Page 3 model parties.

'I was a young lad who thought he knew it all. John Lyall took me to task but the lessons he wanted me to learn didn't get through until it was too late.'

When Alan Devonshire got stretchered off with serious ankle damage during a

1–0 win at Wigan in the FA Cup third round in January 1984, Lyall offered Bobby another chance to show what he could do up the left flank. He did well, kept his place and scored the winner in the next round of the cup in a 2–0 victory at home to Crystal Palace. His outings began to increase in number and he started six of the first seven league games of the 1984–85 season. Then, in the eighth game, a 1–0 defeat at Newcastle United, the emphasis changed from his feet to his skin. 'The early '80s was a very difficult time for black footballers,' he says. 'There were certain grounds where you knew you'd get a rough ride. At Newcastle I had a banana thrown at me. I just ignored it. In fact I had quite a good game that day and remember nutmegging Peter Beardsley.

'It became quite a high-profile incident (the banana, not the nutmeg), with questions raised about it in the House of Commons. I was even invited to speak to the Greater London Council about it, but after talking to John we decided not to dignify the incident by making more of it.'

Barnes found humour a pretty failsafe antidote to racism. He was quoted after the Newcastle game as saying that he didn't like bananas and wished the Geordies had thrown melons instead. His team-mates also tried to diffuse the tension with a joke or two. 'We had one game at Leeds where the lads followed me out for the warm-up and then dashed back up the tunnel to the dressing room without me knowing. Apparently all you could hear around the ground was people booing me!'

Tony Carr recalled a match back in the 1981 FA Youth Cup run in which Barnes repelled a torrent of abuse in the best possible way. 'Away against Cardiff City, Bobby got a hell of a lot of stick from the crowd for being black. It was a real rough and tumble game, but the abuse Bobby got because of his colour lifted him. He played really, really well that night and we won 3–1.'

Barnes made 18 league starts in 1984–85, scoring a priceless winner in May 1985 against Norwich City in a game that secured the Hammers' place in the top flight and helped send Norwich down. That summer, Paul Allen exited to Tottenham, but before Bobby could think about pressing home his claims on the right, Lyall bought Mark Ward from Oldham Athletic. With Devonshire fit again for left-flank duty, the reserves beckoned.

His contribution to the magnificent 1985–86 campaign was a solitary 10-minute substitute appearance in a 2–2 draw at Sheffield Wednesday. Approaching

23, it was time to face up to the fact that he was no longer part of the script. 'My career had gone backwards by then,' he laments. 'I remember John telling me it just wasn't happening for me.'

Bournemouth boss Harry Redknapp made overtures, but Barnes didn't want to uproot from London and instead opted for a humbling £15,000 move to the more commutable Aldershot Town. He would later play for Peterborough, Swindon Town and Partick Thistle, ending his career with more than 100 goals.

No-one was more disappointed in Bobby's failure to blossom at Upton Park than the man himself. But at least as a teenager, when self-confidence got the better of him, he'd had the foresight to take that business studies course. It helped him make the smooth – and, by the way, smooth-headed – transition from football to financial advice when his career ended and would eventually pay dividends with his wide-ranging financial work for the Professional Footballers' Association.

38

THE CARR SHOW: The 1981 FA Youth Cup final

THERE IS A REMARKABLY CONSISTENT PATTERN TO THE TIMING OF boom years for West Ham's youth team. The youngsters always seem to prosper at the same time as the first team is itself experiencing a purple patch. All three of the club's FA Cup final victories have come within a year of FA Youth Cup final appearances, as have two Second Division championships and a second-best ever top-flight position of fifth in 1998–99.

Whether senior success stimulates the youths or vice versa is open to debate, but the pattern certainly adds merit to the belief that a healthy youth set-up is fundamental to a football club's overall well-being. The trend was perfectly illustrated in 1981, Hammers kids winning the Youth Cup as the club completed a fruitful 18-month period in which they beat Arsenal in the FA Cup, won the Second Division title, reached the final of the League Cup and made good progress in the European Cup-Winners' Cup.

A 2–1 aggregate victory over Tottenham Hotspur in the two-legged final (Barnes and Reader the West Ham scorers) was notably achieved with midfielder Paul Allen, who had already won an FA Cup winners' medal. Winger Bobby Barnes had also experienced significant first-team action. Further evidence of how fruitful times were came in the shape of Tony Cottee. Although the 15-year-old associate schoolboy was only on the fringes of the Youth Cup final side, within seven years he had become Britain's most expensive player when Everton signed him for £2.2m.

Victory over Spurs was particularly sweet for Tony Carr, who had taken on full-time running of the youths the previous year. Carr was himself a former Hammers youth striker, having signed apprentice forms in 1966 after captaining East London – with Pat Holland in the side – to victory in the English Schools Trophy. Says Tony: 'I stayed until I was 20 but the bottom line was that I wasn't quite good enough. I ended up taking a different route.

'John Lyall, youth coach at the time, had encouraged me to do the FA preliminary coaching course. A lot of us did it. I went to Barnet but broke my leg and while I was rehabilitating I got a call from John. I'd done my full badge by then, so he asked me back in 1973 to do some coaching twice a week. I took ex-striker Johnny Dick's place. I worked part-time as a PE teacher, then went full-time as youth coach in 1980.'

Following relegation from the First Division in 1978 with a squad noticeable for its lack of youth, Lyall instigated wholesale changes in the area of youth coaching and scouting. His assistant and chief scout Eddie Baily was provided with extra resources to ensure West Ham didn't keep missing out on the cream of Home Counties talent, while Carr's advancement was also part of the overhaul. The youths were also given access to a spanking new gymnasium built at Chadwell Heath. It wasn't the first time – and it wouldn't be the last – that sweeping changes were be made at youth level.

Tony Carr said: 'There weren't a lot of players in the system when Eddie inherited the job from Wally St Pier around 1975. Recruitment generally started about the age of 13 or 14 then and even that was considered young. You can hang your hat on certain boys of that age but for whatever reason they might not progress. You've got to look into your crystal ball to ask what that player is going to be like at 17. Is he going to be able to cope with the demands of professional football and training every day, with the physical demands and the pace of the game? Recruitment is a special art.

'I remember Eddie saying he wanted us to win the FA Youth Cup within five years. To be fair, we just about did that.'

Within 18 months of his full-time appointment, Carr's kids had won the South East Counties League title and appeared in the Southern Junior Floodlit final, as well as the showcase FA Youth Cup. While Barnes was the entertainer of the cup side and Allen already mature beyond his years in the engine room, attacking midfielder Alan Dickens, a 16-year-old Plaistow schoolboy, was widely felt to be the youth team's outstanding prospect. So good, in fact, that West Ham dispensed with a future Liverpool and Eire hero to aid his progress. With hindsight, Carr harboured huge regret about Lyall's decision to offload Ray Houghton to Fulham in 1982. 'The biggest mistake the club made was letting Houghton go. John released him because we had Trevor Brooking and Alan Devonshire in the first team and a very good young player in Dickens coming through.'

Needless to say, five members of the 1981 Youth Cup side would represent West Ham at senior level and Tony Carr would be around for many years to come. He would have to wait another 15 seasons for an FA Youth Cup final appearance and during that time the face of football at that level would undergo massive change. Yet, in the main, the club's uncanny ability to dig up gems in its own back yard would remain the same.

39

LOCAL PRODUCE – DOESN'T TRAVEL WELL:
Alan Dickens

> Born: 3 September 1964; Plaistow, London
> Debut: v. Notts Co (h), 18 December 1982
> Apps/Goals: 231/29
> Final app.: v. Liverpool (a), 23 May 1989

ALTHOUGH THEY WERE NO MATCH FOR LIVERPOOL IN THE 1970s, Manchester United still represented the glamorous pinnacle for many young footballers.

That's where Alan Dickens' talents might have been displayed if he'd not been so loyal to his Cockney roots. 'I was captain of my district side, Newham, and lots of clubs were interested in me,' he recalls. 'In my early teens I was training with West Ham but after I'd played at county level for Essex, Man Utd invited me up during the Christmas and summer holidays.

'I did that for two or three years. Dave Sexton (a Hammer in the 1950s) was the manager at the time. I used to stay in a hall of residence and they had their '80s star Norman Whiteside there too. At 15 they offered me a contract and I had to decide: West Ham or Man Utd? Being a homeboy, coming from the East End, I chose West Ham. They were my local team and the people were always very nice to me.

'Maybe I was kidding myself all along about going to Old Trafford, but I didn't have any regrets. At West Ham I made my debut early and played a lot of games. I could have gone to United and never played.'

Decision made, Dickens buckled down as an associate schoolboy Hammer.

Youth coach Tony Carr noticed early on that self-confidence was not Alan's strong point, but it soon became clear that years of running round the East End streets with a ball glued to his feet had made him a little bit special. The West Ham trademark of one- and two-touch football came naturally to him. Carr regarded Dickens as 'a great talent, an outstanding player', while Hammers kids contemporary Tony Cottee rated 'Dicko' as 'head and shoulders above the rest of us'. Proof of the pudding came when, as a 16-year-old and still at school, he was picked to play in the second leg of the 1981 FA Youth Cup final success against Spurs in May 1981.

By December 1982, Alan, then 18, had shown enough maturity in Carr's South East Counties side to suggest that he was worth a punt in the first team. From not being able to look idols Trevor Brooking and Billy Bonds in the eye as a shy trainee preparing their kits, he was about to join them on the big stage. Playing in place of the injured Alan Devonshire, a dream debut goal came his way after just six minutes of a 2–1 First Division win at Notts County. 'It was only a tap in,' says modesty itself. 'It wasn't on video so I never got to watch it. Tony Cottee made his debut a few days later and his game was on *Match of the Day*!'

The fans soon got to see more of both Dickens and TC as manager John Lyall started to tinker with his ageing side. Both scored in a home 2–1 win over Brighton – Dickens from spectacular distance – and Alan ended an excellent first season with six goals in 15 appearances.

However, any friendly rivalry between the exciting youngsters soon became overshadowed by somewhat unhelpful comparisons between the relaxed style of Dickens and the similarly tall, dark and elegant Brooking. 'I thought Trevor was fantastic,' says Dickens. 'He was the best. But when things weren't going so well for the team, I got the feeling the fans were looking for me to do the kind of things Trevor used to do. Maybe I didn't do that. Trevor possibly got to his best at 26 or 27 years of age. I think I would have got better too as I got older, but I went to Chelsea and it all kind of went pear-shaped.

'I was never very good at taking stick. I used to take it very personally and be hurt by it. Every footballer is going to get it and I should've risen above it.'

As Brooking called it quits in 1984 and Devonshire recovered from an ankle ligament problem, much of the focus of midfield creativity shifted onto the young shoulders of Dickens. Although never a fanatical trainer, Alan worked hard to meet the expectation. Like most of his colleagues he found the 1984–85 season a hard slog, West Ham slumping to 16th having finished 9th and 8th in his previous two seasons. Even so, his efforts were rewarded at England Under-21 level in 1985 with a cap against Finland, as he and Cottee both came off the bench. Ironically, at club level in the summer of '85, a bleach-blond Scot arrived from St Mirren to place his rising profile in jeopardy. 'They bought Frank McAvennie and I'd known on the Thursday before the first game of 1985–86 that I was going to be a substitute. Frank was going to play where I played, with Paul Goddard up front alongside Tony.

'In actual fact I was never confident of playing that season, but in that first game (a 1–0 defeat at Birmingham City) Paul got injured, Frank went forward and I came off the bench into midfield. Things went well from there.'

Both Dickens and McAvennie (twice) scored in the next match, a 3–1 home win over QPR. It was the first of 26 league victories during a remarkable campaign in which Alan missed just a solitary game, scored four goals and made a sack-load as West Ham finished a best-ever third in the First Division. 'I knew what Tony liked and I enjoyed threading those little passes between the back two or between the full-back and the centre-half. We used to work on it in training. You had Dev one side, Mark Ward one side and Frank and Tony up front making runs. It was all so easy. Everyone was behind one another.'

One of Dickens' best performances in a season in which he made 50 starts was in the flawless 4–0 win at Chelsea in March 1986, after which West Ham's title pretensions started to be taken seriously. Little did he realise that three seasons later his career would be going down the pan at Stamford Bridge.

Following such a good campaign, this self-confessed worrier finally felt his place in the starting line-up went without question. Expectation was understandably high in 1986–87, but as an anti-climactic season saw the team revert to mid-table mediocrity, he found himself playing deeper and deeper. That wasn't Alan's style and the change in job description started to affect his confidence. In *Boys of '86*, former centre-half Tony Gale claims the arrival of gung-ho midfielder Stewart Robson from Arsenal also unsettled Dickens. 'Robson wanted to be Roy of the Rovers all the time,' said Gale. 'He was a strong personality and it sent Alan into his shell.' Admits Alan: 'Something disappeared. Maybe it was being told to tackle more, but something went. As the years went by the game changed. Maybe my game had to change too.'

Change came in dramatic fashion after West Ham suffered relegation at the end of the 1988–89 season. Out of contract, Alan had been offered a new three-year deal by Lyall and went away on holiday to mull it over. Believing the Hammers would immediately bounce back from the Second Division, he intended to sign. While he was away, however, Lyall was sacked and in a jiffy Chelsea boss Bobby Campbell – father of Dickens' youth-team colleague Greg – contacted Alan to find out what his plans were.

'I went back to West Ham and Lou Macari had joined as manager. I kept hearing things about how it was going to change down there. Lou was still going to give me the three years, but I went to see Chelsea and in the end decided to sign for them.'

A tribunal fixed Alan's price at £600,000 and off he trotted to west London feeling wanted, but numb. On reflection he admits he made an enormous error of judgement in leaving behind his Upton Park comfort zone. 'I should have asked somebody for advice, but John had just got the sack and there wasn't anybody around. I didn't get any help from anybody. I wasn't sure what to do and there was no-one pulling me towards West Ham. Maybe I just didn't realise what a great thing was going on.'

His naivety in money matters and contracts at Upton Park would also be a source of regret. 'I couldn't believe it when I later read in Tony Cottee's autobiography that he used to go in and ask for more money. I didn't know that's what you had to do. I just thought John said: "This is what you get," which is so stupid.'

He never really settled at Chelsea, where by 1992 he was not so much down the pecking order as off the radar. Training methods were equally dispiriting. 'I couldn't believe the difference compared to West Ham. It was every man for himself and there was a terrible atmosphere there.'

Unable to get any kind of momentum going, Dickens' stock slumped to the extent that he was farmed out on loan, first to West Brom, then to Brentford, to whom he was eventually sold for a small fee. For a born worrier it was all too much and bewildered fall turned into shocking plummet. Colchester United, Chesham, Billericay and Purfleet all had the honour of being added to Alan's curriculum vitae before, in the mid-1990s, he cut his losses. He was shrewd enough to learn 'the knowledge' while playing non-league football and took up cab driving instead. He was barely out of his 20s.

As one of the most effective players in the highest-placed Hammers side ever, Dickens would have nothing to prove to any West Ham fan. Except himself. 'My mum keeps scrapbooks. Sometimes I stop the cab at her house, get them out and remind myself that once I did do something different.'

40

THE POACHER: Tony Cottee

Born: 11 July 1965; West Ham, London
Debut: v. Tottenham Hotspur (h), 1 January 1983
Apps/Goals: 335/145
Final app.: v. Liverpool (h), 29 September 1996

'I'D HAVE LIKED NOTHING BETTER THAN TO HAVE ACHIEVED EVERY-thing I wanted in football with West Ham. But that's the ideal world and, as any Hammers supporter knows, you don't get an ideal world at Upton Park.'

Tony Cottee found himself facing a huge dilemma as the big-hair fashions of the 1980s that had accompanied West Ham's mid-decade success started to recede. The Hammers had challenged for the league championship during the 1985–86 season but had slumped to finish a disappointing 15th the following year. Did he carry on scoring goals for the club he'd followed around the country as a teenage supporter? Or did he swing his shooting boots over his shoulder and take his talents elsewhere in a bid to achieve his career ambition of competing for trophies?

His heart waged a war against his head, as the striker first submitted an unsuccessful transfer request in 1987 and then, having endured another miserable season in which the Hammers avoided relegation only by goal-difference, joined Everton for a British record fee of £2.2m in the summer of 1988. 'There are personal and professional feelings when you're a footballer and you have to separate them sometimes,' says Tony. 'The club was on a downward spiral and I didn't want any more relegation battles. West Ham had been part of my entire life but I wanted to be competing at the top and playing in cup finals.'

Cottee was born with goals in his boots. And they were pre-ordained to be scored at Upton Park. Only born in the district of West Ham as a result of no maternity beds being available in Romford, Tony was always going to follow his father and grandfather's strong allegiance to the Hammers. He saw his first game at the age of six, going home a happy chappy after West Ham had beaten Nottingham Forest 4–2 thanks in part to future idol Bryan 'Pop' Robson, who scored twice. Eight years later, by then a devoted Irons Travel Club member, he followed the team on the road to Wembley and watched as Trevor Brooking stooped to send the FA Cup back to the East End at Arsenal's expense.

By 1980 he'd long established himself as a predatory goalscorer – first with Romford Royal, for whom he scored 198 goals in just three seasons; his school and local sides (an incredible 285 goals in three years); and eventually at district level – although his lack of height was considered by some to represent a major handicap. 'I was always small for my age,' he says. 'At Barking District level they weren't sure of me because of my size and Essex Schoolboys rejected me for their U14 and U15 sides until I eventually got in and scored six goals in my second game for them. Even when I got to West Ham as an apprentice I think they had doubts. From a very early age I knew I could get goals. The easiest thing was to score and the hardest part was the rest of the game. For most players it's the other way round.'

Yet while some of his Essex Schoolboy team-mates were snapped up early by professional clubs, Tony was discovered relatively late, eventually catching the eye of Hammers scout Ronnie Gale during a game for Chase Cross United – formed by dad Clive. 'Ronnie realised he'd seen something a bit different. Eventually that led to me training at West Ham as a schoolboy and then signing apprentice forms.'

Arsenal and Crystal Palace had also taken notice of the young Cottee but he says: 'My parents asked me who I wanted to sign for and I said: "I'm a West Ham fan, what do I want to play for those other clubs for?" Even when I was an apprentice the highlight of the week for me was to play on Saturday mornings in the South East Counties League and then go and watch the first team play in the afternoon.'

Cottee's transition from ardent fan to Hammers hero was almost instantaneous. Within 20 months of arriving at the club in May 1981, he headed home in a 3–0 win against Tottenham Hotspur to cap a sensational first-team debut. 'To suddenly be playing alongside people I'd idolised was surreal and, in terms of emotion and exhilaration on a football pitch, it never got any better than scoring that goal.'

As well as being influenced by youth-team boss Tony Carr, Cottee benefited greatly from the input of manager John Lyall and first-team coaches Mick McGiven and Ronnie Boyce. 'They all took an interest in the young players and I think the fact that John had come through the system himself meant he had a soft spot for the kids,' says Tony. 'He'd keep an eye on you, talk to you and get you involved in training with the first team. It was all about educating you in preparation for the years to come.'

The art of goalscoring, however, is largely instinctive and how much of that can be coached into a player is a topic of great debate. Says Cottee: 'You can't coach somebody to be a natural goalscorer but you can make them a better all-round player. I learned an awful lot under Tony Carr – things such as team play, holding the ball up, working on your first touch and developing passing skills. But to score goals you've got to be in the right place at the right time – and a lot of that is instinctive.'

Cottee also knew how to overcome the physical limitations of being relatively small. 'I knew I wasn't going to win any high balls so I just played to my strengths, trying to make better runs to give other players more options to play the ball to my feet. You have to become clever and I worked that one out very quickly.'

In five and a half seasons, between 1983 and 1988, Cottee scored 117 goals in just 255 games. After finishing runner-up in the Hammer of the Year poll in 1984 and 1985, he collected the trophy for scoring 26 times alongside strike-partner Frank McAvennie during 1985–86. Spring '86 also saw him named the PFA Young Player of the Year as he established himself as West Ham's most prolific marksman since Geoff Hurst. He top-scored in four of his five full seasons, with his best return coming during the 1986–87 campaign when he bagged 28 and made his full England debut.

Despite topping Everton's hit lists in five of his six seasons on Merseyside, Tony endured turbulent times while playing under four managers in Colin Harvey,

Howard Kendall, Mike Walker and Joe Royle. It certainly helped him gain some perspective on the only boss he'd had at Upton Park. 'I don't think I fully appreciated John Lyall until I left West Ham,' he reveals. 'Once I had a few troubles at Everton, I realised that John would probably have handled things better than people there had.'

Contrary to popular view, Cottee had no visions of returning to his spiritual home until a very specific date – 7 March 1994. Tony figured as part of a Premiership XI that played a Hammers side in the Bobby Moore Memorial Match and he reveals: 'I got a fantastic reception from the fans, there was a great atmosphere and it made me realise what I was missing.' Cottee returned to Upton Park with Everton one month later and the former hero turned villain to condemn West Ham to a 1–0 defeat. But he did so while keeping his fingers crossed he'd have many more chances to bust the Boleyn nets – if a Hammers manager would allow him the opportunity.

New boss Harry Redknapp duly obliged in September that year – recruiting him in exchange for defender David Burrows – and the striker instantly made his mark on his second debut for West Ham by getting sent off in a 0–0 draw at Liverpool. He delivered as more usually expected, however, by scoring on his home return in the 1–0 win against Aston Villa the following week.

It was the first of 28 goals in the 80 games he'd play while wearing the Hammers' colours for the second time – a period he views as being successful while feeling downhearted that he became marginalised through Redknapp's introduction of different strikers in 1996. 'I was a bit disappointed because when I returned to West Ham I assumed I'd finish my career there. I felt I was still the best goalscorer at the club.'

An £800,000 move to Selangor of Malaysia in October 1996 was considered too lucrative to resist, although he admits: 'If I'd foreseen the dramatic change that was going to happen in terms of Premiership salaries I probably wouldn't have gone.' Tony's Malaysian sojourn turned into a nightmare, with the season not even kicking off until the following April. 'From a professional point of view it was a total waste of time,' he admits. 'When my wife fell pregnant with twin boys it was a great excuse for me to bail out.'

Cottee resumed his Football League career with Leicester in 1997 and set a record during the 2000–01 season by playing in all four divisions with the Foxes,

Norwich, Millwall and Barnet. His brief spell as player/manager with the latter club ended in disaster when he was sacked shortly before they were relegated to the Nationwide Conference.

That traumatic experience left a sour taste as he announced his retirement but his biggest disappointment, certainly as a player, is that he never had a proper opportunity to shine for England despite winning seven full caps. 'I made six appearances as a substitute and I was taken off in the one game I did start. I'm proud of those caps but I never scored for England and that's the one regret of my career.'

Cottee prefers to reflect on his achievements – after all, he sits fifth in West Ham's all-time goalscoring charts behind Vic Watson, Geoff Hurst, Jimmy Ruffell and Johnny Dick. Yet his undying ambition leads him to admit: 'I got within 21 goals of Ruffell and Dick and it would have been nice to have stayed a bit longer and got into third place.'

41

IN DEFENCE OF DEDICATION: Steve Potts

Born: 7 May 1967; Hartford, Connecticut, USA
Debut: v. QPR (h), 1 January 1985
Apps/Goals: 491/1
Final app.: v. Chelsea (h), 7 March 2001

WHEN STEVE POTTS RAN ONTO THE UPTON PARK PITCH ON NEW Year's Day, 1985, Band Aid's 'Do they Know it's Christmas' was top of the UK singles charts and Madonna was still 'Like a Virgin'. Ninety minutes later, as the 17-year-old disappeared back down the tunnel following the 3–1 defeat by QPR – to be seen just once in the next two years – few surely imagined that the diminutive defender would show Madonna-like staying power by remaining on the Hammers playing staff into the new millennium.

Potts was, in fact, denied a single first-team appearance in 2001–02, the final year of his contract (leaving him stuck on 399 league games), but until then he'd figured in West Ham's team for 17 successive seasons – equalling Trevor Brooking's tally and falling one short of Billy Bonds and Frank Lampard. That triumvirate retired in the 1980s, however, and Steve's achievement should be put into perspective in that he remained loyal during times when players spun through the club's revolving doors with ever-increasing regularity.

'I can understand how the fans might view my length of service as loyalty, but from my own point of view it's just been an honour to be associated with the club for so long,' he says. 'Both the club and football in general have been very good to me and in return I've always given 100 per cent back. If I do something I like to try and do it properly.'

Those that felt that motivation may have been a problem for Steve in the latter part of the 1990s, as he slipped out of the first-choice line-up, often overlooked the fact that he continued to make in excess of 20 appearances per season right up until the summer of 2000. It's a statistic that explains why Potts was content to stay at Upton Park during a period when London clubs such as Crystal Palace, Watford and Charlton were crying out for his kind of top-flight experience following promotion to the Premiership. 'If I hadn't been getting a sniff of the first team it might have been different, but I still had a lot of involvement. West Ham were happy to extend the contract that was due to expire in 2000 and felt I was good enough to be part of the squad – and that was good enough for me.'

Born in the USA to parents from east London and Essex, Steve was brought up in Dagenham after his family returned to England when he was just one year old. At the age of nine he started playing for Dagenham United, a Sunday side put together by Alex Adams, whose son – future Arsenal and England skipper Tony – featured alongside Potts in defence. Steve was starring for the Barking & Dagenham district side when West Ham co-ordinator and local scout Ronnie Gale invited him to attend training sessions with the club. 'I also trained at Arsenal and Fulham but when it came to making a decision I just had a gut feeling that West Ham would be the best club for me. I felt at home there.'

Having represented Essex and London at schoolboy level, Potts signed as an apprentice in 1983 and fell under the wing of youth-team boss Tony Carr. Turning professional at 17, he captained the youths to the South East Counties Division One title in 1985, the season in which he also made his first-team debut. He skippered the reserves to Combination League glory in 1986 and six years later was handed the captain's armband for the first team by manager Billy Bonds.

Inevitably, some felt that Steve's shy personality and easy-going nature – as evident on the pitch as off it – lacked the ingredients necessary to captain at first-team level. As he admits himself: 'I've never been a player who shouts his head off. I guess I got the nod because I'm pretty level-headed, dedicated to my job and fairly sensible.' It's a point confirmed by Tony Carr, who adds: 'Pottsy provided leadership by example. He was a steady, calming influence at the back.'

A touch too calm for former manager Harry Redknapp, it seems. As relegation quicksand threatened to suffocate the Hammers towards the climax of the 1996–97 campaign, a dispute broke out on the pitch between strikers John Hartson and Paul Kitson during a vitally important home game against Everton. West Ham were leading 2–0 – with Kitson netting twice – and were awarded a 49th-minute penalty. A squabble then developed – with each player wanting the other to take the kick – before Kitson eventually fluffed his effort and a grateful Everton scored twice to deny the Hammers two valuable points.

A fuming Redknapp later complained: 'I blamed Steve Potts because as captain he should have taken responsibility. His job is not just about tossing the coin – it's about making sure things are done right on the field.' It was the type of public outburst that helped undermine the relationship between player and manager. 'Things like that should only be said face-to-face behind closed doors,' insists Steve.

Potts had to adapt to the idiosyncrasies of five bosses during his time at West Ham, who had only ever employed nine managers until his departure. John Lyall handed him that shock debut in 1985 and even though Potts only made twenty appearances in his first four seasons, he was content to bide his time. 'In those days it was a natural progression and there was more patience with the young players than there is now. But John was very thorough, a good tactician and the all-round package. Lou Macari was very much a motivational sort of manager. And Billy Bonds was as honest as the day is long. The players really wanted to succeed for him.'

It was during Bonzo's reign that Potts experienced one of the defining moments of his career. With defender Ray Stewart hampered by injury, most of Steve's chances came at right-back but in October 1990 Bonds paid Luton £600,000 for Tim Breacker to fill the berth. Says Steve: 'Maybe I'd started to take things for granted but when the club signed Tim it gave me a big jolt. It could have been the end of my time but I was determined to battle it out.'

Injuries to stalwarts Alvin Martin and Tony Gale subsequently created vital openings for Potts in the centre of defence – where he stayed for the rest of his career. 'I'm not the tallest of centre-halves but I tried to use my brain and read situations.' His reliability and perception in the tackle became his trademarks, easily compensating for the height disadvantage of being just 5ft 7in. As Billy Bonds once said: 'Steve overcame his size by showing much better anticipation and timing than his opponents.'

Potts won his first Hammer of the Year award in the promotion season of 1992–93 (during which he was an ever-present) and followed up with another trophy two years later. It says something about the knowledge of West Ham supporters when a relatively unspectacular player wins such acclaim – after all, he wasn't exactly a 20-goal-a-season man, having netted just once, against Hull City in 1990. But the feeling of appreciation was clearly mutual. 'They are a very loyal group of supporters,' he says of the crowd who sang 'We want Pottsy on the pitch' (in vain) during the final game of the 2001–02 season. 'They're passionate about the club and won't stand for anything less than 100 per cent from people. They've been brought up that way and that's what they expect. It's a special place.'

Surprisingly, the defender looks back on his career with a slight sense of regret – and not just because his last boss Glenn Roeder denied him a farewell appearance. 'I still wonder if I could have done that little bit more. Maybe I'm being a little bit harsh on myself, but perhaps I could have worked harder on certain parts of my game and been better a player for it. Medal-wise there's been nothing to show for my career.'

Steve's international experiences amounted to just 11 England youth caps. But John Lyall paid him a huge tribute around the time of his testimonial match against QPR in August 1997: 'Steve follows on from a group of super professionals such as Bobby Moore, Ronnie Boyce, Martin Peters, Geoff Hurst, Frank Lampard and Alvin Martin – all great servants.' And former team-mate Kevin Keen endorses the view, insisting: 'Pottsy deserves an MBE for his loyalty to West Ham.'

42

THE FIGHTER: George Parris

Born: 11 September 1964; Barking, Essex
Debut: v. Liverpool, 20 May 1985
Apps/Goals: 290/17
Final app.: v. Sunderland (a), 27 February 1993

THE WORDS 'I WAS A SPURS SUPPORTER' ARE ONES THAT SHOULD never pass a West Ham man's lips, but claret and blue fans already aware of George Parris' former allegiances will have long since forgiven the player for his moments of weakness. For Parris may not have been the most stylish of Hammers but he was certainly one of the most committed. 'My strengths were my wholeheartedness and my tackling, although I was also quite a good passer of the ball. I may have kept things simple but I didn't give the ball away a lot,' he insists.

George's determination, dedication, devotion – call it what you will – to West Ham's cause was reflected in more ways than one during his dozen years at the club after signing apprentice forms in 1981. The Barking boy showed great patience during his lengthy stint of reserve-team football prior to making his debut in the final match of the 1984–85 season (Frank Lampard Snr's farewell game). He played in a number of different defensive and midfield positions to keep a shirt on his back, recovered from a broken ankle and knee ligament problems and even survived a mystery heart scare. For a man dubbed 'Chicken George' (after a character in the *Roots* TV series) there was nothing chicken about him at all.

As a schoolboy, Parris rose through the ranks of district (Redbridge) and county

(Essex) football to be discovered by Hammers scout Len Hurford. 'I was about 13 when I got invited to train at West Ham. Most of my county side were already at clubs, so I was one of the last ones to get asked for a trial.' An England U15 international, George signed as a Hammers apprentice around the time he left school and turned professional 18 months later. 'Those first years at the club were a real education,' he says. 'When I first arrived I couldn't kick with my left foot at all – it was basically just to stand on!'

It was always going to be tough for Parris to break into the first team during the early 1980s, with midfielders Trevor Brooking, Alan Devonshire, Geoff Pike, Francois Van der Elst and Paul Allen playing major roles as the club consolidated its position back in the First Division. 'I was playing a lot of reserve-team football and there was a particular period during the 1984–85 season when I was playing really well but not getting a look in.' At one stage it seemed that an escape to Southend United might be on the cards but that fell through and with his contract having expired, George found himself on a weekly deal as the Hammers embarked on what was to become a very special season – for both club and player.

After a spattering of midfield appearances in the latter part of 1985, George's big break came early the following year when a replacement was needed for injured left-back Steve Walford. The Hammers were riding high in the league but the side's momentum had been disrupted by a string of postponed matches. Parris swiftly adapted to the challenge of the new position – one he'd occasionally experienced in the youth team despite being right-footed – and impressed greatly as the team won 11 of its final 14 games to finish a best-ever third. 'We came so close to winning the title,' he says ruefully. 'It was only the fact that we had so many games to play towards the end of the season that undermined us.'

But George had arrived and won many friends in the process. 'The crowd were always behind me. Some people used to give black players stick but I never got that at all and the fact I was a local boy probably helped in that respect.' That may have been the case in respect of his own supporters but Matthew Rush, a team-mate in the early-1990s, remembers that it didn't necessarily apply to opposing team's fans. 'I remember being a young teenager at the club and hearing some of the racist crap George used to get,' says the former winger, who was of mixed race.

The arrival of left-back Tommy McQueen in March 1987 saw Parris briefly relocated into the middle of the park, but he was back in defence when he broke an ankle during a 1–1 draw against Luton the following January. That prompted the signing of the ultra-tenacious Julian Dicks, whose form resulted in George becoming something of a utility man for the rest of his Hammers career (returning from injury at right-back but generally playing in midfield).

The summer of 1989 was depressing on two fronts for Parris: relegation and the dismissal of manager John Lyall. 'He had an immense influence on me – as a coach and father figure. When I was in the youth team we'd have afternoon training sessions in the gym and on many occasions John would come in and spend an hour showing us how to do things. I was a bit annoyed with the way he was sacked, especially after the service he'd given the club.'

The good times returned as the Hammers climbed back into the top flight in 1991. As well as celebrating promotion, Parris was voted the team's best outfield player as he finished runner-up to goalkeeper Ludek Miklosko in the Hammer of the Year poll. And having scored a mere eight goals in his previous five full seasons, the midfielder equalled that figure in one incredible year. 'I scored in four successive games in January and it got to the stage where I was disappointed if I hadn't hit the net,' he says.

Sadly, the 1990–91 season was also to bring George's greatest disappointment in football. West Ham were denied a possible FA Cup final place when referee Keith Hackett made the shocking decision to send off defender Tony Gale for an innocuous foul early in the semi-final against Nottingham Forest at Villa Park. It was 0–0 at the time but the disadvantaged Hammers eventually went down 4–0. A still bitter Parris says: 'I don't know if Hackett still thinks he made the right decision. But I'd like to think that one day he'll be honest and admit he made a mistake.'

As if the following season wasn't dismal enough – West Ham succumbing meekly to relegation amid the Bond Scheme controversy – George required knee ligament surgery following a 3–1 Boxing Day loss at Aston Villa. He then mysteriously collapsed during his comeback appearance as a substitute in the 2–0 home defeat by Arsenal on 14 March. 'I was running back towards our goal when I realised that I wasn't running right and suddenly I keeled over in the middle of the pitch.

'The doctors never did find out the cause, although it was definitely heart-related. I was subjected to lots of tests and it was quite frightening, especially when

I had to go to Harley Street to see the specialist. I'd go home feeling really depressed because he'd say things like: "What would you do if you couldn't play football any more?" I was eventually put on some tablets but because I couldn't do any training my knee started to deteriorate again.'

Somehow Parris showed the character to make a return in West Ham's opening (new First Division) game of the 1992–93 season at Barnsley – but it would be his last campaign at the club. In March 1993 a £100,000 bid was received from rivals Birmingham City and Hammers boss Billy Bonds allowed George the freedom to make a decision. 'My contract was up that season and Billy told me it was in my best interests to at least hear what Birmingham had to say. He was just being honest with me. It was a wrench to leave but at the time it seemed like the right move.'

Within a month of heading to the Midlands, Parris found himself facing his former team-mates in a league game at St Andrews – with West Ham scoring twice in the final three minutes to gain an unlikely 2–1 victory after being behind for most of the match. 'That was a very strange experience, a very scary game,' he says.

Things went rapidly downhill for George in Birmingham. 'Barry Fry replaced Terry Cooper as manager the following season and he didn't fancy me. I went from being captain to not even playing reserve-team football within a couple of months.'

City were relegated to football's third tier in 1994 and Parris saw out the rest of his career in the lower divisions, turning out for Brentford and Bristol City on loan before cementing a new home for himself on the south coast with Brighton. But he did return to Upton Park for a belated and hence poorly attended testimonial game between the Hammers and Ipswich Town in 1995. 'It would have been better if I'd still been at the club but I enjoyed the day and it was an honour to have been at West Ham for such a length of time,' he says.

George found new rewards after quitting the game in his early 30s by acting as a part-time activities organiser at the Ovingdean Hall school for deaf children in Sussex. He says: 'After spending my footballing career with people who had no disabilities, this new responsibility teaches me things such as patience.'

Given the various struggles he faced throughout his West Ham career, it's a commodity Parris needed few lessons in.

43

COUNTRY BOY: Kevin Keen

Born: 25 February 1967; Amersham, Bucks
Debut: v. Liverpool (h), 6 September 1986
Apps/Goals: 263/27
Final app.: v. Cambridge United (h), 8 May 1993

THERE WAS A MOMENT ON THE AFTERNOON OF SUNDAY, 6 JANUARY 2002, that Kevin Keen will remember with fondness for the rest of his life. Running over to one of the corner flags at his Macclesfield Town's tiny Moss Rose ground, Keen was greeted with the kind of warm reception that Hammers fans reserve purely for one of their own. 'That meant a lot to me,' he admitted after his Third Division men had succumbed to a 3–0 FA Cup third round defeat and hence denied Keen the return to Upton Park (via a replay) he so desperately craved. 'It was nice to get applauded like that and means the supporters appreciate what I did for them when at West Ham.'

Twenty-four hours earlier, as 35-year-old Keen prepared for the big game, he hadn't been entirely sure how he'd be received by the travelling Hammers fans. In fact there was just a touch of apprehension in the midfielder's mind as he remembered the difficulties he had in establishing himself with the Boleyn crowd during the late 1980s. 'I think they thought of me as being a bit of a softy,' he confides, 'but I always gave my best and tried to play football the West Ham way. I just wish I'd had the confidence and that little bit of arrogance when I was 19 or 20 that comes with playing 600 games. People like Paul Ince had that then and that made him a better player. And perhaps I feel that I didn't fulfil my potential as a professional footballer because of that.'

Keen's slight build and boyish features often masked his deep-thinking approach to the game. His dad Mike played for Luton, Watford and QPR, and Kevin admits: 'My father was a massive influence on me. He taught me the basic principles of how football should be played and he was a great believer in what we call the West Ham style.'

The youngster's early allegiances were more sky blue than claret and blue, however, with Keen supporting Manchester City because his idol Colin Bell played for them. But it was his home town of Wycombe that provided him with the earliest of platforms. In 1981 Kevin was a member of the High Wycombe U15 side that won the English Schools Trophy, while the following year he became the youngest player – at 15 years and 209 days – to appear in the first team for Wycombe (then a Southern League side managed by his father). 'Winning the English Schools Trophy was a big thing because nobody came to Wycombe to look for kids. We were considered country bumpkins but it encouraged a lot of interest,' he says.

Kevin played three games for Wycombe on a non-contract basis but by then he'd caught the eye of West Ham, having been discovered by youth scout Mike Dove at an U12s tournament on the Isle of Wight and then tracked for a few years by scout Charlie Faulkner as he collected England schoolboy caps. At the age of 16 Keen had a dilemma – to stay on at school to study for A-levels while playing for Wycombe or serve an apprenticeship at West Ham with a view to turning professional. He plumped for the Hammers, eventually turning pro in 1984, although he admits: 'It was a difficult first couple of years, being away from home and staying in digs.

'Youth-team boss Tony Carr was a huge influence during those early days. You don't necessarily realise it at the time but you're being taught the basics that will keep you going for the rest of your career. Watching the likes of Alan Devonshire and Trevor Brooking in training was a delight.' After winning 15 England Youth caps and helping West Ham's reserves win the Combination League from a central midfield position, Kevin eventually found himself being moved out onto the flanks. 'I think manager John Lyall, probably when I was about 18, thought I might be a bit small to play in the centre at a time when football was very robust.'

Lyall may not have regularly coached the youngsters, relying more on the likes of Tony Carr and first-team coaches Ronnie Boyce and Mick McGiven, but his presence was always felt. Says Keen: 'John was always explaining the value of being at West Ham, of being a professional footballer. He was very much a father figure and the whole ethos of the club revolved around him.'

West Ham finished third in Division One in the summer of 1986 but in the next few seasons the first team went into decline. At the age of 19 Keen made his debut as a substitute in a 5–2 home defeat by Liverpool in September 1986 and during the course of the next three years he made 72 appearances. The 1988–89 season culminated in relegation, with spring defeats on Merseyside banging the final nails in the Hammers' coffin after the corpse had shown signs of life with four successive victories. Says Keen: 'I missed a penalty at Everton which goalkeeper Neville Southall saved. We lost 3–1 but after playing in a 2–1 win at Nottingham Forest I was left out of the last game at Liverpool. I was very disappointed and I held a bit of a grudge about it. After seeing us lose 5–1 to go down it left a very dull, dry ache. Relegation was a massive blow for me.'

In retrospect, going down wasn't such a disaster for Keen. Under Lyall's replacement Lou Macari, then Billy Bonds, he became a virtual ever-present and his finest form was seen in the two promotion seasons of 1990–91 and 1992–93 as the Hammers yo-yoed between the top two divisions. 'I played in every game when we came up the second time and created a lot of goals. We won 5–1 at Bristol City in September and I was involved in every goal – including theirs when I cocked up.' Indeed, Keen's name seemed to be mentioned in the build-up to virtually every goal in the club's end-of-season video and the fans were sufficiently won over to make him runner-up in the Hammer of the Year poll.

Sadly, it appeared the club were less convinced of his worth as they returned to the top flight in 1993, allowing his contract to expire and then offering only marginally improved terms. 'West Ham didn't have a lot of money after the disaster of the Bond Scheme the previous year,' he says, 'and when you'd come through the ranks it seemed that contracts weren't as extravagant as they were for players who'd been bought by the club.

'Billy Bonds called me into his office the day before our final game of the season – at home to Cambridge – and I said: "Look, Bill, don't talk to me now, I want to concentrate on tomorrow's game." Two days after winning promotion I sat down with him and he made me the offer. He said he knew it wasn't great, especially as

I'd had a good season, but told me to see what happened during the summer and if anybody came in for me he'd see what he could do. It really kicked me in the teeth. I can remember driving home with team-mate Martin Allen and feeling distraught. It was going to be my tenth season and nothing was even mentioned of a testimonial – until Wolverhampton Wanderers came in.'

Keen visited the West Midlands to look around the First Division outfit and was sufficiently impressed. 'They made me feel very wanted and had great plans. I discussed the situation again with Billy and secretary Tom Finn but my mind was already made up, although I must admit I had a tear in my eye. I didn't really want to go. Leaving West Ham was a huge decision for me but at that time it was the right thing for me and my family.'

It's an undoubted source of regret for Keen that he never played top-flight football again following his £600,000 move. Just over a year after leaving Upton Park he was heading even further north to renew his relationship with former boss Lou Macari at Stoke City, where he played under six managers before arriving at Macclesfield in September 2000. He even became caretaker boss of the Third Division club for six games a few months before West Ham arrived for the televised FA Cup clash. And speaking just before the game with his former side, Keen admitted to hoping that he could use his Hammers education in some kind of coaching capacity after hanging up his boots.

'I'm a very honest person. Young lads know that what I say is not bullshit. I think I've got a decent knowledge of the game – because of my roots, my dad and West Ham.'

Just six months later, those credentials were considered attractive enough for West Ham to appoint him as the club's new Under-17s academy coach, as successor to the recently departed Peter Brabrook. So Keen made his return to Upton Park after all, once again working under the umbrella of youth chief Tony Carr, who said: 'Kevin is young, enthusiastic, has his A licence in coaching and, of course, is steeped in West Ham United. He knows the club through and through and everything that we stand for.'

44

THE MAN YOU LOVE TO HATE: Paul Ince

Born: 21 October 1967; Ilford, Essex
Debut: v. Newcastle United (a), 30 November 1986
Apps/Goals: 91/11
Final app.: v. Stoke City (a), 10 August 1989

THERE WERE ABOUT 60 SECONDS REMAINING ON THE CLOCK WHEN a huge cheer emerged from the Boleyn Ground, almost rivalling the explosion of sound that had greeted Hammers striker Frederic Kanoute's match-winning goal around 15 minutes earlier. The visit of Middlesbrough to Upton Park on 23 February 2002 had seemed one of the least attractive fixtures of West Ham's Premiership campaign, until fans once again realised that it would allow for some 'enthusiastic banter' with former idol Paul Ince. Yet, the man labelled 'Judas' by some angry Hammers supporters – following the grave indiscretion of posing in a Manchester United shirt prior to his controversial defection in 1989 – was determined to make his mark.

Watching the persistence of this glowering, growling midfielder go unrewarded in his side's 1–0 defeat would have been enough for many locals. But seeing him needlessly talk himself into the referee's notebook – following team-mate Ugo Ehiogu's dismissal – pretty much trowelled the icing on the cake.

As well as confirming that Paul continued to be considered Public Enemy No. 1 by the more unforgiving supporters, the 'Incey-dent' once again reinforced the fact that the former Hammer seemed to find it impossible to avoid confrontation and controversy when it came to clashes with his old club.

Just five months earlier he'd been critical of West Ham teenager Jermain Defoe for simply stating the obvious, the striker reckoning it might be a good time to play Boro, who'd lost their opening four league games. Paul's insistence after his team's 2–0 win that 'I would not be having young players saying that kind of thing' seemed a bit rich given his own past indiscretions. At the same time, his claim that 'apart from Bobby Moore, I'm the most decorated player to come out of West Ham' was misinterpreted to cause further friction. Way back in February 1994, his hotly anticipated return to Upton Park with Manchester United saw him have the last laugh with a late equaliser in a 2–2 draw, but the smile was wiped off his face a year later when the Hammers held the Reds 1–1 to deny them the championship.

Observing Ince derive motivation from the discord, it is almost possible to believe he secretly enjoyed his role as 'The Man You Love To Hate'. But then it seems that an element of conflict has long existed in his life. 'He's always been Mr Angry,' says his former Hammers youth-team boss Tony Carr. 'He was difficult, between the ages of 16 to 18, because he saw everybody as his enemy. He would always fight authority.

'But he's always had a great desire on the football pitch. Paul was destined to be a top player because of the ultra-confidence he has in his ability. With the type of background and upbringing he had, he's done fantastically well to become a top professional and captain his country. His wife Claire – his girlfriend when he was an apprentice – has obviously been a steadying influence on him and he's a real family man now. That's something he didn't really have as a child and I've got nothing but praise for what he's achieved.'

Educated at Mayfield Boys in Goodmayes (a few years beneath another future Hammer, George Parris), Ince showed promise with Essex Schoolboys before joining West Ham in 1984 as a YTS scholar. A year later he turned professional, with manager John Lyall providing a correcting influence as the youngster occasionally ran with the wrong pack off the field. Remembers coach Ronnie Boyce: 'Paul was a bit of a rogue as a teenager. He had so much confidence that he was always going to be a success – as long as he didn't go off the rails. But John would always know what he was up to.'

Unlikely as it may have seemed, Ince formed a great friendship with youth-team colleague Steve Potts. The former has admitted to being 'a bit cocky as a youngster', while the latter's placid personality makes it difficult to imagine the pair establishing any kind of rapport. 'Maybe it's because we are such opposites,' offers Potts. 'Our girlfriends were friends when we were both coming through the ranks and they still are. I've always liked Paul – he makes me laugh and is a real character.'

Tony Carr recalls one memorable occasion in the late 1980s, after both players had made the first team, when boisterous Ince attempted to drive Potts round the bend – literally. 'We were all driving down to Basildon to train on an artificial pitch prior to playing a game at QPR. They were both in the car ahead of me when Paul, being a bit flash, overtook everybody in the outside lane, hit a lump of ice, crashed into someone, rolled the car over and ended up in the ditch. Incey broke his ribs, Pottsy smacked his eye and they both missed the game the next day. John wasn't too pleased about that one.'

Ince had made his league debut as a substitute at Newcastle in November 1986 and impressed manager Lyall enough during his dozen games that season to be trusted as an emergency sweeper during 1987–88 as an injury crisis bit deep. But it was his midfield form in 47 games during the following relegation campaign that won him his eventual move to Old Trafford. His two goals in the sensational 4–1 Littlewoods Cup fourth round victory against Liverpool in November 1988 catapulted his name into the public consciousness, while his 25-yard strike in the 1–0 win at Aston Villa the following March was described by Lyall as 'the goal of the season'.

Outraged that his mentor Lyall was sacked by the club following the drop into Division Two, the England U21 international and Hammer of the Year was so keen to quit Upton Park that he allowed himself to be photographed in a Manchester United shirt, believing that a deal would be struck while away on holiday. Agent Ambrose Mendy and photographer Lawrence Lustig had also assured him that the shot would never see light of day if the move failed to materialise. Yet a breakdown in communication resulted in the picture being published in the *Daily Express*, much to the horror of Hammers fans who subsequently made it plain during the opening game of the 1989–90 season that the player's position at the club had become untenable.

United eventually landed the midfielder in September 1989 for a bargain £800,000 plus further instalments (to a maximum of £1.7m) after a medical raised fears relating to a pelvic injury. The suspicion that it was all a bit of a ruse to get

Ince on the cheap was intensified as the untroubled player went on to play such a key role in the Reds' emergence as football's dominant force in the next decade. The flames of fury were fanned further when an ill-judged comment about 'moron' Hammers fans was blown up by the press. Says Tony Carr: 'Paul didn't handle his departure in the best way but he was a young lad and he was influenced by people who, had he been older, he possibly wouldn't have listened to so much.'

The problem for many West Ham fans was that there was no sign of an apology from Ince about committing the ultimate sin of posing in another club's shirt. Even his mate Steve Potts admitted: 'I think the supporters would have just liked an explanation.'

That moment eventually came some eight years later (by which time the self-styled 'Guv'nor' had won five trophies – including two league championships – before leaving United in 1995 for Inter Milan and then returning to England in 1997 with Liverpool) when interviewed by Tony McDonald for *Hammers News Magazine.* 'I didn't really want to have the picture taken but I went along with it. I was still very young at the time and didn't really know what was right and wrong,' he admitted. 'I can understand the reaction of the fans because it wasn't a nice thing to do. It's something I regret and I just hope the supporters accept that people make mistakes.'

The fact that the England international (who earned 53 full caps and in 1993 became the first black player to wear the captain's armband) continued to receive abuse during subsequent visits to Upton Park with Liverpool and then Middlesbrough suggested that wasn't necessarily the case. Football fans have long memories and there's little doubt that Ince will forever be considered – by the Upton Park cognoscenti, at least – as the most notorious homegrown Hammer of all time.

45

THE AGE OF INNOCENCE: Stuart Slater

Born: 27 March 1969; Sudbury, Suffolk
Debut: v. Derby County (h), 3 October 1987
Apps/Goals: 174/16
Final app.: v. Nottingham Forest (h), 2 May 1992

CONSUMED WITH REGRET ABOUT EVER LEAVING UPTON PARK, STUART Slater was scrabbling around for a foothold in Australian and non-league soccer within seven years of leaving West Ham aged 23. Such a notion was simply inconceivable during a spell at the start of the 1990s when Stuart's electrifying pace and footwork lit up the Boleyn Ground.

His former Hammers coach Mick McGiven must have thought as much a decade later when the two met up during Slater's stint with Conference side Forest Green Rovers. 'I had to get a shirt signed by the Chelsea players for the Forest Green chairman,' Slater says. 'I knew Mick was a coach at Chelsea so I went to see him. I went through these doors and there were all their star players having dinner: Jimmy Floyd Hasselbaink, Gianfranco Zola, Graeme Le Saux . . . Mick turned to them and said: "Now this was a player, boys." I was thinking: "Hang on a minute. I really was up there with these sort of players once."'

Slater was raised in rural Suffolk a million miles up the A12 from the East End. His grandparents drove a caravanette around as they followed his progress in the local junior leagues and it was around the vehicle's foldaway table that their skinny grandson was recruited as a schoolboy Hammer. After another fine performance for Colchester's Langham Lions alongside future Spur Jason Dozzell, striker Stuart shook persistent scout Ronnie Gale's hand and agreed to join West Ham, in spite of overtures from his favourites Ipswich Town.

Slater lodged at Gale's Hainault, Essex, home during summer training sessions, moving in permanently as an apprentice in 1986. His first year was a tough one. 'I struggled a little bit. We played in the FA Youth Cup against Tottenham and some younger boys from Lilleshall, the national football school, were in our side. I was played out of position on the right and got subbed at half-time, while my best mate, a lad called Peter, was on the bench.

'Peter actually quit after that game. He didn't see any point in carrying on. I had the same impression, thinking: "If they think more of the Lilleshall boys, what's the point?" But I decided to stick it out.'

His resolve paid off. Within a year he had become the undisputed star of the youths, banging in goals and revelling in the training ground emphasis on expression. 'The coaches wanted you to keep it on the deck, play one-twos, make blindside runs. They'd say: "Don't overdo it but if you can beat somebody then go for it." It's a one-off club that allows you to do that. John Lyall, the manager, once said I was the one setting the standards the others needed to match. It was getting to the stage where they were saying: "Just give Stuart the ball and he'll do something with it."

'John had that aura about him that was hard to describe,' says Slater, who would link up with his mentor again after Celtic sold him to Ipswich Town in 1993. He would later play for Watford and Leicester City before, hampered by a knee injury, he slipped quietly into semi-pro football. 'If you lost a game and you weren't looking him in the eyes, he'd know straight away what was up with you.'

Youth boss Tony Carr also recognised Slater's huge potential, but saw a sensitive kid whose confidence could be knocked with frightening ease. 'Stuart had natural dribbling skills and great pace,' says Carr. 'The two linked together were a devastating combination. But he didn't take criticism too well.'

Still an apprentice, Stuart replaced Stewart as he came on as a substitute for right-back Ray on his debut at home to Derby County in October 1987. In the first game of the following season, having been offered a professional contract fully six months before his peers, the little marksman made his first start. A clash of heads with Southampton's Russell Osman resulted in Slater being withdrawn after just a minute's play, but the new No. 9 won Man of the Match awards in his next two games. For an Upton Park crowd infuriated by £600,000 David Kelly's fumblings up front, the home-grown boy's sprightly enthusiasm was a real tonic, especially when he converted an Alan Devonshire cross to earn a 1–0 win at Charlton in the FA Cup fifth round.

By the end of that torturous 1988–89 season, which resulted in Lyall's sacking, Slater was one of the few reasons for the supporters to feel any kind of optimism, as the 5–1 relegation-confirmer at Liverpool proved. 'I had a virus and after about 60 minutes it looked like I was going to be brought off. The bench had my number up but ended up putting the placard in the bag and pulling someone else off because the supporters were going absolutely mental chanting my name.'

Slater bagged nine goals in 49 starts in 1989–1990. He made it into the England Under-21 squad as a striker in 1990, making three substitute appearances, but although he insisted his forte was playing up front, it was his jinking approach play that left the bigger impression. After Lyall's replacement Lou Macari sensationally quit in February 1990, his successor Billy Bonds saw a new role for the mercurial talent. For the second leg of the Littlewoods Cup semi-final (Oldham having humbled West Ham 6–0 in the first game), Bonds played Slater behind a front two of Kelly and Leroy Rosenior. 'We won 3–0 and all had a good game, but a few matches later Bill decided he couldn't keep that system and played me wide left. I played really well, but thought to myself: "What have I let myself in for? They'll think I'm a natural left-winger."'

Slater might not have fancied the proposition, but soon everyone was drooling over his wing wizardry. Breathtaking displays of skill and verve came in the Second Division, most notably in a 5–0 Boleyn bashing of Sheffield United in March 1990, but the defining moment came when he made mincemeat of the Everton defence in an FA Cup quarter-final the following year. Every trick and every dribble came off and to cap it all he cracked home West Ham's second from 20 yards in the 2–1 home win.

Goodison boss Howard Kendall gushed afterwards that Slater would become the first £3m player, while former Evertonian Bruce Rioch went even further by likening him to Portuguese legend Eusebio. With Upton Park cries of 'Slater for England!' ringing in his ears, Stuart joined his chief service-provider Ian Bishop in two England 'B' parties. The perfect audition for the full side should have been the FA Cup semi-final versus Nottingham Forest, but despite hitting the woodwork late on, he was as subdued as every other Hammer once Tony Gale received his marching orders and Forest cruised to a 4–0 win.

In 1991–92, the club having returned to the top flight, all eyes were on him – including those of managers reportedly keen to lure him away from Upton Park. Ironically, while Bonds was busy quelling transfer gossip, his prize asset's form fell away badly. Unsettled by all the speculation and troubled by an Achilles injury, Slater's attacks lacked zeal and he failed to score in 51 outings. Winning just nine league games all season, West Ham finished bottom but the success-starved supporters didn't take kindly to the thought of Slater leaving, regardless of his form. 'At the end they turned on me because they thought I was deserting the ship. There were always stories in the press saying I was leaving and I wasn't happy. I probably wasn't a strong enough character to say the things I wanted to say.'

When the inevitable happened, it left Stuart shell-shocked. He would harbour deep regret about how his £1.5m exit from Upton Park was handled. Liam Brady, Stuart's hero and a late-1980s team-mate, had by then moved into the business side of football and started handling the youngster's contract negotiations. But when Brady accepted the Celtic manager's post in the summer of 1992, things took a strange twist. Says Stuart: 'Liam put me on to his mate. We had a contract meeting at Upton Park – Billy Bonds was there, one of the Cearns family from the board, the club secretary and my agent, Liam's mate. They offered me a great contract and I was like: "Oh my goodness, what an offer!"

'My agent, without even asking me, said: "No, we are not signing that." I was too young and naive to say anything. He just said he'd get me a better club, better international prospects and more money.'

Celtic fitted the description. Before he knew it Slater was travelling north to discuss terms with Brady. Naturally, part of him was elated that he was the subject of a record outlay by such a huge club. But a bigger part wanted to be back in his nan's caravan shaking hands with Ronnie Gale. 'When I went up on the Thursday to talk to Liam I took my mum with me as she knew he could wrap me around his little finger. They needed me to sign before the European deadline and I was umming and aahing. Then, about 6 p.m. on the Friday, he persuaded me. I flew back home that evening and cried all weekend. My dad was getting to the stage where he was going to phone Liam up and just say: "Look, Stuart wants to stay at West Ham."

'To play for Celtic was a great honour,' he says, 'but there was only one club suited to my game and that was West Ham. I had so much respect for Bill. He turned down all these bids and wanted to build the team around me. Deep down I knew I didn't want to leave. West Ham had offered me the biggest contract in their history. They thought I'd turned it down, but I didn't have a say.'

PART FIVE

The '90s – A Decade of Two Halves

46

THE BARREN YEARS: 1988–93

WITH THE EARLY 1980s HAVING BEEN REASONABLY PRODUCTIVE FOR
the Hammers' youth system, a disappointingly fallow period followed – mirroring
the decline and turbulence of the club at first-team level.

In the seven years that divided the first-team debuts of Stuart Slater in 1987 and
midfielder Danny Williamson in 1994 – during which the club was twice relegated
and employed three different managers – West Ham fans saw just one homegrown
Hammer break into the first team, winger Matthew Rush in 1990. Something had
clearly gone wrong, with the production line simply not delivering the quality or
quantity of young players required.

A trend had already been set, with the 1980s producing less local talent than
the 1970s, which had in turn produced much less than the 1960s. That can partly
be attributed to chief scout Wally St Pier's retirement in 1975 – successor Eddie
Baily (the former Tottenham player and coach) had an illustrious act to follow.
Youth recruitment was already becoming far more competitive and it appears that
West Ham simply weren't playing the game as well as they might.

Says Tony Carr, who'd first started coaching the club's youngsters on a part-
time basis in 1973: 'It was a lot easier to attract players in the 1960s because it was
more of a local thing. There may have only been two or three clubs fighting for the
same players. But it all became more intense and when there's more competition
other factors come into play, with different kinds of promises and incentives being
offered. There was a lull in the sense that perhaps we were still "old school" in our
approach and it took us a while to wake up to the fact that our recruitment drive
had to be a lot more fierce.'

It's a point supported by former coach Ronnie Boyce, who eventually succeeded
Baily as chief scout in 1991. 'West Ham were one of the last clubs to have a family-

orientated board and there was a time when we were missing out on the kids, partly because we were hanging on to past traditions. The quality of kids wasn't coming through as it had done in the past and maybe that meant we weren't doing things that other clubs were doing. Whether some of those things were legal or not, I don't know.'

West Ham's scouting structure also needed reshaping to accommodate the changing nature of youth recruitment in the late 1980s. Centres of Excellence were being established, with clubs now recruiting boys from the age of 11 or 12, while Baily – still officially carrying the official title of chief representative inherited from St Pier – had far too much on his plate. Explains Tony Carr, who took responsibility for the club's new Centre of Excellence in the late '80s: 'On the one hand Eddie was scouting for first-team players for manager John Lyall, while on the other he was still in charge of youth recruitment. The job had grown far too large and responsibilities needed to be divided.

'The likes of Kevin Keen, Paul Ince and Slater had made their debuts around 1986–87 but had been in the system for a few years. But where were the 14-year-olds in 1987 that were going to come through? That's what I was asking because there was an obvious decline in quality. That's when I called a meeting with John and Eddie.'

Baily appointed part-time scout Len Hurford as the club's first youth development officer, while Carr took charge of the reserve side to enable the set-up to accommodate recently retired defender Billy Bonds as the new youth-team coach in 1988. Hurford resigned in the early 1990s before new first-team boss Bonds invited former Hammer Jimmy Neighbour to take charge of youth development. By that time Ronnie Boyce had replaced Baily, who'd retired, as chief scout. Says Boyce: 'Eddie's ideas had been good, although the scouting network wasn't as developed as it would be later on. But most of the scouts he had were good and we continued to work well.'

But there were to be plenty more changes following the arrival of Harry Redknapp as Billy's assistant in 1992. Says Carr, who resumed direct control of the youth team following former defender Paul Hilton's brief spell as Bonds' successor: 'When Harry came in alongside Bill he felt youth development wasn't as good as he would have liked. Jimmy Neighbour resigned after one or two disagreements with the management and Jimmy Hampson took over.'

Hampson had established his youth development credentials with Wimbledon and Charlton and arrived at Upton Park in 1993, initially working alongside Neighbour and then succeeding him as Redknapp started to put his own ideas into place.

47

EASY COME, EASY GO: Matthew Rush

Born: 6 August 1971; Hackney, London
Debut: v. Hull City (h), 6 October 1990
Apps/Goals: 52/5
Final app.: v. Blackburn (h), 30 April 1995

BEFORE FALLING OUT OF FAVOUR WITH MANAGER HARRY REDKNAPP, Matthew Rush was the only homegrown player to make any impact at the start of the 1990s. Like Stuart Slater before him, Rush was a rocket-heeled winger. Like midfielder Danny Williamson – the next youth-team product four years down the line – his professional career would be cruelly cut short by injury.

Rush believes the dearth of talent at the end of the 1980s and early '90s was merely bad luck, rather than poor workmanship with regards to youth development. 'Sometimes you get a bunch of talented kids, sometimes it's barren,' he says. 'There were some talented ones even when I was there. There was a lad called Tony Macklin who was a fantastic ball player but his attitude was disastrous. It's about getting a combination of things right.'

The son of an Irish mother and a West Indian father, Matt was born in the East End but his family headed through the Rotherhithe Tunnel when he was a youngster and settled south of the Thames in Deptford – Millwall country. As a schoolboy player, Rush was in for a torrid time once his siblings got wind of interest in him from the 'orrible 'ammers. 'When one of them heard I'd signed apprentice forms (in 1988) for West Ham his face just dropped,' says Matt, whose brother Marcus was also briefly on the club's junior books. 'I came on as substitute when West Ham played at the old Den in 1991. The Millwall fans were all warning me not to play well, so when I rattled down the wing and fired in a shot that hit the crossbar I could hear them chanting: "Oi Rushie. We know where you li-iive, we know where you li-iive!" To be fair I was a local lad so there was an underlying respect, even though I was playing for 'The Scum'.'

Hammers coach Tony Carr saw bags of potential in the tricky starlet, even if he appeared too easy-going at times. 'If he was any more laid back he'd fall over,' Carr said. Rush wasn't quite so relaxed during a bizarre early confrontation with manager John Lyall. 'He offered me out for a fight in the showers. He came over and said: "Hey Rushie, you're quite a big lad for your age. Come on, let's see how tough you are." I was just a kid at the time, thinking: "Oh my God, the manager wants to beat me up." I guessed he was only jesting, so I laughed at him and fortunately for me he laughed back!'

Lyall and his successor Lou Macari had come and gone in the hot-seat by the time Billy Bonds blooded Rush as a substitute early in the Second Division promotion season of 1990–91. His chief contribution in the 7–1 mauling of Hull City at home was accidentally knocking an opponent out with a stray elbow. Although appearing just six times all season, Matt made a big enough impression to earn two Eire Under-21 caps thanks to his mum's roots.

The following season saw the yo-yoing Hammers relegated from the old First Division for the second time in four seasons. The fans got another glimpse of Rush's talents in April 1992 when, in only his second start of the season, he surprised everyone by heading two goals in a 4–0 home thumping of Norwich City.

With Billy Bonds relying more on wily experience than sporadic flair in his successful quest to get West Ham back into the top flight at the first time of asking, Rush's sole first-team activity in 1992–93 came in the Anglo-Italian Cup. After a dour 0–0 home tie against Pisa in December 1992, he was wishing he hadn't been picked for that competition either. 'This individual spent all game spitting, pulling and scratching me. Towards the end I got past him and was one-on-one with the keeper. Next thing I know I'm being dragged back by my shirt. I snapped, which was very unlike me. Everyone else was as surprised by my reaction as I was.' More cynical fans viewed Matt's retaliatory kick and clench of fists in self-defence – as a group of Italian players turned on him – as the highlight of a belittling 'European' campaign.

Unable to get a look-in in domestic competition, early in 1993 he spent ten games on loan with First Division rivals Cambridge United, against whom the Hammers would secure promotion on the last day of the season. Yet despite the uncertainty that came with being farmed out and lagging behind Mark Robson in the right-wing pecking order, generally speaking Rush was enjoying life as a professional footballer – even if it differed vastly in content from that of his team-mates.

Not for Rushy a lunch-time trip to the bookies then back to the mock-Tudor mansion in Epping. He was 'Metropolitan Man', perfectly at home with people who didn't know their Dicks from their elbows. 'I'd be out five nights a week,' he says. 'My friends owned clubs and there were always parties to go to. We'd go to the theatre and the ballet quite a lot. I designed a loft space in a warehouse conversion in Wapping with my girlfriend. I had 2,000 sq. ft to play with. Friends used to ask if I practised corners in my lounge. It always amazed me that footballers earned an obscene amount of money, yet watched football on TV all the time and ate kebabs. Once I must have mentioned that I went to see *The Nutcracker Suite* or something, because I got a really sound ribbing.'

London's in-crowd continued to see rather more of Rush than did West Ham fans. Niggling injury and competition for places restricted him to just one substitute appearance in the first half of the club's first Premiership campaign in 1993–94. Rather than leave him to fester in the reserves, boss Bonds felt it best to send his under-achieving winger out on loan again, this time to lowly Swansea City. The trick worked, Matt's superior skills proving a major factor as Swansea progressed to the semi-finals of the 1994 Autoglass Trophy. Recalled to Upton Park in March 1994, he missed out on Swansea's success in the final – but felt rejuvenated and hungry. A wonderful 25-yard strike in his first game back, a 2–1 home win over Ipswich, was proof of that.

Bonds could see the difference and in the close-season started to make noises about a new contract. So too did Kevin Keegan. The Newcastle United boss, mightily impressed by Rush's endeavours in Wales, wanted to add him to a squad that was already bristling with attacking talent. 'I had a meeting with Keegan and his assistant Terry McDermott,' recalls Matt. 'I had no intention of leaving West Ham but I met them purely out of respect. Keegan actually offered me a contract, but Bill offered me one too and, being a London boy, I just didn't want to leave – at that time anyway.'

That was at the start of the summer of 1994. By the end of it Bonds, Rush's idol, had gone and Matt faced the uphill task of impressing new manager Harry Redknapp, a man he'd always found it difficult to warm to when assistant boss. 'I'd signed a three-year contract with Bill, but I would have signed for ten if he'd wanted. I'd trusted him completely and it's quite rare in football that you trust a manager. He was always fair and full of encouragement.

'Then Harry took over – a man who I'd never had the most solid of relationships with. I might score or play really well, but then be left out for cock and bull reasons. It could've been personality or anything. There was no bad blood between us, but something wasn't right.'

It was probably fair to say that Harry's problem was with the inconsistency which dogged Matt's performances, rather than his penchant for ballet, and Rush admits: 'It's true my form was up and down. I was an out-and-out winger who didn't come inside too much, so I was totally reliant on being fed the ball. All I'd ever be thinking was: "I'm going to get the ball and beat the guy in front of me." If it didn't happen a couple of times I'd maybe force it too much, which would be detrimental.'

After 18 starts and two goals in 1994–95, he became one of the first to enter Redknapp's revolving transfer door, spinning out in a daze at Second Division Norwich in the summer of 1995. Just three days after his £350,000 transfer to Carrow Road, he badly ruptured his knee, repercussions from which would eventually force him to retire aged 27 while with Oldham Athletic.

Matt immediately enrolled on a sports science degree and in 2001 took up a post as a teacher at a sports college in Manchester. Tony Carr's verdict on this happy-go-lucky player suggests his Upton Park college report would probably have read something like: Matthew has lots of ability but too often appears distracted. Must stop grinning and try harder. Says Carr: 'Matthew always had a smile on his face. But he was frustrating. You always felt he could give more, but he'd only go so far.'

48

THE INVISIBLE MAN: Danny Williamson

Born: 5 December 1973; West Ham, London
Debut: v. Arsenal (a), 30 April 1994
Apps/Goals: 58/5
Final app.: v. Chelsea (h), 12 March 1997

'I'LL NEVER TAKE ANYTHING FOR GRANTED. I'VE ALREADY SEEN enough to make me realise that you can never know what's just around the corner in this game. I intend to make the most of it while it lasts.'

So said Danny Williamson in February 1996, having established himself in West Ham's midfield nearly two years after making his first-team debut. There was no doubting his determination to take his opportunity with both hands, for within a week of uttering these words the 22-year-old had scored twice in two matches – at Chelsea and at home to Newcastle United – to help extend the Hammers' winning streak to a record five successive Premiership games.

Yet his youthful spirit would be crushed within 18 months. Following a season disrupted by ankle injuries, he made a £4m price-tagged move to fallen giants Everton, but the brakes were put on his new career before it even got out of first gear. He played just 17 games for the Merseysiders before succumbing to a foot ligament injury that would virtually imprison him in his new club's treatment room for the next three years. With his fight for fitness ultimately proving to be in vain, his contract with Everton was terminated in September 2000 and, at the age of just 26, Danny was tragically forced to retire from football.

'It's very sad,' says Harry Redknapp, under whom Williamson played all but three of his 58 West Ham games. 'Danny was a young player with terrific potential and it was very disappointing to see his career come to a premature end.'

It had been Redknapp's predecessor Billy Bonds who'd handed the youngster his first-team debut, as an 87th-minute substitute in a shock 2–0 win at Arsenal at the tail end of the 1993–94 season (West Ham's first in the Premiership). A week later, in a 3–3 draw with Southampton, Williamson became the first homegrown Hammer to score on his home debut since Tony Cottee in 1983. Ironically, it was Cottee whom Danny had chosen to be pictured with when signing schoolboy forms with West Ham many years earlier. It was a dream come true for the kid who had ardently cheered on the Hammers from the North Bank of Upton Park. 'My father Alan used to take me to games when I was younger and we'd get down to the ground before the gates opened to make sure of getting a good view,' he remembers.

Pulling the strings in West Ham's midfield during the mid-1980s was the stylish Alan Dickens, with Williamson reflecting: 'Dickens was my hero. I idolised him and it broke my heart when he joined Chelsea in 1989. He was a great inspiration to me.' By that time Plaistow-based kid Danny had progressed through the Newham and Essex Schoolboy ranks to sign forms with West Ham. He also went for a trial at north London rivals Arsenal but insists: 'You know what it's like when all your mates are Hammers fans. I went to Highbury once but didn't ever go back.'

Arsenal's loss was West Ham's gain as Williamson signed up for a two-year apprenticeship in 1990. Youth-team boss Tony Carr remembers: 'I had a lot of time for Danny. He was a bit similar to former midfielder Alan Dickens but had a little more oomph about him. Some people questioned whether he had the pace to play at the top level but I always felt his footballing ability would make up for any lack of mobility.'

After turning professional in 1992, Williamson was loaned out to non-league Farnborough Town (managed by future Hammers chief scout Ted Pearce) and then to Third Division Doncaster Rovers where he made his league debut in October 1993. The fact that West Ham boss Billy Bonds happily allowed him to become cup-tied during his 16-game spell at the Belle Vue hardly gave him confidence of making a first-team breakthrough upon his return south. He later admitted: 'I sometimes wondered: "Are they putting me out on loan just to get rid of me?"'

While he played in the final three games of the 1993–94 season, signing off in style with West Ham's first goal in that six-goal thriller against Southampton, the signs of a decent run in the side during the following campaign looked ominous after the £1m-plus arrivals of midfielders John Moncur and Don Hutchison. Along with the small matter of an ankle injury, it was no surprise that Danny was restricted to just four appearances during 1994–95.

Although he scored against Leeds just five minutes into the 1995–96 campaign (West Ham eventually going down 2–1 at home), Danny had to show patience before getting a recall for a game at Bolton Wanderers in November. He made his mark in emphatic style, running with the ball for all of 70 yards before scoring West Ham's final goal in a fine 3–0 win. 'It was a great feeling to see the ball go in. Now I feel my life's going somewhere again,' he said afterwards. In all, Danny played 33 times in a season that saw the Hammers gain a top-half finish for the first time in ten years. And Williamson certainly played his part, with Harry Redknapp reflecting: 'He was an outstanding passer of the ball. He had a terrific shot on him and I always thought he was going to be a very good player.'

However, Danny lost momentum in the 1996–97 season, with another ankle injury restricting him to just 18 games. An attempted comeback as a substitute against Chelsea on 12 March resulted in the player going to hospital for surgery. Hammers' physiotherapist John Green explains the problem: 'There's a bone at the back of the ankle called the *os trigonus*. It's a nugget of bone that was larger than usual with Danny and caused problems when his foot was in a position to strike the ball. The operation he had prior to leaving West Ham was to have the *os trigonus* removed.'

Given his enforced absence from the side, Williamson's move to Everton in August 1997 came as something of a surprise. Green remembers: 'Danny was in our medical room, at a very late stage of his recuperation, when Harry rang me. I was just about to say that Danny was ready to resume training when Harry told me that Everton manager Howard Kendall wanted to speak to him.'

With defenders Julian Dicks and Richard Hall sidelined through injury, Redknapp was desperate for a left-sided centre-half and suggested that Everton's David Unsworth could be used as part of a deal taking Williamson north. Says Harry: 'Everton asked me about Danny and so I said: "Give me Unsworth and money." Howard said: "Leave off, David's an England international," but I managed to get the deal done.' With Unsworth travelling to London along with a cash payment of £1m, it was understandable that Redknapp would insist at the time that it was 'business the club had to do'.

Bizarrely, both players found themselves making debuts against their former clubs as West Ham travelled to Goodison Park for a league fixture on 23 August. Predictably, the Hammers lost (2–1). Almost as predictably, Unsworth got homesick for Merseyside after just one season in London and returned (via an ill-conceived £3m stop on the M6 at Aston Villa) to Goodison. Perhaps most predictable of all, Williamson fell victim to injury and never played another first-team game for Everton after appearing against Wimbledon in December 1997.

Physio John Green, who'd initially kept in touch with Danny, remembers the trouble the player was experiencing at that time: 'He had a lot of problems with the planter fascia which is basically the foot's equivalent of the palm of your hand.'

Some assumed that West Ham must have had an inkling that Williamson's long-term career had already been in jeopardy, despite him passing Everton's medical. Harry Redknapp refutes the suggestion, insisting: 'How would I sell somebody not 100 per cent fit? I didn't know he had a dodgy ankle.'

John Green presents a more detailed case, stating: 'It's a very tenuous argument to say the later problems were linked to the original operation. Usually with the *os trigonus*, you have the operation and it's over and done with. But problems with the planter fascia can develop when you've been out for a while with a completely unrelated injury.'

Green initially tried to offer Danny assistance, declaring: 'Our podiatrist tried to help him but Everton were reluctant to let him come down for treatment. It caused a few problems and I wasn't really in a position to help him any further unless Everton allowed it.'

In August 1999 Williamson travelled to Munich in Germany to see specialist Dr Hans Muller Wohlfahrt. Says Green: 'I'm not sure if Everton were happy with him going and I think he may have funded the visit himself.' Soon afterwards – clearly homesick in Liverpool – Williamson declared: 'This has been the hardest year of my life. I've been injured, the manager who signed me was sacked [Howard Kendall making way for Walter Smith], I have no family or friends with me and it has been a terrible experience.'

And it was to get worse, with Danny's planter fascia problems leading to growths on his heels that would eventually force him to throw in the towel. After his Everton contract was terminated, nine months early, he became something of an invisible man, quietly returning south and spending a brief period studying at the Ardleigh Green Technical College in Havering before hiding behind his curtains at his new home just outside Romford in Essex. He kept in contact with few people at West Ham, although Tony Carr insists: 'I'd be very happy to talk to Danny about coaching youngsters. He'd be more than welcome if he'd like to get in touch.'

49

CONTROVERSIAL TIMES: The Mid-1990s

ONCE HARRY REDKNAPP REPLACED BILLY BONDS AS MANAGER IN August 1994, he set about trying to improve West Ham's scouting and coaching departments. And that meant making changes of personnel – some of them not at all popular with those around the club who believed that stability and loyalty within the backroom team represented a major cornerstone of West Ham's traditional philosophies.

At the end of 1995, having had three years since his return as Billy's assistant to assess the roles performed by members of the staff, Redknapp sacked chief scout Ronnie Boyce, reserve-team boss Paul Hilton and training ground co-ordinator/scout Ronnie Gale.

The Hammers boss defended his axing of those with such lengthy associations with the club, insisting: 'It's my responsibility to make decisions. People come and go at every other football club, so why shouldn't it happen at West Ham? If I don't get the job done, I'll get the sack – it's as simple as that.'

On further reflection Harry is adamant that he made the right decisions, although it wasn't easy pushing Boyce – who'd remained faithful to the Hammers for 36 years – out of his latest role. Admits Redknapp: 'It was difficult. I liked the fella and he'd been a terrific servant to the club, but I just felt a change was needed.

Sometimes people can be around at a football club for too long.'

Ted Pearce – a long-time associate of Redknapp who'd managed non-league Farnborough Town to an FA Cup third round replay against the Hammers in 1992 – arrived as Boyce's replacement, while former Swansea boss Frank Burrows succeeded Hilton. 'Paul was a good lad and I had nothing against him,' says Harry, 'but I knew Frank very well, he'd had management experience and felt he'd help improve the whole set-up.'

On the youth development side, Jimmy Hampson had already succeeded Jimmy Neighbour (towards the end of Billy Bonds' reign) and his more forceful methods suited Redknapp's ideals perfectly. Says Tony Carr, who in the late 1990s would become director of the youth academy: 'Jimmy took hold of the youth scouting system by the scruff of the neck. Billy Bonds had started to put things in place and when Harry took over he carried on that philosophy and demanded that we be more aggressive.'

If Redknapp had been appalled by the attitude of some first-team players when he arrived as Bonds' assistant following relegation in 1992, he was equally dismayed with the lack of potential at youth-team level. 'I found it incredible that we hadn't produced any kids for years,' he says. 'The standard was very poor and I felt we needed to upgrade that. The club was never going to have lots of money to spend in the transfer market so the only way forward was to develop the youth policy.'

Frank Lampard Snr – who returned to the club as assistant manager when Harry took over – agrees that change was necessary. 'I'd been going back to coach youngsters and could see what was happening. The players weren't coming through. It's like any business – you're only as good as who you employ and we obviously didn't have the right scouts out there.'

The club had missed out on hot local talent such as David Beckham and Sol Campbell (signed by Manchester United and Tottenham Hotspur respectively) and Lampard says: 'There were lots of good players around and if you can't get Newham-based boys to join the club, what can you do? We missed the boat on so many players in the early '90s.'

West Ham's youth development prospects were dealt a huge blow when their Centres of Excellence were controversially closed in the mid-'90s as a result of infringements of Football Association regulations. Incredibly, the man who reported some of the club's illegal activities was former Hammers midfielder Geoff Pike, whose first-team career spanned a dozen years.

In his new capacity as one of the FA's youth monitors, Pike witnessed a youth game at Chadwell Heath that was in breach of the rules. Explains Tony Carr: 'We put on an 11-a-side game to look at some boys when we should only have played small-sided games. It was fairly innocent as far as we were concerned. I would describe it as a minor infringement of regulations.'

Pike confronted Carr and Jimmy Hampson on the pitch touchline and the net result, following an FA review, was that West Ham were fined an undisclosed amount and banned from signing young players for an entire year. Additionally, the FA suspended Hampson for the same period. Says Carr: 'Jimmy obviously felt very aggrieved by it. It was a real blow for the club. It was like swinging a sledgehammer to crack a nut and we felt that Geoff played a big part in that.'

West Ham managing director Peter Storrie subsequently banned Pike from the club's ground and training facilities, considering him persona non grata. But many years later, having eventually repaired his relationship with the Hammers, Pike was surprisingly allowed to put forward his defence in the club's official magazine.

He told *Hammers News*: 'There were lots of other things that the FA allegedly took into account when they closed down the club's coaching centres. The FA had a file on West Ham that was four or five inches thick.'

The likelihood is that the Hammers would not have been alone in overlooking some of the rules as they sought to keep pace with other Premiership clubs in the increasingly competitive area of youth recruitment. But while the episode caused some embarrassment for the club, the message was clear: West Ham were not going to be left trailing behind.

50

FAMILY VALUES: Frank Lampard Jnr

> Born: 20 June 1978; Romford, Essex
> Debut: v. Coventry City (h), 31 January 1996
> Apps: 186/38
> Final app.: v. Leeds (h), 21 April 2001

IT WASN'T MEANT TO BE LIKE THIS. YOUNG HEARTBEAT OF WEST Ham's gifted midfield; 7 goals and 19 appearances for England Under-21s; an £11m superstar at Chelsea; a Man of the Match performance in the 2002 FA Cup final; 7 full caps. Ever since his starring role for the brilliant Hammers youth team of the mid-1990s, Frank Lampard Jnr's career had looked set fair on participation in the 2002 World Cup finals. Yet when England boss Sven-Goran Eriksson finally revealed his squad for Japan and South Korea in May 2002, Lampard's name was not among the list of 23.

There were two key factors conspiring against Frank. One was his style of play. Absolutely nothing wrong with being efficient and industrious, but that little extra 'something' which had made him stand out for the Under-21s had rarely if ever revealed itself at full international level. The second, probably more crucial factor, was an alleged indiscretion committed eight months earlier. Just days after the devastating terrorist attack on New York's World Trade Center on 11 September 2001, Lampard and some of his new Chelsea chums were reported to have behaved with drunken disregard in front of American tourists stranded in the UK at a west London hotel. Eriksson had no choice but to ignore him for his squad for the immediate World Cup qualifier against Greece and, although he reinstated Frank after the furore had subsided, the player would have to have done something pretty exceptional in an England shirt to make amends. It appears he failed to do so.

Lampard was by no means the only high-profile midfielder forced to watch in despair as the likes of West Ham's Joe Cole and Trevor Sinclair posed in their smart new World Cup suits on the steps of the Far East-bound England jet. But none of his counterparts carried anything like the level of expectation thrust on him courtesy of his ancestry.

Dad Frank Snr is a West Ham icon, number two in the all-time appearances list. Uncle Harry Redknapp (Frank Snr's wife and Harry's wife are sisters) is one of the most popular managers in the club's history. Cousin Jamie is a former Liverpool hero and England regular. 'There was quite a lot of pressure,' Frank Jnr told *Loaded* magazine in 2001, 'although I don't regret for a minute how much Dad pushed me. He could see I had talent and he's a hard man who tells you what he thinks. I'd cry sometimes because of the stick he gave me, but I'm glad of it now.'

Says his father: 'Frank's been brought up in the football world. That's all he knew. When I was a kid I had West Ham, Leyton Orient and Southend knocking on my door. But he had Arsenal and Tottenham and he wanted to come to West Ham. It gave me great pleasure that he came through at the club.'

In fact, Lampard trained with Tottenham's juniors as well as West Ham's before pledging himself to the Upton Park club. In January 1999, when Spurs unsuccessfully tabled a £4.3m bid for him, Frank explained: 'Players were coming through from their youth ranks and making it in the first team. That wasn't happening at the time at West Ham. It was touch and go, but as a West Ham fan through and through, my heart said the Hammers.'

Within a year of signing apprentice forms in 1994, the powerfully built teenager had become the dominant midfield presence in a youth side that, while paying dividends under new manager Harry Redknapp, suggested that prospects had already started to improve under former boss Billy Bonds. The first sign of major progress came with a sensational South East Counties League Cup final victory over Chelsea at the end of 1994–95. Trailing 5–2 after a disastrous home leg, West Ham thumped Chelsea 4–1 in the return to level things at 6–6. Lampard it was who secured the win with the deciding spot-kick in a penalty shoot-out.

With Frank's great friend Rio Ferdinand establishing himself in defence, the

Hammers youngsters played even more gripping football during 1995–96 – winning 18 successive games along the way. Lampard spent a character-building loan period with Swansea City before Christmas, but was back to help the youths clinch the South East Counties League title in April 1996 with a 3–2 home win over Tottenham – Frank scoring twice. Days later West Ham lost 4–1 on aggregate in the club's sixth FA Youth Cup final appearance against a Liverpool side featuring Michael Owen. Almost inevitably, Frank scored West Ham's consolation goal in the second leg at Anfield.

Amid all this frenetic activity, Redknapp handed the precocious 17-year-old a first-team debut at home to Coventry City soon after his return from Swansea and both Rio and Frank made substitute appearances in Alvin Martin's farewell appearance in the last game of the season. To cap it all, the pair were invited to train with England's Euro '96 squad. Young Lampard was on Cloud Nine, but a storm was brewing in E13.

If 1996–97 was a demanding one for West Ham – the first team flirting with relegation and getting knocked out of the FA Cup and Coca-Cola Cup by Wrexham and Stockport County respectively – it wasn't without its difficulties for Lampard either. He made 16 appearances – 11 as substitute – but the transition proved tough. If the team had spent more time going forwards than backwards, things might have been different, but Frank struggled to adapt to the circumstances. Sections of the crowd cruelly took their frustrations out on the anonymous new kid, with angry accusations of family favouritism the common theme. Twaddle, retorted Redknapp, who later told the club magazine: 'Some silly people were thinking it was all a family act. None of them knew what they were looking at but I certainly did.' Adds Frank Snr: 'I can remember them slagging Mooro off in the Chicken Run. I said to Frank: "Everyone gets it, don't worry."'

The final calamity in his first full season in the first-team squad came when he broke his leg in a 0–0 draw at Aston Villa in March 1997 (injury being the only reason he ever left the pitch early). Fit again for the start of 1997–98, the popularity pendulum swung back the other way as Lampard scored in a 2–1 opening-day win at Barnsley. Where others might have wilted under early criticism, he looked more eager than ever to prove his doubters wrong. With his perfectly timed runs into the box and the hardest shot at the club, Frank bagged ten goals, including a hat-trick at home to Walsall in the fourth round of the Coca-

Cola Cup. That total was just one fewer than regular central-midfield incumbents John Moncur and Ian Bishop had managed between them in four seasons and was a welcome relief at a club with fond traditions of employing scoring midfielders.

Frank added six more goals in the following campaign as West Ham finished fifth. And having earned his first England Under-21 cap in November 1997 against Greece, boss Peter Taylor made him captain. He relished the responsibility and showed his gratitude by scoring a goal every other game during Taylor's reign.

Lampard's dream of joining Ferdinand in the full squad was realised in April 1999, although Kevin Keegan chose not to play him in the 1–1 friendly against Hungary. 'Friendly' was also the operative word for Frank's performance in a 5–1 home defeat by Leeds the following month, when he was the only West Ham player to survive the full 90 minutes without a yellow or red card. At the end of the 1998–99 season, and in spite of almost constant tabloid rumours about him being offloaded to Aston Villa or Spurs, Lampard sounded happy with life at the Boleyn. 'I'd say my all-round game has improved. I feel more comfortable and stronger, both mentally and physically.'

Thirteen more goals were smashed home in 1999–2000. His fan base improved considerably as he hit home in a 1–0 victory over Spurs on the opening day and he notched four goals in West Ham's Intertoto/UEFA Cup campaign. Best of all, he earned his first full cap in a 2–1 home friendly win over Belgium. 'We always felt Frank was going to be a top player because it was clear he had the ability and the attitude to go to the very top,' a proud Redknapp told *FourFourTwo* magazine.

Missing much of pre-season through an ankle injury, Lampard started 2000–01 slowly. He also found himself playing deeper to accommodate the flair of Joe Cole, although he still bagged nine goals. But two things above all precipitated his eventual departure from the club. In November his pal Ferdinand was sold to Leeds for a record £18m, then, in May 2002, after a disappointing season, his father and uncle were dismissed. Without hesitation, Frank decided his position was untenable.

Where a host of bids had previously failed, Chelsea succeeded and Frank, 23, headed west with some strong words for the club he and his family had called home. 'I have always been ambitious enough to want to move on to . . . a club where I would have a better chance of winning things,' he told *The Mail on Sunday*. 'In a way, they forced the decision but I'm sure it would have come anyway

. . . It was a terrible experience, the sort of thing that colours your opinion on whether or not you want to be around the club.'

Adds Frank Snr: 'It made sense for everybody. The club got a lot of money for him. I think by going to Chelsea, playing with some world-class players, he's learning more about the game. I think that's why the last couple of England managers have had him in the squad, because they know he's got the ability to take things on board.'

Frank's willingness to do just that would be the key to reinforcing his international credentials as England entered the qualifying stages of the 2004 European Championships.

51

A CLASSIC MODEL: Rio Ferdinand

Born: 8 November 1978; Camberwell, London
Debut: v. Sheffield Wednesday (h), 5 May 1996
Apps/Goals: 157/2
Final app.: v. Leeds United (a), 18 November 2000

WITH RIO FERDINAND DISPLAYING AN IMMACULATE SENSE OF CLASS and style, it was little surprise that Hammers boss Harry Redknapp would repeatedly describe him as a 'Rolls Royce of a footballer'. Yet there were many key questions asked during Rio's years at the club. Where should he best be parked in the team? Would he be tempted to live life in the fast lane and in what direction would that take his career? How long would he keep pulling up onto Upton Park's forecourt? And did his eventual one-way journey up the M1 to Leeds effectively result in Redknapp heading out of West Ham's exit gates?

Ferdinand would first need to make a trip through the Blackwall Tunnel, having spent his early life on a council estate in south London's Peckham – synonymous with a yellow Reliant Robin adorned with 'Trotter's Trading' rather than gleaming Rollers. It's the sort of place where there's a healthy trade in 'borrowed' car stereos and Rio is the first to admit that, had it not been for the strict influence of mum Janice (who gave birth to him at just 17), he could well have found himself on the road to nowhere. 'Some of the lads I used to hang around with at my old school ended up inside,' Rio says. 'But thankfully I've always had my football to concentrate on and a strong family that kept me from going astray.'

Initially showing an enthusiasm for gymnastics (winning an Inner London schoolboy championship) as well as football, 11-year-old Ferdinand was spotted by coach Dave Goodwin shortly after joining Blackheath Bluecoat School. In charge of the Blackheath and District Schools sides, Goodwin was immediately impressed by the youngster's maturity. 'There were three main things that stuck out – his ability to pass the ball, the sheer vision he displayed and the way he organised the midfield,' he said.

Ferdinand acknowledges Goodwin as having the biggest single influence on his early playing years, helping to keep him focused while attracting the interest of professional clubs through his relationships with West Ham youth development officer Jimmy Hampson and Middlesbrough boss Lenny Lawrence. Rio also spent time with QPR (with whom his second cousin, England international striker Les, made his name) and Millwall, but it was the Hammers who got the nod when it was time to sign YTS forms in 1993. Youth boss Tony Carr remembers: 'He liked what we had to offer, liked the people and felt he could develop as a player here.'

Ferdinand's early days as a midfielder were not without a few problems, however. Young team-mate Frank Lampard Jnr recalls: 'Rio had a terrible time when we were about 15. Sometimes kids can outgrow their body and become all gangly – and that happened to him.'

A turning point came in the 1995 South East Counties League Cup final, in which Ferdinand scored during an incredible 4–1 second-leg win at Chelsea (resulting in a 6–6 aggregate score followed by a victorious penalty shoot-out). Lampard feels that Rio 'arrived that day', while manager Harry Redknapp confirms that his youngster did indeed make an impression. 'My dad rang me up, saying: "What a player you've got in your midfield!" I said: "Who's that, Frank Lampard?" And he says: "No, a tall dark boy." From then on we knew we had a player.'

Ferdinand's move into defence (as he turned professional at the end of 1995) came about as a result of the progressive thinking of Tony Carr. 'I attended a course at Lilleshall where [former Scotland manager] Andy Roxburgh appeared as the UEFA technical director. Andy said that a European philosophy was to play with three centre-backs, using a midfield player – who was comfortable with the ball and had reasonable defensive qualities – in the middle of the back three. The idea would be to encourage that player to break out with the ball from the back.

'I immediately thought: "That's Rio!" I came back home and said to Harry Redknapp: "Do you mind if I change the playing system of the youth teams to 3–5–2?" He gave me the go-ahead and we were really successful with it, winning the South East Counties League in 1996 and getting to the FA Youth Cup final [which saw the Hammers go down 4–1 to Liverpool over two legs]. To be honest, Rio wasn't sure at first if he wanted to play there. But all the ingredients were there – height, pace, great agility and mobility, as well as great technical ability. And that switch was the making of him.'

After his first-team debut as a 17-year-old substitute in the final game of the 1995–96 season, he furthered his education with an 11-game loan spell at Second Division Bournemouth in the early part of the next campaign. Returning to Upton Park, Rio quickly established himself as a defender who oozed confidence and composure – and the West Ham fans loved him for it. They voted him Young Hammer of the Year in 1997 and Hammer of the Year in 1998 as he became the fulcrum of a three-man central defence in the wake of Croatian international Slaven Bilic's departure.

The Bobby Moore comparisons were inevitable and, after graduating through England's youth and U21 ranks, the only question was how many full caps he would eventually win with his country. His full England debut during 1997–98 was delayed by two months after he was convicted of drink-driving but manager Glenn Hoddle still took him to France as part of his World Cup '98 party – although he failed to make an appearance.

Ferdinand is the first to admit he lost momentum during the 1999–2000 season ('I probably became a bit complacent,' he was quoted in newspapers as saying). But while he was guilty of the occasional lapse in concentration, few made allowances for the fact that he'd held things together alongside half a dozen different centre-halves (including hardmen Neil Ruddock, Stuart Pearce and Igor Stimac) as injuries disrupted the defence.

Whatever the circumstances, he failed to sufficiently impress new England boss Kevin Keegan who omitted him from his Euro 2000 squad. Rio duly took himself off to the Cyprus clubbing resort of Ayia Napa with team-mate Frank Lampard, among others, for some dancin' and unorthodox romancin'. The *News of the World* subsequently ran a front-page story, with the headline 'Video Shame of England Soccer Stars', exposing the players for having generated some saucy cinematography with a camcorder and some good-time girls.

No matter. By the start of the 2000–01 campaign a whole host of top European clubs – including Barcelona and Real Madrid – were said to be knocking on West Ham's door to acquire Ferdinand's services. But Leeds United were knocking loudest, making a series of bids to test the Hammers' resolve. On Harry Redknapp's insistence West Ham rejected several £15m offers, but he effectively named his price on 11 November 2000 when declaring: 'I know Rio won't be here forever. If we got £18m we would have a problem.' Ferdinand's performance in a shock 1–0 win at Leeds the following week convinced the ambitious Yorkshire club to stump up that exact figure, setting a new British transfer record and a world-record fee for a defender.

His former youth boss Tony Carr understandably had mixed feelings. 'Part of me said: "What a fantastic amount of money, you can't turn that down," while the other half said: "It's a shame we can't produce and keep our own players."' Rio himself admitted to the press: 'I never wanted to leave West Ham. It was my intention to achieve my ambitions at Upton Park but they needed the money. I owe the club a hell of a lot.'

Less than six months later, on 21 April 2001, Ferdinand was warmly received in his new colours and wearing the captain's armband when Leeds arrived at Upton Park for a league fixture. As the script dictated, he scored a rare goal in his side's 2–0 win, although he looked almost embarrassed to have inflicted damage on his former colleagues. 'I didn't think it was right to get too excited. That is why I didn't celebrate,' he said.

Tony Carr asked Rio for his new shirt as a souvenir, but was one of many. 'He said I could have it the next time Leeds came and when they returned for our first home game of the 2001–02 season Rio found me and handed it over, which was nice.'

By that time Harry Redknapp had been sacked as Hammers boss after a dispute with the club's chairman about money. Asked how he felt when selling Ferdinand, he admits: 'I was gutted but £18m was a difficult offer to refuse.' But the question was always going to be how much of that figure would be handed back to Redknapp to spend on new players. With only around £6.5m initially being spent on transfer fees (for six new players including defenders Christian Dailly and Rigobert Song), it was little wonder that West Ham fans started to sarcastically refer to the impressive new Dr. Martens Stand as the 'Rio Ferdinand Stand'.

Harry had admitted at the time of the sale that 'his loss makes my job a lot tougher'. And predictably, having lost his most important player, Redknapp's side had a disappointing season (finishing 15th) which culminated in a row over transfer funds. Just how different things would have been had Rio stayed at West Ham would be a topic of much debate.

Ferdinand's value subsequently increased substantially after the 2002 World Cup finals, in which he truly came of age. For many, he was England's most impressive player as they reached the quarter-finals and the tournament ended with the 23-year-old being linked with a sensational move to Manchester United.

Rio subsequently handed Leeds a transfer request and United ultimately agreed a transfer fee of £33m – smashing the British transfer record and once again establishing the youngster as the most expensive defender on the planet. In the same week, Rio's 17-year-old brother Anton, a YTS boy with the Hammers, signed a three-year professional contract with the club. Let's hope the kid's made of the same stuff.

52

GREAT EXPECTATIONS: Joe Cole

Born: 8 November 1981; Islington, London
Debut: v. Swansea City (h), 2 January 1999
Apps/Goals: 109/8 (at end of 2001–02)

THURSDAY, 9 MAY 2002, WAS A SPECIAL DAY FOR JOE COLE. FIRST IT was confirmed that the attacking midfielder had been included as the youngest member of England manager Sven-Goran Eriksson's squad for the World Cup finals in Japan and South Korea in the summer. Then he received congratulations in person from the Queen during Her Majesty's Golden Jubilee tour in which she formally opened West Ham's new Dr. Martens Stand. The glare of the media spotlight was as intense as ever but, like everything else the 20-year-old had encountered in his short life, it was all taken in his stride with those magical feet of his never straying too far from the ground.

'To make a player you've got to make the person first and there are lots of people who've played a part,' he says. 'My family have been a massive influence on me and they should take a lot of credit for where I am today. It's more important to be a good person in life, rather than just a good footballer. Everyone makes mistakes but my family have provided great support.'

Joseph John Cole will always be grateful to mum Susan and stepfather George, who provided the stabilising force after his natural father Christopher Rooks left home just a few months after his birth. He grew up on an estate in Camden, north London, instinctively falling in love with soccer and spending all his spare time with a ball at his mercy. 'I used to go out in the street after school and spend hours kicking a ball against the wall with both feet. I suppose that's how I built up my skills,' he says.

That dazzling footwork would quickly make Cole the most exciting youth prodigy of his generation. But while the kid obviously had a God-given talent, there were other figures – apart from his family and Him upstairs – who played key roles in his development. These include Jimmy Hampson, West Ham's youth development officer chiefly responsible for bringing Cole to the club as a schoolboy; Keith Blunt, a coach at the Lilleshall School of Excellence where Joe spent two crucial years away from home; and Hammers youth-team boss Tony Carr, under whom he played a key role in the FA Youth Cup success of 1998–99.

Remembers Carr: 'I first set eyes on Joe when he was 11 and even then I knew he was special. He had all the tricks. Some time later he was playing in a trial match and I'd been on to manager Harry Redknapp to come and have a look at this lad. The match was only five minutes old when Harry said: "Someone find a copper who can handcuff that kid to the gates. Don't let him out of here."'

Cole's enthusiasm for the game was relentless, with Carr recalling the time in 1996 when the Hammers travelled to Liverpool for the second leg of the FA Youth Cup final at Anfield. 'Jimmy Hampson said he wanted to bring Joe up to the game along with his parents. They said: "Do you mind if young Joe comes out onto the pitch before the game and has a kickabout?" No problems. Anyway, I came down for breakfast at the hotel, sat by the window and the ground outside was covered in frost. I had to do a double-take because there was Joe, doing tricks with the ball on the grass. He just couldn't sleep.'

Having trained under coach Peter Brabrook at Chadwell Heath as an associated schoolboy, attacking-midfielder Cole spent the final two years of his academic education at Lilleshall in Shropshire. Dad George initially had doubts about Joe being away from home and has admitted that the homesick teenager struggled at first. But Cole now claims to remember those times with great fondness. 'It was just the best time,' he says. 'To be away from home between the ages of 14 to 16 made me a stronger person and kept me away from other temptations in London. And from a football point of view it helped me to focus on working towards the team and how to influence a game. Keith Blunt taught me a lot about discipline and doing the right things.'

By now there was no shortage of professional clubs on his trail. Manchester

United boss Alex Ferguson had already taken the youngster to Wembley for the 1996 FA Cup final on the team bus, handing him a Reds shirt and apparently saying: 'One day you'll be wearing one of these.'

Remembers Harry Redknapp, who agreed to allow the youngster to play the field to keep his family happy: 'There was a time when he was spending time with other clubs and when Joe told me he was off to Man Utd for a few days I had some sleepless nights. But his dad always told me not to worry; Joe loved West Ham and would be back.'

Jimmy Hampson, meanwhile, would regularly travel to Shropshire to monitor the youngster's progress at Lilleshall and would later take responsibility for his interests, as would the PFA. Says Cole: 'Jimmy always made me feel so welcome at West Ham. The club had such a warm vibe to it and it made me feel as if I belonged. It just felt right.'

By the time Joe graduated from Lilleshall in 1998, he'd established himself as an England Schoolboy superstar – acknowledged by an explosion of media interest and sensationalistic hyperbole. An *Evening Standard* article in February of that year – nearly 12 months before his first-team debut – was titled: 'This 16-year-old is said to be the greatest prospect in England.' In it West Ham's director of football Peter Storrie confirmed that Cole's professional contract was already registered, adding: 'We had to fight everybody off but I like to think it was our successful youth policy that helped swing things our way.'

Cole publicly put pen to paper on the Upton Park pitch prior to the Hammers' 1–1 draw with Chelsea in November 1998 and the same month saw men's lifestyle magazine *Maxim* duly declare: 'West Ham have acquired the future of English football – and its name is Joe Cole.' The *Daily Mail*'s Jeff Powell described the player as 'the best prospect since the Great Gold Rush', while the *Daily Star* pictured him in their news pages after *Company* magazine had included him in their listings as to 'What's Hot for 1999'. The poor lad still hadn't made his debut – although that followed in early January when he came on as a substitute in a 1–1 FA Cup third round draw with Third Division Swansea City (Joe becoming the second youngest outfield player in Hammers history – after Paul Allen – at 17 years and 55 days). His first Premiership outing followed just eight days later, in a 4–1 defeat at Manchester United.

Cole made nine first-team appearances during the 1998–99 season (in which he won the club's Young Hammer of the Year award) while also playing all ten FA Youth Cup games for Tony Carr's victorious side. Reflects Carr: 'I think Joe has dealt with the hype remarkably well. The frustrating thing was that when he left school in 1998, he broke two toes while on holiday with his family. So before he'd even kicked a ball for us in a full-time capacity he was out for three or four months and that was terribly frustrating for the kid.'

From 1999 onwards the hopes and dreams invested in Cole continued to pile up, but he insists that he's learnt to deal with the pressure. 'There's always been great expectations of me and there always will be,' he says. 'But it works both ways really. I've only got to do something small and people make a big deal of it and say it's brilliant. And if I make a little error it's made out to be a massive mistake.'

The major issues of debate for pundits and punters alike concerned exactly where Joe best fitted into the West Ham side and when the full England team should have started to exploit his talents. Boss Redknapp initially saw Cole as a free spirit and loved his creativity, but began to sacrifice the player for away games because of doubts about his defensive attributes. England boss Kevin Keegan, who'd invited Joe to train with the national squad as a 17-year-old in 1999, had even considered him for the Euro 2000 championships ('I was dying for him to play regularly for West Ham,' he admitted). But if the lack of games hadn't made Keegan's mind up, a broken leg – courtesy of a challenge from Derby's Rory Delap during a league game in April – certainly did. And during season 2000–01 Redknapp was talking of Cole needing to 'learn a position' while again occasionally relegating the player to the substitute's bench as the Hammers struggled.

Redknapp's assistant Frank Lampard could sympathise with the youngster but knew that he would possibly have to make compromises to develop his overall game. 'It's a shame because when Joe was a kid he didn't have to run back,' he says. 'But now he's playing in a team with formation and structure, there are going to be games when he's got to be less typically Joe Cole and a bit more orthodox.'

That maturity started to reveal itself under next Hammers boss Glenn Roeder – who frowned upon the 'free spirit' concept – during the 2001–02 campaign that saw Joe deployed in traditional midfield positions. A troublesome foot injury sidelined him for the first few months and it was then Roeder's intention to teach Cole a new discipline on the left flank. However, a change of tactics for a game at

Manchester United in December saw Joe return to a more familiar (and preferred) central role. He was inspirational in a shock 1–0 victory at Old Trafford and remained in the middle for most of the season, his form earning him a ticket to the World Cup finals.

His first full England cap (following a number of U18 and U21 outings) came as a substitute in the 4–0 friendly win against Mexico in May 2001 and further cameo appearances were made in World Cup warm-up games against Holland, Italy and Paraguay. The media reacted hysterically to Cole making a mistake in England's 2–1 defeat by Italy in March. But a starring performance in the 4–0 win against Paraguay a month later ensured his inclusion in the World Cup party, with Swedish boss Eriksson describing him as 'one of the best technical players we have'.

Joe travelled to Japan and South Korea with England fans hoping he'd get the opportunity to produce some magic, although he returned with a slight sense of disappointment having been restricted to just 16 minutes of action as a substitute against Sweden. West Ham supporters, meanwhile, were conscious of the fact that success on the international stage would only have increased the chances of Cole following in the footsteps of Rio Ferdinand and Frank Lampard to more lucrative pastures away from Upton Park.

But they could take comfort from his insistence: 'I'm not going to leave until the club wants to sell me. If you want to be a legend like Trevor Brooking then you've got to stay at one club and show loyalty.'

53

ONE OF THOSE NIGHTS:
The 1999 FA Youth Cup final

YOUTH GAMES DO NOT ORDINARILY ENTER A LIST OF THE BEST TEAM performances ever witnessed at Upton Park. But then the second leg of the 1999 FA Youth Cup final was no ordinary youth game.

Few in the spellbound 24,000 crowd, with millions more watching on Sky TV, could have predicted such an astonishing feast of entertainment as West Ham's youngsters swept Coventry City aside 6–0 after beating them 3–0 in the first leg. Sky commentators Martin Tyler and Brian Marwood sounded genuinely shocked at the standard of football they were seeing. 'There's quality oozing from every pore of every player,' observed Tyler, not a man associated with cliché or exaggeration.

For manager Harry Redknapp and his back-up team, there was immense satisfaction on several levels. Firstly, this victory more than made up for defeat at the same stage against Liverpool three years previously. Then there was the pride in knowing that the youngsters were about to scoop an historic 'Double'. Season 1998–99 was the first since the brave new world of the FA Youth Academy system had replaced the antiquated regional youth leagues (in West Ham's case, the South East Counties League). And just three days after the FA Youth Cup final victory, the kids were crowned the first ever winners of the FA Premier Academy Under-19 championship, too, with Gary Alexander (later sold to Swindon without making a single first-team appearance) scoring a last-minute winner in a play-off final against Sheffield Wednesday.

The new 'vocationally-aware' system was devised by ex-Leeds boss Howard Wilkinson, the technical director of the FA. Clubs were now required to appoint a director of football, a director of the academy and a director of youth development; at West Ham the positions were filled by Peter Storrie, Tony Carr and Jimmy Hampson respectively (with former Charlton man Jimmy Tindall succeeding the last as youth development officer). As Carr explained at the time: 'Clubs will take full responsibility for the whole of a lad's football education and monitor his academic studies. The scheme is a partnership between each boy's school and the club. [West Ham] have to provide a classroom at their training ground and appoint a full-time education and welfare officer.'

Bearing in mind that West Ham had won the last ever South East Counties Championship in 1997–98 (going 21 league and cup games without defeat from the start of the season to mid-January) and would go on to win the FA Premier Academy U19 title again in 1999–2000, the achievements of Redknapp and his staff at the turn of the new millennium were quite astounding, especially given the arid state of the Hammers' youth system at the beginning of the 1990s.

On the night of 14 May, though, it was all about seeing young players play the beautiful game beautifully, and in Joe Cole – half-footballer, half-Harlem Globetrotter – West Ham had the most talked-about face of tomorrow in the British game. Having appeared nine times in the first team by the time of the final, classy Cole's unfeasible tricks had already won him a substantial fan base. In the second leg against Coventry, the Hammers played superbly as a team unit, but two boys in particular – Geordie playmaker Michael Carrick and right wing-back Adam Newton – appeared, like Cole, to have the world at their feet.

Proving once again how unpredictable football can be, Newton struggled to impose himself higher up the ladder and was transferred to Peterborough in May 2002. In contrast, Carrick and Cole became automatic first-team choices within a year or so and full England internationals by 2001.

At the final whistle, the glow on the faces of West Ham's playing and coaching staff – not least youth bosses Carr (Under-19) and Peter Brabrook (Under-17) – suggested they knew they had just been a part of something rather special. Six of the very best, no less . . .

● After just three minutes (kick-off having been delayed 15 minutes by crowd congestion), Carrick and Newton combine to set up the first goal, the former's raking 40-yard pass being headed down by Newton at the far post for striker Bertie Brayley to stroke home. Brayley, Newton and defender Stevland Angus had scored the goals at Highfield Road in the first leg. With Shaun Byrne injured in that match, Sam Taylor came in at left wing-back.

● On 27 minutes, just after Cole caused audible gasps in the crowd by juggling and twisting to lose his man-marker, Newton tears down the right wing, slips inside two players and curls in a beauty off both posts for number two. West Ham goalkeeper Stephen Bywater, a £300,000 signing from Rochdale as a 16-year-old, has barely touched the ball, but a year later he will be the Hammers' hero as his penalty shoot-out saves see off Arsenal in the U19 Premier Academy title play-off.

● Six minutes later, striker Richard Garcia bags a third from the penalty spot as Coventry start to capitulate. Garcia and fellow Australian, midfielder Michael Ferrante, validated the establishment in 1998 of two schools of excellence Down Under. Based in Perth and Sydney, they were the initiatives of Peter Storrie, who recognised the benefits of casting the youth net way beyond the Thames Estuary.

● Five minutes after the break, Brayley – who swapped Aston Villa's youth set-up for West Ham's – slots home a cute Carrick cut-back to make it 4–0. Coventry keeper Chris Kirkland – two years later the subject of an £8m transfer to Liverpool – looks wistfully in the direction of the M1.

● With Cole continuing to dance his way through City's defence and captain Izzie Iriekpen – celebrating his 17th birthday – Alvin Martin-like at the back alongside Tyrell Forbes, the ecstatic crowd starts a Mexican wave. On 75 minutes Carrick, now playing with a smile as wide as the Tyne Bridge, breaks down a Coventry attack on the halfway line, swaps passes with Garcia and scores from eight yards.

● With just a couple of minutes remaining, Carrick feints past his marker, spots a run by Garcia and plays another defence-splitting pass for the Aussie to make it 6–0 on the night and 9–0 on aggregate – a record score for an FA Youth Cup final. Another famous party night begins on Green Street, E13.

54

H'WAY THE LAD: Michael Carrick

Born: 28 July 1981; Wallsend, North Shields
Debut: v. FC Jokerit (h), 24 July 1999
Goals/apps: 82/4 (at end of 2001–02)

WEST HAM HAVE A LONG TRADITION OF DRAWING PLAYERS FROM England's Northeast. Indeed, one of the first to make the long trip south was an outside left by the name of Christopher Carrick, way back in 1904. It is a testament to the enduring appeal of the club's youth system that, with Newcastle United (certainly) and Middlesbrough and Sunderland (arguably), being deemed 'bigger' clubs, the Hammers can still tap into a talent pool at the other end of the country.

Very nearly 100 years after Chris Carrick was born in Stockton, Teesside, namesake Michael emerged into a footballing family a little further north in the tough Newcastle district of Wallsend. Dad Vince had been good enough to make it to reserve level at Middlesbrough and it was Boro who first picked up on Michael's talents after he started to shine for the famous Wallsend Boys Club – breeding ground of England internationals Alan Shearer and Peter Beardsley, to name but two. 'I only lived two minutes down the road,' says Michael. 'There was a five-a-side league and a Sunday side, plus judo, pool, table tennis and all sorts of stuff going on. Everyone around there goes to Wallsend Boys.

'Scouts from all over came on a Sunday to watch the 11-a-side. Most of the lads go to Newcastle, Sunderland and Middlesbrough. I was at Middlesbrough until I was 12 or 13, then I did the rounds, went on trial with about a dozen clubs. My summer was spent travelling around the country.'

Four glowing scout reports on Carrick – then more of an attacker than a midfielder – were reportedly sent to Newcastle United, but the club on his doorstep inexplicably ignored him. In contrast, a report compiled by one of West Ham's representatives in the north had the desired effect and St James' Park's oversight became Upton Park's gain. From the age of 14 he trained with the Hammers during school holidays, then at 16 the move from the Northeast to the Southeast became permanent. Youth boss Tony Carr – who a few years later would also see Michael's kid brother Graeme join as an apprentice – says it is a migration with significant, if perplexing, precedents.

'Well it's always been done, hasn't it,' says Carr. 'Alan Shearer went to Southampton. How did he get down there? The Charlton brothers went to Leeds and Manchester United. Michael always felt that he'd be under too much peer pressure from his mates by staying in Newcastle. He came down here, liked what he saw and the rest is history.'

Carrick's conversion to digs life and 'southern' ways proved a test early on. 'I did miss home quite a lot. I was used to seeing my family and mates every day and I'd speak to them all the time on the phone. But you adapt. Playing football every day takes your mind off it.'

In 1998, he and six other trainees moved into a hostel-style house owned by the club. The friendships he established there boosted his confidence immeasurably, while physical weaknesses earlier identified by boss Harry Redknapp rapidly gave way to six feet of strong-limbed, technically brilliant midfield maestro. As the superb 9–0 aggregate 1999 FA Youth Cup final victory over Coventry City proved, Michael was loving life at West Ham; the gleeful grin he wore for much of the game as his gilt-edged passes carved open City's defence was evidence of that. 'All the lads were really good mates,' he says, 'and most of us lived together. We got on so well we were just having a laugh on the pitch and everyone was playing brilliantly.'

The House of the Rising Sons had another reason to celebrate four days before Michael's 18th birthday, when he was given a run-out in an early round of the Intertoto Cup at the beginning of the 1999–2000 season. His Premiership debut came via a substitute appearance at Bradford City in August, before Harry Redknapp's learning curve saw him go out on loan, first with Swindon Town, then later with Birmingham City. 'At Swindon I played six games and scored a couple [one a brilliant effort against Charlton following a move started by Carrick in his own half]. They were bottom of the First Division at the time but it was a really good experience. In a way it made me more determined than ever that I didn't want to play at that level.'

Returning to Upton Park around Christmas, Carrick made his first Hammers start in the opening game of the new millennium – at none other than Newcastle United. 'That was some experience,' he says. 'It was all my dreams come true, although it turned out to be a hard game. We ended up getting a 2–2 draw and I kept seeing all my mates and people I'd gone to school with in the crowd, which was a bit weird.'

Michael continued to turn out for Carr's superb Under-19s that season, scoring two goals in a 6–6 Premier Youth Academy play-off final against Arsenal. The Hammers won on penalties to retain the championship.

Having totalled eight Premiership appearances in 1999–2000, Young Hammer of the Year Carrick consolidated his position in the first team during the following campaign with some imperious displays among his 33 league games. And in an FA Cup fourth-round tie in January 2001, both his profile and that of fellow youth products Cole and Frank Lampard received an unexpected boost. Amid ominous circumstances, West Ham's angelic midfield took on world stars Roy Keane, David Beckham and Ryan Giggs of Manchester United – and won. 'We went back there after being beaten 3–1 a few weeks before,' says Michael. 'A lot of people were saying we were only turning up for a day out, so to get the win in the way we did

[Paolo Di Canio calling United keeper Fabian Barthez's bluff for the only goal of the game] was a big test for the lads.

'That game is up there with the best of them. And to go back there and get the same result in the Premiership the following season was just amazing.'

By then a regular at Under-21 level, Michael's alarming maturity was rewarded with a call-up to the full England squad – Sven-Goran Eriksson's first – for a friendly versus Spain in February 2001. A hamstring strain ruined the script but Carrick came back to earn his first cap as a sub against Mexico three months later.

With Cole out injured at the start of the following season and Frank Lampard Jnr sold to Chelsea for £11m, Michael's name dominated the column inches devoted to 'West Ham's bright future'. Against Lampard's new employer Carrick, always willing his try his luck from a distance, scored West Ham's first from 20-yards in a 2–1 win in October to bolster his reputation.

Ever keen to find a story where none existed, the media started to imply that Carrick, not 'boy wonder' Cole, was set to become the key midfield influence at Upton Park. Their contrasting styles – Joe a whirling dervish, Michael a composed passer – were duly dissected with a fine-tooth comb. 'It's quite funny actually. People make out we are rivals, but we are good mates and we just have a laugh about all this nonsense that "he's better than me and I'm better than him". We are just playing the game the way we enjoy – it's others that put you in a certain spotlight.'

New boss Glenn Roeder preferred to praise rather than pit peer against peer. 'Michael is truly a modern-day midfield player. He can play short, long, off his right foot, off his left foot and he is almost impossible to close down. There is no doubt that as each season goes on his influence on the team is going to grow.'

The abundance of attacking talent at Roeder's disposal saw Carrick influence the side from more of a holding midfield role as 2001–02 progressed. A berth in Eriksson's 2002 World Cup squad was looking a distinct possibility until he sprained knee ligaments just after Christmas, while eight weeks out with a groin injury pushed him further into the England shadows. Perhaps more surprising than his eventual exclusion from the squad was the manner in which he found out. 'It was after training at West Ham. The fitness trainer came up and told me after seeing it on the telly. I didn't get a phone call or anything. I didn't really know what to expect, having never been in that situation before.'

But he confesses: 'I never really thought I'd be in to start with. It would be easy to blame the injury problems, but I think I've had enough games to prove myself. If Sven wanted to take me, he'd have taken me regardless.'

Carrick had the consolation of being named in the Under-21 squad, having sensationally booked the side's passage to the 2002 European Championships the previous November with the deciding goal against Holland in a 3–2 aggregate play-off match at Derby. But in the last game of the domestic season, a home victory over Bolton, the injury curse hit again to cause Michael further groin – and heart – ache.

While his immediate international ambitions caved in, those in the know had little doubt that this assured performer would play a key role for England in years to come. And Frank Lampard Snr's comparison of Carrick with one of Upton Park's most illustrious homegrown sons speaks volumes about his promise. 'Michael's got great awareness, he lets the ball do the work and I'd liken him to Martin Peters. He'll go on to be a top player.'

55

IRON IN THE FIRE: Jermain Defoe

Born: 7 October 1982; Beckton, London
Debut: v. Walsall (a), 19 September 2000
Apps/Goals: 40/15 (at end of 2001–02)

FEW THINGS STIR A WEST HAM SUPPORTER'S SOUL MORE THAN THE unearthing of a homegrown Cockney striker equipped to score 20 goals a season. Until Jermain Defoe arrived on the scene in September 2000 with a confidently taken debut goal, the club hadn't had one of those since Tony Cottee in the early 1980s. Like Cottee, Defoe appeared compact, fast, instinctive and hungry. Yet the truth, of course, was that West Ham hadn't unearthed him at all – that honour went to Charlton Athletic.

Up to the age of 16, Defoe attended Charlton's School of Excellence as an associate schoolboy. Then, in 1999, he took the controversial decision to turn professional with West Ham. 'The main reason I left,' Jermain says, 'was that I'd seen the Rio Ferdinands and Frank Lampards come through the West Ham ranks. I suppose I wanted a piece of that. I just missed out on the FA Youth Cup final [West Ham thrashing Coventry 9–0 over two legs] but I was at the second game. After that I guess I made my decision. I thought to myself: "They've got all these players here; it will be great for me if I can be a part of that."'

Outwardly, manager Harry Redknapp was matter-of-fact about West Ham's gain and Charlton's bitterly disappointing loss. 'It can happen to anybody. West Ham lost a couple of kids, with one going to Manchester United.'

But having nurtured Defoe, Charlton were naturally upset and took their grievance to the Football Association. They were subsequently awarded a compensation package rising to around £1.4m based on Premiership and international appearances. It was to be a sum – and a saga – that stuck in the craw of Addicks boss Alan Curbishley, himself a former West Ham prodigy. 'That was hardly compensation for a player in the Premiership who had been with us for six or seven years,' blasted Curbishley. 'He's got to play 50-odd games for West Ham for us to get near the £1.4m and if you play 50 games in the Premiership you're worth more than that.'

That feelings ran high was understandable; Defoe had been the talk of football wherever he had performed, even in the playground of his junior school, St Joachim's, in the East End district of Custom House. Remembers former teacher Robin Sorflaten: 'We used to talk about him in the staff room, about the ability he had. He was too good for the boys of his age. I refereed a match once that he played in and he had to be taken off at half-time because he was outplaying everybody else.

'Jermain had a sort of glow about him. He was very focussed on becoming a footballer and loved to be called 'Wrighty' after Ian Wright.' To Defoe's delight, the legendary former Arsenal and England striker was on West Ham's books when he joined the club. 'I used to stay behind after training with him and work on my finishing,' says Jermain. 'It was really a dream come true.'

He graduated from his junior school side to the remarkably productive Sunday league outfit Senrab (a backward spelling of the East End street after which the side took its name). 'Premiership players like Lee Bowyer, John Terry, Ashley Cole and Ledley King all came through from there,' Defoe says. 'Obviously we used to get scouts coming down all the time. We used to train at the leisure centre in Beckton so it was local for Charlton as well as West Ham.'

In 1997, Charlton enrolled 14-year-old Defoe at Lilleshall, the FA's National School of Excellence in Shropshire. 'You'd come home from school and go straight out to training,' says Jermain. 'After that you'd have homework to do but you'd be so knackered. Joe Cole was there at the time. I lived with him for a year so got to know him well.' Two years on and he joined Cole at Upton Park. Jermain was an immediate hit, his goals – including two in the play-off final against Arsenal – rocketing the Under-19s to the Premiership Academy title in 1999–2000, their second championship on the trot.

At senior level, Harry Redknapp had the lavish skills, if not the abundant goals, of Paolo Di Canio and Frederic Kanoute to enjoy, but the temptation to give the exciting Defoe a run-out in the first team proved overwhelming. A Worthington Cup tie at Walsall in September 2000 seemed a suitable test bed and the 17-year-old sprang off the bench on 75 minutes to instant effect. 'At the time I came on it was 0–0, so to win the game [Jermain volleying home the only goal of the game] with my family in the crowd was a special moment.'

Any hopes his family had of seeing more of the same were dashed the following month when Redknapp's masterplan for Defoe saw him leave on a near-season-long loan to Second Division Bournemouth. It would prove to be arguably the most remarkable loan spell ever, if not one of obvious early appeal to Jermain. 'When Harry first asked me if I fancied going out on loan to Bournemouth, I thought: "Well . . .?" So I spoke to Rio Ferdinand [the defender spent a loan period with the Cherries in 1996–97] about it and he said it would be good for me. I thought if that's the case I've just got to do it. I went there for a month, enjoyed it and stayed there for the rest of the season.'

Showing rare consistency in one so young, Defoe netted 19 times in 29 starts, a spree that saw him level former Liverpool striker John Aldridge's record of scoring in ten consecutive league games. Meanwhile, back at West Ham, a marked shortage of goals was resulting in a worrying flirtation with relegation as the club limped to 15th place and Redknapp lost his job.

In 2001–02, the clamour for Redknapp's successor Glenn Roeder to grant Defoe a place in the starting line-up intensified as the season wore on. In October, with West Ham living up to their billing as candidates for the drop, late substitute Defoe scored the Hammers' third and his first Premiership goal in a valuable 3–2 away win at Ipswich Town. Roeder's intention that season was to use him sparingly so as not to risk burn-out, but as Jermain's performances started to overshadow that of the senior strikers, the decision began to irk many supporters, Tony Cottee among them. 'What manager John Lyall did with me,' said Cottee, 'which is different from what Glenn has done with Jermain, was play me for eight or nine games, give me a rest, put me in, then give me another rest. Defoe's the best finisher at the club. He should be the first striker on the team-sheet.'

England Under-21 boss David Platt went even further. Having seen Defoe dazzle with a goal on his debut for the U21s at Leicester in a 3–0 friendly win over Mexico in May 2001, plus two more at Reading in a 4–0 friendly victory against Holland three months later (Jermain making history again by scoring the fastest ever international goal by a substitute after just three seconds), Platt could barely contain himself. 'I think he is absolutely without weakness,' enthused the former England captain. If Roeder feared such compliments would go to Defoe's head he needn't have worried. Says Jermain: 'I read it in the papers but I didn't really think about it too much. Obviously it's nice for someone like David Platt to say something like that. He's been there and done it and all the players have got so much respect for him.

'Every time the U21s meet up I'm just really looking forward to it,' adds the striker, whose elevation to the big time came too late for the 2002 World Cup, but just right for the European Under-21 Championships the same summer. England flopped at the first stage in Switzerland, but Jermain got yet another goal, against the host nation just three minutes into the first game, to add to his international tally.

West Ham's climb up the table in the winter and spring of 2001–02 coincided with Defoe's increased exposure as he benefited from injuries to Di Canio and Kanoute and left experienced reserves Paul Kitson and Titi Camara trailing in the pecking order. To rub salt into Charlton's wounds, in November 2001 he smashed home West Ham's fourth goal in a 4–4 thriller to silence his disgruntled baiters at The Valley. The undisputed highlight of the season came at Manchester United the following month, the 5ft 7in. striker out-jumping his markers to head home a superb Di Canio cross and seal a second improbable 1–0 win at Old Trafford in little more than ten months. 'With over 67,000 there the atmosphere was unbelievable. It was a great, great moment,' he says.

Defoe grabbed four more goals that season in the FA Cup, including an outlandish volley from an acute angle in the 3–2 fifth round defeat at home to Chelsea. It was his other goal in that tie which convinced Tony Cottee of his true merit. 'It was palmed out by the keeper and he was in the right place at the right time, four yards out, to tap it home. As good as Di Canio and Kanoute are, they don't score those type of goals.' Suddenly, rewards began to rain in as heavily as plaudits. By notching his tenth goal of the season in the Chelsea game, Defoe was reportedly awarded a 500 per cent salary increase, from £3,000 a week (plus £3,000 a goal) to £18,000 per week.

Unapologetic about using his top scorer primarily as a substitute, Roeder stuck to his beliefs that the next season, 2002–03, would be the one in which he could 'take him off the leash and let him go'. Jermain, who finished the season with 14 goals, seemed happy enough with his lot. 'I'm not one of those players who go and knock on the manager's door or open my mouth and say things I shouldn't. I'll just keep on working hard and let my football do the talking.'

Given his meteoric rise, Defoe's decision to leave Charlton three years earlier had been totally vindicated. Despite his misgivings about the affair, Alan Curbishley remains a big fan – and a backer of Roeder's cautious stance. 'Jermain has got a lot going for him and is still very young,' says Curbishley. 'He shouldn't think that not being involved in the first team or being on the bench is a backward step, because he's got to have everything in his locker to go on and be a Premiership player for the next ten years.'

Hammers fans, so used to seeing the club's favourite sons sold on to other clubs, will be praying that all of those ten years will be spent with West Ham.

56

BUBBLING UNDER:
Some that didn't make it and a few that might

THERE ARE MANY HOMEGROWN HAMMERS WHO, DESPITE FAILING to amass the 25 appearances required to warrant a chapter in this book, have nevertheless played their part in the fortunes of the club since 1958. Some were flair players whose talents burnt out alarmingly quickly. Some got frustrated and left through lack of first-team opportunity. Others suffered injury or, quite simply, didn't have enough about their game. Quite which category Emmanuel Omoyinmi fitted into is open to debate, but it's probably fair to say his demise at West Ham was the most controversial of the lot.

Manny came to prominence as a member of the youth side which in 1996 won the South East Counties League title and reached the FA Youth Cup final. The little winger's finest moment with the first team came as a substitute against Crystal Palace when he salvaged a point with two goals in a 3–3 draw at Selhurst Park in May 1998. It was again as a late substitute in a home Worthington Cup quarter-final victory (via a penalty shoot-out) over Aston Villa in December 1999, that his Hammers career went out of the window.

Having already appeared in an earlier round of the competition while on loan at Gillingham, he was ineligible to play – a fact that escaped manager Harry Redknapp, club secretary Graham Mackrell and, most curiously, the player himself. Villa's beady-eyed administrators were not so absent-minded. A complaint was made to the Football Association, the game was replayed and West Ham, losing 3–1, stumbled out in a daze. So did Omoyinmi, who when queried by Redknapp about why he'd happily sat on the bench in the first game simply said he 'didn't think'. A free transfer to Oxford United quickly followed.

Thankfully, Manny's demise had no ill-effect on the through-put of youth players. Striker Richard Garcia (who scored in every round of the 1999 FA Youth Cup success), midfielder Grant McCann (a full Northern Ireland international), defenders Adam Newton and Shaun Byrne (also capped by Northern Ireland) and goalkeeper Stephen Bywater (like Newton, an England Under-21 star) all debuted in Manny's wake. Each would be more than happy to emulate the career success, if not the Upton Park fortunes, of Ray Houghton. Rejected by John Lyall after just one substitute appearance in 1981–82, Houghton later became a massive favourite for Liverpool and Eire.

The most unfortunate one-hit wonder was surely defender Paul Marquis, whose 60 seconds of action and single touch of the ball as a 90th-minute sub at Manchester City in 1994 made his the shortest post-war West Ham career. Goalkeeper Neil Finn's only appearance was also against City. At just 17 years and three days young, the YTS trainee was sensationally drafted in on New Year's Day 1996 due to an injury crisis. Finn disappeared into non-league football before he'd made it out of his teens, but entered the record books as the youngest West Ham player ever to appear in the Premiership.

Derek Woodley was another unlucky member of the flash-in-the-pan brigade. The promising winger notched a brace on his debut in a 3–1 home win over Luton Town in 1959, yet managed just 13 games before he was sold to Southend United in 1962. Left-back Eddie Presland announced his arrival in 1965 with West Ham's first goal in a 2–1 win against Liverpool at Upton Park. It doesn't get much better than that and it didn't for Essex boy Eddie, whose Boleyn career was finished five games later.

Forwards Mick Beesley (v. Everton in 1960) and tricky Nigerian Ade Coker (v. Crystal Palace in 1971) were two other debut scorers quickly shown the door, while Roger Hugo had a goals-per-game ratio of 66 per cent to take with him to Watford after scoring in two of his three appearances in 1963–64.

George Cowie was an elegant young Scottish midfielder of immense promise who, in the late-1970s, captained his country's youth team at the same time as his club-mate Paul Allen skippered England's. Through injury and competition for places, Cowie's Hammers career fizzled out after just nine appearances.

Three Hammers products of the late 1960s that didn't quite make the grade would play a fundamental part in nurturing some of the brightest talents at the club. East Ham-born striker Roger Cross (first-team coach after returning to the club in 1998) scored once in eight games, while prolific schoolboy scorer Tony Carr (future head of youth coaching) missed the first team by a whisker. Paul Heffer, a defender whose career was cut short by injury, would later work under Carr in the late 1990s as coach to the Under-15s/16s.

Inside-forward Johnny Cartwright may have struggled to establish himself as a player (making just five appearances between 1959 and 1961) but he enjoyed enormous success as a coach, managing the England youth side and then assisting Arsenal boss Don Howe in the mid-1980s.

Frank Lampard Jnr was always at pains to explain that family connections counted for little at West Ham. Clive Charles and Billy Lansdowne Jnr would vouch for that – together they racked up just 29 appearances in the 1970s in contrast to brother John Charles and dad Billy Lansdowne Snr who appeared 202 times between them in the 1950s and '60s. Clive Charles went on to become a leading figure in US soccer, while Lansdowne Snr worked for a time as youth and reserves coach at Upton Park.

From the 1990s, there was a smidgeon of action for forwards Simon Clarke, Lee Hodges and Lee Boylan, midfielders Paul Kelly and Simon Livett and Aussie defender Chris Coyne, while keeper Steven Banks' involvement was limited to a single Anglo-Italian Cup appearance.

In the 1980s, capable Republic of Ireland U21 striker Eamonn Dolan (19 apps) and 1981 FA Youth Cup winners Keith McPherson and Everald La Ronde were unlucky not to progress further. Midfielders Dale Banton and Warren Donald, striker Greg Campbell and injury-stricken full-back Mark Smith also experienced little more than their allotted 15 minutes of Hammers fame.

Briefly appearing in the 1970s were winger Joe Durrell, defender Phil Brignull and striker David Llewelyn, while from the late '50s and '60s there was fleeting action from goalkeepers Colin Mackleworth, Alan Dickie and Stephen Death, defender Bill Kitchener and attackers Trevor Dawkins, Trevor Hartley and Andy Smillie (23 appearances but just three goals).

57

THE TOMORROW PEOPLE: 2002 and beyond

RIO FERDINAND CALMLY COLLECTS THE BALL ON THE EDGE OF HIS OWN penalty area, steps confidently forward and finds Frank Lampard, who plays a short pass to Michael Carrick. The midfielder runs into the opposition's half and sends an intelligent ball out to Joe Cole who's darted into space on the right flank. Cole dances past one defender, skips past another to move inside and fires the ball into the six-yard box before Jermain Defoe pounces to ruthlessly dispatch it into the back of the net. Cue mass celebrations as the Hammers qualify for Champions League football . . .

Fiction could well have been fact if West Ham had succeeded in holding onto its best homegrown talent in later years. But the challenges that face the club will always remain; can they continue to produce top-class players and how long will they be able to hold onto them?

In 2001–02 manager Glenn Roeder took the Hammers to seventh in his first year in charge and insisted that he would need to keep the likes of Cole, Carrick and Defoe if the club were to progress. 'Of course there is always a danger that a club like Manchester United or Arsenal will want to sign them,' he said, 'but at the moment I think Upton Park is the perfect environment for these players.'

Director of youth academy Tony Carr openly declares that his ambition is to see five or six homegrown Hammers in the same first team, but recognises the harsh realities that make that unlikely. 'My heart says one thing but my head knows that things can't necessarily be that way,' he says. First the club needs to continue producing such talent and the signs in 2002 were looking positive. Declared Carr: 'A Premier League document said that West Ham's youth development system is second only to Manchester United's. So I'm very proud of that.'

Interestingly, United boss Sir Alex Ferguson described the Premier League

Academy system as 'a waste of time' and it was suggested that after the 2002–03 season it could possibly be restructured as a single U18 competition to reduce costs. One definite change at West Ham in the summer of 2002, however, was the departure of U17 coach Peter Brabrook following a five-year full-time association upon his return to the club with whom he won an FA Cup winners' medal in 1964. 'Obviously my age was a consideration because they wanted a younger person in,' said the 64-year-old as he reluctantly waved goodbye.

That 'younger person' would ultimately be confirmed as 35-year-old former Hammer Kevin Keen, who'd gained his coaching licence while seeing out his playing days at Third Division Macclesfield Town.

Brabrook left behind a group of youngsters that included Anton Ferdinand and Graeme Carrick (brothers of Rio and Michael respectively) while there were high hopes for 2002 Young Hammer of the Year Glen Johnson. With restrictions now preventing clubs from signing kids who live beyond a certain distance, Tony Carr emphasises that the club's 'recruitment drive has got to be concentrated within our locality' – as it was back in the 1960 and '70s.

But the increasingly demanding arena of youth development in the new millennium is here to stay, with Carr admitting: 'There's now a much greater pressure on youth systems to produce. We used to work quietly in the background but now I'm not as relaxed as I used to be. I feel it's a must that we succeed now.'

Certainly, it can be argued that West Ham's dependence on a healthy youth production line has never been greater. As well as enjoying the obvious benefits on the pitch, the combined £29m sales of Rio Ferdinand and Frank Lampard in 2000 and 2001 have helped bring financial stability while helping to fund team rebuilding during times when spiralling wage bills have prompted football to question the road it's heading down.

The influx of foreign talent has irrevocably changed the face of the British game but fans at Upton Park will forever remain hopeful that their side will always include a handful of homegrown Hammers who'll bleed claret and blue blood for the club's cause.